William Everett examines the musical across continents, genres and languages in the seminal year of 1924, when the constellation of current and future stars aligned to create works of artistic brilliance and great popularity. For the first time in critical musical theatre scholarship equal treatment is given to cultural capitals across the Atlantic such as Madrid, Buenos Aires, New York, London, Berlin, Vienna and Milan, and to the multitude of genres that comprise musical theatre. Everett casts his net widely to include the usual characters – the Astaires, the Gershwins, Coward, Kern, Hammerstein, Romberg – and also less well-known figures, such as Sissle and Blake, Florence Mills, Emmerich Kálmán and Amadeo Vives – all of whom are part of the history of the musical in 1924. Beautifully researched and engagingly written, this is a virtuosic tour de force.

John Koegel, Professor of Musicology, California State University

Coming hot on the heels of a number of books scrutinizing a particular year in western culture, William A Everett's decision to cast 1924 as the *Wunderjahr* of the musical is inspired. What a time it was! He surveys it all: musical comedies, lavish and intimate revues, zarzuelas and operettas, featuring the rise of the Astaires and the Gershwins and the heyday of numerous stars. The shows opened in New York, London, Paris, Madrid, Milan, Vienna, Berlin and Budapest; their settings ranged from the Canadian Rockies to Damascus by way of Greenwich Village or the Thames; and their improbable but often socially probing plots encompassed infidelity, bootlegging, drug dealing, sex working, people trafficking and personal journeys from riches to rags and back again. They showed it all – which might mean anything from complete stage nudity to the misplaced inclusivity that now spells racism. Everett, duly sensitive to the contexts of both now and then, is an expert guide to all the glamour and a complete master of the literature and such primary sources as still survive. Is it OK still to enjoy those nostalgic or jazz-age songs he refers to, many of which today's online resources allow us to hear and verify for ourselves? Read, listen and decide.

Stephen Banfield, Stanley Hugh Badock Professor of Music Emeritus, University of Bristol

In the timeline of musical theatre history, there are certain years that stand out in large, bolded typeface as turning points for the form. In 1957, *West Side Story* and *The Music Man* both entered the canon as two very different examples of a changing form. In 1964, *Funny Girl, Fiddler on the Roof* and *Hello, Dolly!* represented a glorious sunset for the Golden Age of the genre and hinted at the direction it would take in the next decades. In *The Year that Made the Musical*, William Everett convincingly demonstrates that 1924 has been overlooked as another such pivotal year when the changes and developments that might ordinarily play out over a decade were compressed into a single twelve-month period.

Doug Reside, Curator, Billy Rose Theater Collection, New York Public Library for the Performing Arts

Musical theatre in 1924, the single year addressed in this innovative book, consisted of comedies, revues and operettas, and was characterized by transnational influences, transfers and migrations. By using a comprehensive approach to a defined period, Everett provides a fascinating cross-sectional perspective on the interactions between countries, politics and the production of musicals.

Millie Taylor, Van den Ende Chair of the Musical, University of Amsterdam

The Year that Made the Musical

1924 and the Glamour of Musical Theatre

———

WILLIAM A. EVERETT

University of Missouri–Kansas City

CAMBRIDGE
UNIVERSITY PRESS

Shaftesbury Road, Cambridge CB2 8EA, United Kingdom

One Liberty Plaza, 20th Floor, New York, NY 10006, USA

477 Williamstown Road, Port Melbourne, VIC 3207, Australia

314–321, 3rd Floor, Plot 3, Splendor Forum, Jasola District Centre,
New Delhi – 110025, India

103 Penang Road, #05–06/07, Visioncrest Commercial, Singapore 238467

Cambridge University Press is part of Cambridge University Press & Assessment,
a department of the University of Cambridge.

We share the University's mission to contribute to society through the pursuit of
education, learning and research at the highest international levels of excellence.

www.cambridge.org
Information on this title: www.cambridge.org/9781009316514

DOI: 10.1017/9781009316545

First published 2024

Printed in the United Kingdom by CPI Group Ltd, Croydon CR0 4YY

A catalogue record for this publication is available from the British Library

A Cataloging-in-Publication data record for this book is available from the Library of Congress

ISBN 978-1-009-31651-4 Hardback

To Lynda, Bridget and Bruno

Contents

The plates will be found between pages 124 and 125

Plates

Figures

Acknowledgements

Researching and writing a book relies on the assistance and goodwill of many people. My sincere thanks to all who have been part of this journey to uncover and recover so many of the musical theatre events of 1924. First are all the people who, when I told them about this project, asked 'Why 1924?' They helped me define and continually refocus my responses on why this particular year held such tremendous interest and was so pivotal in the world of the musical theatre.

To the amazing librarians and archivists: thank you! These include the extraordinary staff at the British Library, the Bristol Theatre Collection (Jill Sullivan), the Shubert Archive (Mark Swartz, Sylvia Wang and Arielle Dorlester), the Music Division at the Library of Congress (Paul Sommerfeld), the New York Public Library – New York Public Library for the Performing Arts (Doug Reside, Curator of the Billy Rose Theatre Collection, and especially Annemarie van Roessel, Assistant Curator of the Billy Rose Theatre Collection), the Schomburg Center for Research in Black Culture and the Astor Reading Room at the Stephen A. Schwarzman Building, Michael Owen of the Ira and Leonore Gershwin Trusts and the University of Missouri–Kansas City's Miller Nichols Library Interlibrary Loan department. I want to take a moment to also thank the cloakroom attendants and security officers, whose kindness and service is greatly appreciated. Special thanks to the New York Public Library for honouring me with a Short-Term Research Fellowship that made it possible to spend two weeks consulting materials in their brilliant collections.

At the University of Missouri–Kansas City, special thanks go to former dean Diane Petrella, former interim dean Andrew Granade and business officer Heather Swanson for their support and help with travel requests and reimbursements. I would also like to specifically acknowledge my gratitude to John and Roberta Graziano, and, of course, Gomer, for their hospitality, and to the staff at various cafes in Manby, Louth and Lincoln, where I spent many, many hours editing the manuscript.

Special thanks go to Kate Brett and Alex Wright at Cambridge University Press for their enthusiastic support of this project. To Abi

Sears and Nigel Graves at Cambridge University Press, Bharathan Sankar at Integra and the superb copyeditor Helen B. Cooper, many thanks for your help in bringing this book to fruition. Thank you also to all the wonderful and smart friends who have answered questions, asked questions, provided advice and encouragement, read portions of the manuscript and shared materials related to this magnificent year, including Brian Valencia, Dominic Broomfield-McHugh, Dominic Symonds, George Burrows, John and Roberta Graziano, John Koegel, Luca Cerchiari, Massimiliano Vitiello, Matteo Magarotto, Matteo Paoletti, Micaela Baranello, Orly Leah Krasner, Patricia and Frank Whyles, Paul Laird, Péter Bozó and Pierre Fargeton. Finally, thanks to my beloved wife Lynda and to Bridget and Bruno, our canine companions, for their love and support.

Chronology

1923

February

7   *Wildflower*, starring Edith Day, opens at the Casino Theatre in New York, where it plays until 29 March 1924, for a striking 477 performances.

May

30   *Stop Flirting*, a reworking of *For Goodness Sake*, featuring Adele and Fred Astaire, opens in London at the Shaftesbury Theatre, where, after moving twice, it closes on 15 December after 224 performances, then goes on tour in anticipation of returning to London the following spring.

July

2   George M. Cohan's *Little Nellie Kelly*, an American import, opens at the New Oxford Theatre in London, where it plays until 16 February 1924 for 263 performances before touring.

August

20   *Artists and Models*, the Shubert-produced revue famous for varying degrees of on-stage nudity, opens in New York at the Shubert Theatre, where it plays until 23 March 1924 before transferring to the Winter Garden Theatre, where it lasts until 17 May for a total of 312 performances.

September

3   *Poppy*, a musical comedy featuring W. C. Fields, opens at the Apollo
     Theatre in New York, where its highly successful 346-performance
     run lasts until 28 June 1924.

4   *London Calling!*, a revue produced by André Charlot and featuring
     songs by Noël Coward, who also appeared in the production along-
     side Gertrude Lawrence, opens in London at the Duke of York's
     Theatre, where it plays in various guises well into 1924.

5   *The Beauty Prize*, a musical comedy with book and lyrics by George
     Grossmith, Jr and P. G. Wodehouse and music by Jerome Kern, and
     starring Dorothy Dickson, Grossmith and Leslie Henson, begins its
     214-performance run at the Winter Garden Theatre in London, where
     it closes on 8 March 1924.

22   *Catherine*, an operetta-infused musical about the Russian Empress,
     with José Collins in the title role, opens at the Gaiety Theatre in
     London for a 217-performance run, closing on 24 March 1924.

October

17   *Doña Francisquita*, one of the most popular Spanish zarzuelas, opens
     at the Teatro Apolo in Madrid, leading to productions throughout
     Spain and South America in 1924.

20   Florenz Ziegfeld's *Follies of 1923* opens on Broadway at the New
     Amsterdam Theatre, where its star-studded glamour dazzles audi-
     ences for 233 performances, closing on 10 May 1924.

29   *Runnin' Wild*, a successor to the landmark Black musical *Shuffle
     Along*, written by its two lead actors, Flournoy Miller and Aubrey
     Lyles, opens at the New Colonial Theatre, where it plays 228 perform-
     ances, closing on 28 June 1924, and popularizing the Charleston
     dance on Broadway.

November

6   *Stepping Stones*, a fantasy extravaganza starring Fred Stone and his
     daughter Dorothy (in her stage debut), opens at Charles Dillingham's
     Globe Theatre in New York, where it plays 241 performances until 31
     May 1924, after which it goes on tour.

20   The Shubert-produced revue *Topics of 1923*, featuring Alice Delysia in
     a series of lavish gowns, opens at the Broadhurst Theatre, from where

it transfers to the Winter Garden Theatre on 14 January 1924 for the remainder of its 154-performance run.

23   *Il paese dei campanelli* (The Land of the Bells), an Italian operetta by Carlo Lombardo with music by Lombardo and Virgilio Ranzato, opens at the Teatro Lirico in Milan and eventually becomes a cornerstone of the Italian operetta repertory, with productions throughout 1924 and beyond.

27   *One Kiss*, an adaptation of the popular French *opérette Ta bouche*, with its sexual elements tamed by Clare Kummer, opens at the Fulton Theatre, where it plays ninety-five performances, closing on 16 February 1924.

December

2   *Dinah*, a Black musical starring Gertrude Saunders and introducing the Black Bottom dance, opens at the Lafayette Theatre in Harlem, where it continues to play into 1924.

20   *Madame Pompadour*, an adaptation of Leo Fall, Rudolph Schanzer and Ernst Welisch's Berlin original starring Evelyn Laye, begins its 469-performance run in London at Daly's Theatre, closing on 31 January 1925.

25   *The Rise of Rosie O'Reilly*, with book, lyrics and music by George M. Cohan, opens at the Liberty Theatre in New York, where it plays ninety-seven performances until 15 March 1924.

25   *Mary Jane McKane*, with music by Vincent Youmans and Herbert Stothart, opens at the Imperial Theatre, where it closes on 3 May 1924, after 151 performances.

26   *Almond Eye*, an Orientalist musical comedy, opens at the New Scala Theatre in London for a mere twenty-four performances, closing on 12 January 1924.

31   George M. Cohan opens at the Hudson Theatre in the title role of his latest play, *The Song and Dance Man*, for ninety-six performances, closing in March 1924.

31   Eddie Cantor stars in *Kid Boots*, which opens at the Earl Carroll Theatre in New York and clocks up 479 performances before closing on 21 February 1925.

1924

January

2   *Puppets*, a revue produced by André Charlot, opens at the Vaudeville Theatre in London, where it plays 254 performances before closing on 26 July.

9   *André Charlot's Revue of 1924* opens in New York at the Times Square Theatre with the US debuts of Gertrude Lawrence, Beatrice Lillie and Jack Buchanan, proving the commercial viability in New York of a distinctly English style of revue, with its 298-performance run that lasts until 20 September before going on tour.

15   An Italian-language version of *Madame Pompadour*, prepared and produced by the Compagnia Regini Lombardo, opens in Milan at the Teatro Dal Verme.

18   *Le leyenda del beso* (The Legend of the Kiss), a landmark in the Spanish zarzuela repertory, opens at the Teatro Apolo in Madrid.

21   *Lollipop*, a musical comedy by Zelda Sears and Vincent Youmans, opens at the Knickerbocker Theatre, where it plays for 152 performances, closing on 31 May.

21   *Sweet Little Devil*, a musical comedy starring Constance Binney, with music by George Gershwin, lyrics by Buddy De Sylva and book by Frank Mandel and Laurence Schwab, opens in New York at the Astor Theatre, moves to the Central Theatre and closes on 3 May after 120 performances.

25   *The Three Graces*, an English-language adaptation of Franz Lehár's *La Danza delle libellule/Der Libellentanz* (Dance of the Dragonflies), opens at the Empire Theatre in London for 123 performances.

30   The musical comedy *Moonlight* opens on Broadway at the Longacre Theatre for a 174-performance run that lasts until 28 June.

February

12   George Gershwin's *Rhapsody in Blue* has its premiere in Paul Whiteman's 'A Concert of Modern Music' at Aeolian Hall, New York, which also features jazz-band arrangements of music by Victor Herbert and Rudolf Friml, among others.

19   *The Chiffon Girl*, a rags-to-riches musical comedy, opens at the Lyric Theatre in New York and moves to other theatres before closing on 17 May after 103 performances.

28   *Gräfin Mariza* (Countess Maritza), an operetta with an evocative score by Emmerich Kálmán, opens at the Theater an der Wien in Vienna and becomes a classic in the operetta repertory.

March

4   *The Whirl of the World*, a large-scale revue produced by Albert de Courville, opens at the Palladium in London, where it plays 627 performances, and, after the usual changes in cast and material, closes on 21 March 1925.
8   *Cloclo*, an operetta with music by Franz Lehár, opens at the Bürgertheater in Vienna.
20   *Leap Year*, featuring the talents of comedian George Robey and the dazzling Gertrude Hoffman Girls, opens at the Hippodrome in London, where it plays 471 performances before closing on 20 December.
20   *Temple Belles*, with music by Richard Rodgers, lyrics by Lorenz Hart and direction by Herbert Fields, plays a single performance at the Park Avenue Synagogue in New York.
23   *The Prisoner of Zenda*, with music by Richard Rodgers and lyrics by Herbert Fields, is performed by the Benjamin School for Girls in New York, with future lyricist Dorothy Fields in the title role.
25   The Spanish zarzuela *Doña Francisquita* opens at the Teatro Victoria in Buenos Aires, Argentina, to inaugurate its South American tour.
27   *Vogues of 1924*, featuring the multiply talented Odette Myrtil, opens at the Shubert Theatre in New York and closes on 12 July after 114 performances, some of which are in a second edition billed as *Vogues and Frolics*.
28   Adele and Fred Astaire return to the London stage in *Stop Flirting*, their massive success from the previous year, at the Strand Theatre, for 194 performances, bidding farewell on 30 August, shortly after which they return to New York.
31   *Paradise Alley*, another rags-to-riches musical comedy, opens on Broadway at the Casino Theatre, moves to the Vanderbilt Theatre, and plays a total of sixty-four performances before closing on 24 May.

April

8   *Sitting Pretty*, a Broadway musical by 'Wodehouse, Bolton and Kern' of Princess Theatre fame, about a set of identical twins, opens on

Broadway at the Fulton Theatre, transfers to the Majestic Theatre and closes on 28 June after ninety-five performances.

16   *Our Nell*, a historical-themed musical about Nell Gwynne, opens in London at the Gaiety Theatre, starring José Collins.

19   *Cartoons*, a revue that features animated cartoons alongside live action, opens at the Criterion Theatre in London.

21   A revival of *To-night's the Night* opens at the Winter Garden Theatre in London with two of its original stars, George Grossmith, Jr and Leslie Henson, for 140 performances, closing on 16 August.

May

1   The revue *Come In* opens at the Queen's Theatre in London, where, despite substantial rewrites during its first week, it closes on 24 May after twenty-eight performances.

2   *Gosse de Riche* (Rich Kid), with a score by Maurice Yvain, opens in Paris.

5   *Peg o' My Dreams*, a musical version of *Peg o' My Heart*, opens at Jolson's 59th Street Theatre in New York and moves to the Imperial Theatre, where it closes on 31 May after just thirty-two performances.

12   *Plain Jane*, a literal rags-to-riches musical comedy, opens on Broadway at the New Amsterdam Theatre, where it proves itself a summer success and ends its New York run on 4 October after 168 performances.

12   *Toni*, a Ruritanian musical comedy featuring the dancing of Jack Buchanan, opens at the Shaftesbury Theatre in London for its 248-performance run, closing on 13 December.

13   *The Melody Man* – not a musical, but rather a play about musical style by Herbert Fields, Richard Rodgers and Lorenz Hart, and starring the producer Lew Fields – opens at the Central Theatre in New York, where it plays for eighty performances.

19   *I'll Say She Is*, a revue disguised as a musical comedy, featuring the Broadway debuts of the Marx Brothers, opens at the Casino Theatre, where it plays 313 performances, closing on 7 February 1925.

20   *Innocent Eyes*, a Shubert-produced revue, opens at the Winter Garden in New York, where it plays for 126 performances before going on tour.

20   *The Grand Street Follies*, a revue produced by the Neighborhood Playhouse in the Lower East Side, begins its 172-performance run, closing on 30 November.

21   *Round the Town*, a revue with material written mostly by journalists, opens on the Century Roof in New York and closes after thirteen performances.

21   *The Punch* Bowl, a revue that features an extended 'Punch and Judy Up-to-Date' sequence, opens in London at the Duke of York's Theatre, where, after transferring to His Majesty's Theatre, it closes on 22 August 1925, after 554 performances.

22   The Broadway revue *Keep Kool* opens at the Morosco Theatre and moves twice during its 148-performance run, closing on 27 September.

28   A revival of *The Merry Widow* opens in London at the Lyceum Theatre, where it charms audiences for 216 performances, closing on 29 November.

June

3   The lacklustre bedroom farce *Flossie* opens at the Lyric Theatre in New York, where it closes on 28 June after just thirty-one performances.

3   *Elsie Janis at Home* opens at the Queen's Theatre in London for a limited run.

11   The London revue *Yoicks!* opens at the Kingsway Theatre, where, with changes in material and performers, it closes on 14 February 1925, after 271 performances.

24   Ziegfeld's *Follies of 1924* opens at the New Amsterdam Theatre in New York, where it plays 295 performances until March 1925.

27   *The Street Singer*, a musical comedy starring Phyllis Dare and Harry Welchman, opens at the Lyric Theatre in London for 360 performances, closing on 3 May 1925.

30   The 1924 edition of *George White's Scandals* opens at the Apollo Theatre in New York, where it plays 196 performances, closing on 13 December.

July

3   *Midsummer Madness*, an experimental work starring Marie Tempest, opens at the Lyric, Hammersmith in London for 115 performances.

21   A British rags-to-riches musical comedy, *Tilly*, opens at the Empire Theatre in Leeds, after which it tours until early November.

30 *The Odd Spot*, a revue featuring Binnie Hale, opens in London at the Vaudeville Theatre, moves to the Little Theatre and closes on 25 October following 106 performances.

August

11 *Marjorie*, a musical comedy with a plethora of creators, opens at the Shubert Theatre on Broadway, where it plays 144 performances, closing on 13 December.
13 The musical comedy *No Other Girl* opens on Broadway at the Morosco Theatre, where its fifty-six-performance run ends on 27 September.
20 *The Dream Girl*, a fantasy-like work with music by Victor Herbert and book and lyrics by Rida Johnson Young, opens at the Ambassador Theatre in New York, where it plays for 117 performances until 29 November.
25 *Bye, Bye, Barbara*, a musical comedy whose name says it all, opens at the National Theatre in New York and closes on 6 September after just sixteen performances.

September

1 *The Chocolate Dandies*, a musical comedy with a score by Noble Sissle and Eubie Blake, opens at the New Colonial Theatre in New York, where it plays ninety-six performances, closing on 22 November.
1 The musical comedy *Top Hole* opens at the Fulton Theatre, moves to different theatres, closes on 29 November after 104 performances and returns to Broadway for sixteen additional performances during the Christmas and New Year holidays.
1 *Stepping Stones* returns to Broadway at the Globe Theatre, where it plays until 4 October.
2 *Rose-Marie*, the second-longest-running Broadway musical to open during the decade, opens at the Imperial Theatre, where its 557-performance run lasts until 16 January 1926.
2 The small-scale revue *The Co-Optimists* opens in its eighth incarnation at the Palace Theatre in London, where it plays 207 performances, closing on 7 March 1925.
3 *Be Yourself!*, a musical comedy starring Jack Donahue and Queenie Smith, opens in New York at the Sam H. Harris Theatre, where it closes on 22 November after ninety-three performances.

3   The Shubert-produced *Passing Show of 1924* opens at the Winter Garden Theatre in New York for 106 performances, closing on 22 November.

4   *Great Music*, not a musical but a play about a year in the life of a composer dramatized to the sounds of his own symphony, opens on Broadway at the Earl Carroll Theatre for forty-four performances.

4   The American import *Poppy* opens in an anglicized version at London's Gaiety Theatre for 188 performances, closing on 14 February 1925.

8   *Springtime*, an adaptation of Franz Lehár's one-act operetta *Frühling*, opens at London's Empire Theatre as part of a larger variety programme.

10   *Earl Carroll's Vanities* opens on Broadway at the Music Box Theatre, then moves to the producer's eponymous theatre, where it closes on 3 January 1925 after a total of 133 performances.

11   *Primrose*, a sprightly English musical comedy with a score by George Gershwin, opens at London's Winter Garden Theatre for 255 performances, closing on 25 April 1925.

16   *The Greenwich Village Follies* opens at the Shubert Theatre in New York, where, including a move to the Winter Garden Theatre, it plays for a total 131 performances, closing on 3 January 1925.

17   *Hassard Short's Ritz Revue* opens at the Ritz Theatre in New York, where it plays 109 performances, closing on 20 December.

23   *Charlot's Revue* opens at the Prince of Wales Theatre in London for a 518-performance run.

23   Lyricist Howard Dietz makes his credited Broadway debut in *Dear Sir*, with music by Jerome Kern, which closes on 4 October after just fifteen performances.

October

2   A revue produced by Albert de Courville in the style of Charlot, *The Looking Glass* opens in London at the Vaudeville Theatre for its fifty-six-performance run, closing on 15 November.

6   Ed Wynn opens in *The Grab Bag* at the Globe Theatre in New York for 184 performances, before it closes on 14 March 1925.

15   *Artists and Models of 1924* opens on Broadway at the Astor Theatre and moves to the Casino Theatre in February 1925, where it plays until 23 May 1925, for a total of 519 performances.

15 Edwin Justus Mayer's *The Firebrand*, not a musical but a play with a song with lyrics by Ira Gershwin and music by Robert Russell Bennett, opens in New York at the Morosco Theatre, where it lasts until May 1925 for 261 performances.

18 The Hungarian version of Emmerich Kálmán's *Gräfin Mariza*, *Marica grófnő*, opens at the Király Szíház (King's Theatre) in Budapest and quickly becomes part of the core Hungarian operetta repertory.

31 *Patricia*, a musical comedy starring Dorothy Dickson, opens at Her Majesty's Theatre in London, where its run, including a transfer to the Strand Theatre, lasts for 160 performances.

27 *André Charlot's Revue of 1924* begins its post-Broadway tour in Boston, featuring Beatrice Lillie and Gertrude Lawrence.

29 *Dixie to Broadway*, starring the dazzling Florence Mills, opens at the Broadhurst Theatre on Broadway, where it plays seventy-seven performances, closing in January 1925.

November

4 *Annie Dear*, featuring Billie Burke in the title role and with book, lyrics and music by Clare Kummer, opens on Broadway at the Times Square Theatre, where it runs for 103 performances, closing on 31 January 1925.

6 *Peter Pan*, starring former Ziegfeld favourite Marilyn Miller and produced by Charles B. Dillingham, opens at New York's Knickerbocker Theatre for 125 performances.

10 *The First Kiss*, a heavily revised English-language version of Pablo Luna's 1916 Spanish zarzuela *El asombro de Damasco*, opens at the New Oxford Theatre in London, where it plays six weeks before going on tour.

11 The New York production of *Madame Pompadour*, adapted by Clare Kummer, inaugurates the Martin Beck Theatre, where it closes on 17 January 1925, after eighty performances.

24 The musical comedy *My Girl* opens on Broadway at the Vanderbilt Theatre for a strong 291-performance run, closing on 1 August, 1925.

25 The musical comedy *The Magnolia Lady* opens at the Shubert Theatre in New York for a forty-seven-performance run, closing on 3 January, 1925.

25 The Russian–French revue *Le Chauve-Souris* opens in London at the Strand Theatre for a limited four-week engagement.

December

1   *Lady, Be Good!*, starring Adele and Fred Astaire as a sibling dance duo and with a score by George and Ira Gershwin, opens in New York at the Liberty Theatre, where it plays 330 performances until 12 September 1925.

1   *Princess April*, yet another rags-to-riches musical comedy, opens in New York at the Ambassador Theatre, where its twenty-four-performance run ends on 20 December.

1   The fourth and final edition of Irving Berlin's *Music Box Revue* opens in New York at the Music Box Theatre, where it closes on 9 May 1925, after 184 performances.

2   *The Student Prince in Heidelberg* opens in New York at Jolson's Theatre, eventually becoming the longest-running Broadway musical to open during the decade at 608 performances.

20 The famed Moulin Rouge reopens in Paris, following reconstruction after a devastating fire in 1915.

23 *Eva and Topsy*, a musical reworking of *Uncle Tom's Cabin*, opens at the Sam H. Harris Theatre on Broadway after a long and successful tour starring the Duncan Sisters and plays 165 performances until 9 May before returning to the road.

25 The musical comedy *Betty Lee* begins its Broadway run at the 44th Street Theatre, where it closes on 21 March 1925, after ninety-eight performances.

26 A fund-raiser for the Mineola Home, *Vanity Fair of 1924*, plays two performances (the second the following day) in the grand ballroom of the Waldorf-Astoria Hotel in New York.

29 *Seenianya Ptitza* (The Blue Bird), a Russian touring revue, opens in New York in repertory at the Frolic Theatre, above the New Amsterdam Theatre, where it is succeeded by a revised edition for a total run of eighty performances, closing on 7 March 1925.

Abbreviations

BL   British Library
BNA   British Newspaper Archive
LC   Library of Congress
LCP   Lord Chamberlain's Plays
M&M   Mander & Mitchenson Theatre Collection, Theatre Collection,
        University of Bristol (UK)
NYPL   New York Public Library

PART I

From One Year to the Next

1 | Legacies

New Year's Day, 1924. The American siblings Adele and Fred Astaire are in Birmingham, England, where audiences have been flocking to see them in *Stop Flirting*, the show that made them stars when it played in London the previous year. Evelyn Laye was establishing herself as London West End royalty in the title role of *Madame Pompadour*, while José Collins was continuing her reign as Empress Catherine of Russia in *Catherine*. In New York, three stars of the London stage – Gertrude Lawrence, Beatrice Lillie and Jack Buchanan – were preparing for their Broadway debuts in *André Charlot's Revue of 1924*. Eddie Cantor, a recent star of Ziegfeld's *Follies*, was revelling in the glow of his opening night performance in *Kid Boots* the previous evening. The dazzling Marilyn Miller, who had become a star thanks to Florenz Ziegfeld, had just gone through a very public departure from the powerful producer and, with her husband, was staying with actor John Barrymore in California, having attended his New Year's Eve party.[1] Nella Regini and Carlo Lombardo, managers of a prominent operetta company in Italy, were basking in the success of their original Italian operetta, *Il paese dei campanelli* (The Land of the Bells), and finalizing their next venture, an Italian version of the same *Madame Pompadour* that was thrilling audiences in London.

Although the musical theatre industry was enjoying renewed prosperity after the combined effects of the Great War and the Great Influenza Epidemic of 1918–1920, the remarkable events of 1924 truly stood out. This was an overlap of the old and the new, the past coming into the present and pointing toward the future. New stars were emerging as established ones were returning to the limelight, if they ever left. The same could be said for songwriters, librettists and producers. Genres such as the revue were likewise changing as impresarios were seeking new directions for their shows while maintaining, to varying degrees, the branding that had made them famous. The critic Brett Page wrote of this dynamism in September: 'There is no need

---

[1] Warren G. Harris, *The Other Marilyn: A Biography of Marilyn Miller* (New York: Arbor House, 1985), 120.

today to speak of 'the good old days of the stage'. The best days are here these flying minutes!'[2]

Musical theatre legends of the past were seeing their names on marquees and playbills in 1924. Among them were the illustrious West End star Marie Tempest, the Viennese operetta composer Franz Lehár, the Black songwriting team of Noble Sissle and Eubie Blake, the venerable composer Victor Herbert and the former vaudevillian Fred Stone. They were joined by an illustrious group of relative newcomers, several of whom, like the Astaires and Florence Mills, were making their debuts as lead performers on Broadway. Others were seen in supporting roles on stages in the USA and Europe, such as the Austrian film actor Hans Moser and the African American dancer and activist Josephine Baker.

The year was likewise significant for many of the creators. George Gershwin had three musicals open in 1924: two in New York and one in London. In February he introduced his *Rhapsody in Blue* in Paul Whiteman's legendary 'Experiment in Modern Music' concert. Sigmund Romberg and Rudolf Friml each had what would become their longest-running operetta (though neither was actually called an operetta at the time) open on Broadway: Romberg's *The Student Prince in Heidelberg* (aka *The Student Prince*) and Friml's *Rose-Marie*. These became the longest and second-longest-running musicals of any sort to open on Broadway during the decade.

It was also a time of passing. In Italy, the deaths in 1924 of opera composer Giacomo Puccini and actress Eleonora Duse had profound reverberations throughout the music and theatre realms, while in the USA the death of Victor Herbert marked the end of an era.

World events, some of which would have horrific consequences, were also taking place. In Germany, the American-led Dawes Plan, which restructured Germany's war reparations debt, was signed on 16 August 1924. The legislation provided further stability for the German currency and an ease in unemployment. As Peter Ross Range remarks, 'A corner had been turned; Germany seemed to be on the upswing.'[3] At the same time, Adolf Hitler was in prison writing *Mein Kampf*, and his trial for high treason (from 26 February to 1 April) attracted massive attention from the international media.[4] The decisive events of that year, according to Range, 'soon

[2] Brett Page, 'Broadway: A Glimpse of the New Plays, Picture Hits, Operas and Their Stars', syndicated column, *Birmingham News* (Alabama, USA), 28 September 1924, newspapers.com.
[3] Peter Ross Range, *1924: The Year that Made Hitler* (New York: Little, Brown and Co., 2016), 116.
[4] For more on the trial, including Hitler's testimony, see Range, *1924*, 125–183.

became part of the growing Hitler myth' and became incorporated into legend.[5]

In the United Kingdom, on 22 January, the Labour Party came to power for the first time under Ramsay MacDonald. MacDonald was a former coal miner, and this was the first time a working-class person had ever served as prime minister. Though the party was defeated in a general election in November, Labour proved it was 'fit to govern' and instituted some changes to help working-class people and improve public spaces. Not surprisingly, social class continued to be a significant plot point and character-defining trait in musicals of various sorts.

In the USA, Calvin Coolidge was president, having succeeded Warren G. Harding, who died in office the previous year. On 20 March, the state of Virginia passed the Virginia Sterilization Act of 1924, which became a model for eugenics- and racism-based sterilization, especially after its constitutionality was upheld by the US Supreme Court. The law allowed for the sterilization of institutionalized individuals deemed as 'afflicted with hereditary forms of insanity that are recurrent, idiocy, imbecility, feeble-mindedness or epilepsy'.[6] This overt endorsement of eugenics, or 'selective breeding', through which proponents believed that negative traits could be eliminated from the human gene pool, had a huge following in the 1920s. That same day, Virginia passed the 'Racial Integrity Act', which made it illegal for a white person in Virginia to marry anyone except another white person. Texas legislation from the same year excluded Blacks from voting in Democratic primaries in the state – a law declared unconstitutional and overturned by the US Supreme Court in 1927.[7] It would not be until forty years later that Virginia's Sterilization and Racial Integrity Acts were officially overturned by the US Supreme Court with the 1967 *Loving* v. *Virginia* case.

Against this racist backdrop emerged what became known as the Jazz Age. The cultural contrasts and contradictions were profound. With the Jazz Age came a sense of vitality, newness and invention. This sense of invention was certainly present in the realm of musical theatre.

The sexualized body and risqué humour were likewise being intensified and curtailed. Eddie Cantor made it one of his New Year's resolutions for 1924 to stop telling off-colour jokes in his performances, and Ed Wynn's

---

[5] Range, *1924*, 258.

[6] 'Virginia Sterilization Act of 3/20/1924'; document image available at https://dnalc.cshl.edu/view/11213-Virginia-Sterilization-Act-of-3-20-1924.html, accessed 2 December 2023.

[7] Gerald Leinwand, *1927: High Tide of the 1920s* (New York: Four Walls Eight Windows, 2001), 157.

The Grab Bag was lauded for not including anything that would make anyone blush. On the other hand, several series of revues, such as *Artists and Models*, played on the problematic commodification of the female body in various states of undress, as did some of the marketing for the Viennese operetta *Gräfin Mariza*. Sexual allure was at the heart of the Italian operetta *Il paese del campanelli* and was also featured prominently elsewhere.

This emphasis on the physical body coincides with the popularity of sport and physical fitness in the 1920s. In the USA, as John Bush Jones puts it, 'Both participatory and spectator sports caught the public imagination as never before.'[8] Golf was especially popular, with an estimated 2,000,000 golfers playing on 5,000 golf courses around the USA.[9] Sport also had its social implications, particularly in the British context, where, as Ben Macpherson asserts, 'a game of cricket or tennis on a village green . . . has come to be viewed as an idyllic embodiment of British civility'.[10] Values of 'fair play and camaraderie'[11] reigned supreme. Such sporting attitudes are reflected – or thwarted – in the numerous sport-themed musicals that were playing in 1924, including *Kid Boots* (golf), *Plain Jane* (boxing), *Top Hole* (golf again) and *Betty Lee* (foot race).

Musicals never play in temporal or geographical vacuums but form part of a continuum, one that is filled with various twists, turns and diversions. This was certainly the case in 1924. Echoes of the previous decade (and even earlier) rippled into the present and intrepid visions of the future were constantly bubbling and gurgling. More recent musicals continued to make their mark, among the most important of which was *Shuffle Along*.

Shuffle Along and Its Legacies in 1924

When *Shuffle Along* opened at the 63rd Street Music Hall on 23 May 1921, it was the result of a coming together of two pairs of Black creative artists: the vaudeville duo of Flournoy Miller (1885–1971) and Aubrey Lyles (1884–1932), and the songwriting team of Noble Sissle (1889–1975) and Eubie Blake (1887–1983). Miller and Lyles crafted the book and starred in

---

[8] John Bush Jones, *Our Musicals, Ourselves: A Social History of the American Musical Theatre* (Lebanon, NH: Brandeis University Press, 2003), 54.
[9] Jones, *Our Musicals, Ourselves*, 54.
[10] Ben Macpherson, *Cultural Identity in British Musical Theatre, 1890–1939: Knowing One's Place* (London: Palgrave Macmillan, 2018), 191.
[11] Macpherson, *Cultural Identity in British Musical Theatre*, 191.

the new endeavour, which included some of the classic routines they had already made famous in their stage personas of Steve Jenkins (Miller) and Sam Peck (Lyles). Sissle and Blake's sparkling songs provided a dynamic, often syncopated soundworld for the production (see Plate 1).

The story centred around a mayoral election in the fictional town of Jimtown, where the two candidates, Steve Jenkins and Sam Peck, run the local grocery store. Steve wins and appoints Sam chief of police. Corruption abounds until Harry Walton (played by Roger Matthews) comes along with a promise to clean things up. The town celebrates him in the show's hit song 'I'm Just Wild about Harry'. There's also a love story between Harry and Ruth Little (played by Gertrude Saunders) that provides the impetus for the duet 'Love Will Find a Way' and Ruth's 'I'm Craving for that Kind of Love'.

Writing in *The Gift of Black Folk: The Negroes in the Making of America*, published in 1924, the eminent Ghanian American historian, author and activist W. E. B. Du Bois (1868–1963) described how white authors were depicting Black men at the time: '[T]oday he is slowly but tentatively, almost apologetically rising – a somewhat deserving, often poignant, but hopeless figure; a man whose only proper end is dramatic suicide – physically or morally.'[12] In doing so, he was also describing how Black men needed to be depicted if a musical – even if created and performed by Blacks – was going to draw white audiences. Such is the case with Steve, Sam and Harry in *Shuffle Along*. To their white audience, Steve and Sam's forced departures from Jimtown constitute their social suicides, while Harry represents what Du Bois calls an 'exceptional case'[13] not only because of his professional integrity but also – more importantly – because he is the show's romantic leading man. To have a Black character who was not a comic but rather one who experienced real human emotion was something novel on white stages.

Shuffle Along looked simultaneously forward and backward. Theatre historian David Krasner sees the musical as combining an artistic goal to depict 'progressively minded musical characters with integrity and capable of romance' with a commercial need 'to appeal successfully to white nostalgia for minstrel humor and Dixie'.[14] It is the latter dimension that

[12] W. E. B. Du Bois, *The Gift of Black Folk: The Negroes in the Making of America* [originally published 1924] (Garden City Park: Square One, 2009), 138–139.

[13] Du Bois, *The Gift of Black Folk*, 139.

[14] David Krasner, '*Shuffle Along* and the Quest for Nostalgia: Black Musicals of the 1920s', in *A Beautiful Pageant: African American Theatre, Drama, and Performance in the Harlem Renaissance, 1910–1927* (New York: Palgrave Macmillan, 2002), 240.

is evident in such racist practices as blackface. (Black artists as well as white ones did this as part of performance expectations for white audiences.) There were songs with racially demeaning titles such as 'If You've Never Been Vamped by a Brown Skin, You've Never Been Vamped at All', which Miller and Lyles performed in blackface backed by the female chorus.

The foxtrot was one of the most popular dances in 1921, and it is no coincidence that 'I'm Just Wild about Harry', written for *Shuffle Along*, is a foxtrot. The step is thought to have begun with Harry Fox (1882–1959), a vaudeville performer. In the early twentieth century, there were strict rules about women moving about on stage if they were not fully clothed. Fox's idea was that the scantily clad women would remain still, and he would trot around them, at one step per beat, hence fox's trot or foxtrot. Dancer, choreographer and dance historian Robert Hylton describes the foxtrot, once it entered the domain of white ballrooms, as a 'smooth partner dance characterized by long, flowing movements. . . . [I]t proved to be a great accompaniment to the sounds of ragtime.'[15] The syncopation of ragtime, where the emphasized beats in the melody do not necessarily align with those in the lowest-sounding part, the bass line, along with a pronounced emphasis on uneven rhythmic figures (also called 'dotted rhythms' because of how they are notated) became among the most distinguishing features of popular musical theatre song in the 1920s. These so-called jazz rhythms inspired a slew of new dances drawn from Black culture that white dancers performed in ballrooms, on boardwalks and on stage.

This appropriation forms a critical part of what Matthew D. Morrison calls Blacksound, which he defines as 'the sonic and embodied legacy of blackface performance as the origin of all popular music, entertainment, and culture in the United States.'[16] Considering that *Shuffle Along* featured Black actors in blackface as well as songs that became hits in the white commercial marketplace through recordings and live performances, and especially how 'I'm Just Wild about Harry' became associated with US President Harry S. Truman in the 1940s and 1950s, what Morrison writes about Blacksound as an analytical tool can be applied to many of the musicals that were playing in 1924.

Shuffle Along was an unqualified success in the white theatrical market-place and a key player in the legacy of Blacksound. The musical's popularity

---

[15] Robert Hylton, *Dancing in Time: The History of Moving and Shaking* (London: British Library, 2022), 78.

[16] Matthew D. Morrison, 'Race, Blacksound, and the (Re)Making of Musicological Discourse', *Journal of the American Musicological Society* 72, no. 3 (2019): 789.

inspired a string of Black musicals that perhaps oversaturated the white theatrical market to the point where, by late 1923 and into 1924, Black musicals were no longer holding the same drawing power for white audiences they once did.[17] As a result, Black artists wanting to write for white Broadway were having to create shows that would be funnier and faster than anything else on offer.[18]

Sissle and Blake and Miller and Lyles did just that. The creators of *Shuffle Along* wanted to capitalize on the sensation they themselves helped create. They did not do this as a foursome, however, for each team went its separate way. Sissle and Blake continued touring with *Shuffle Along*, doing their best to sustain the show's momentum. Miller and Lyles, meanwhile, signed on with the ambitious young producer George White (1891–1968), one of several white impresarios who wanted to capitalize on the popularity of Black musicals. The result was *Runnin' Wild*. For their new show, Miller and Lyles came up another misadventure featuring Steve Jenkins and Sam Peck. The duo is again forced to flee Jimtown, ending up in St. Paul, Minnesota, where they almost freeze to death in the harsh winter, before returning to Jimtown disguised as mediums. For the songs, White engaged the top-notch Black songwriting team of composer James P. Johnson (1894–1955) and lyricist Cecil Mack (1873–1944).

Mediums and spirituality were extremely important cultural themes in the 1920s. Especially after the deaths of millions during the Great War and the influenza pandemic that followed, making contact with the dead reached fever pitch in the decade. Among the most famous promoters of spiritualism was Sir Arthur Conan Doyle (1859–1930), creator of Sherlock Holmes. Doyle's *The Coming of the Fairies* (1922) and *The Land of Mist* (1926) reflect widely held beliefs of the time. Steve and Sam, therefore, are playing into a very lucrative subterfuge.

Runnin' Wild began its pre-Broadway tryout at the Howard Theatre in Washington, DC on 23 August 1923, and opened on Broadway at the New Colonial Theatre on 29 October 1923, where it continued until late June 1924. The New Colonial Theatre was a recently converted vaudeville house at 62nd Street and Broadway, north of the Times Square area and somewhat removed from the principal Broadway houses.

The score included many delights, but the two standout songs were 'Old Fashioned Love' and 'Charleston'. The moderately paced 'Old Fashioned

---

[17] For a discussion of some of these shows, see Allen Woll, *Black Musical Theatre: From 'Coontown' to 'Dreamgirls'* (Baton Rouge: Louisiana State University Press, 1989), 75–84.

[18] Richard Carlin and Ken Bloom, *Eubie Blake: Rags, Rhythm, and Race* (New York: Oxford University Press, 2020), 186.

Love' is a lyrical gem performed in the show by a vocal trio. Of the three singers who introduced it – Ina Duncan, Adelaide Hall and Arthur Porter – only Adelaide Hall (1901–1993), a member of the original *Shuffle Along* cast, went on to have a major singing career (see Figure 1.1). Concerning the song itself, by February 1924 no fewer than four different renditions had been recorded. Its popularity and appeal were immense. Leading the way was the white popular singer Frank Crumit, who recorded it on 7 September 1923, while the show was still in tryouts. An example of a white singer taking a song from Black creators and removing its context, an aspect of Morrison's Blacksound paradigm, Crumit's version was released in November, shortly after *Runnin' Wild* opened on Broadway.[19] In December, another white singer, Cliff Edwards, also known as 'Ukelele Ike', recorded the song and famously included scat singing in his rendition.

Figure 1.1 Adelaide Hall, one of the stars of *Runnin' Wild*.

[19] Columbia A3997.

Black artists also recorded 'Old Fashioned Love.' In the recording made by Alberta Hunter and the Elkins-Payne Jubilee Quartette, the quartet's close harmonies add poignancy to the song's nostalgic tone, and none other than Sissle and Blake recorded it in what became a showpiece for Blake's fine pianism and Sissle's splendid tenor voice.[20]

The show's most famous and influential dance number, 'Charleston', was – somewhat surprisingly, given its future fame – overlooked by critics early on. The dance appears at the end of the first act and was led by the teenager Elisabeth Welch (1904–2003), playing the same Ruth Little character who had been the romantic lead in *Shuffle Along* (see Figure 1.2). Welch, like her co-star Adelaide Hall, would go on to become one of the most important popular singers of the twentieth century. Both women, African Americans, spent most of their lives and careers in the United Kingdom, where they were regarded as national treasures. In addition to leading 'Charleston', Welch sang as a member of the 'Song Birds Quartette' in Act 2, offering her a chance to display her vocal talents as well as her terpsichorean ones.

When *Runnin' Wild* opened, the Charleston was already well on its way to becoming an embodiment of the entire 1920s. Though *Runnin' Wild* was not the first Broadway musical to feature the dance (there's debate on which show can actually claim that title, but *Liza* from 1922 is a likely contender[21]), it was this particular musical, in the words of the Black cultural historian, author and activist James Weldon Johnson, that 'started the dance on its world-encircling course.'[22]

The Charleston, according to Hylton, 'is not the most complicated of dances. ... it is all about style: a full-bodied rhythmic dance that oozes character, head to shoulders, torso, knees, feet and everything in between.'[23] Part of its immense popularity developed because, as Hylton states, it 'was a dance for people of all abilities.'[24] Like most dances, it has multiple origin stories, but what these tales have in common are the dance's

---

[20] Cliff Edwards recorded his version on 10 December 1923 (Pathé Actuelle 021097), Alberta Hunter and the Elkins-Payne Jubilee Quartette in February 1924 (Paramount 12093) and Sissle and Blake on 8 January 1924 (Victor 19253–A).

[21] Marshall Stearns, *Jazz Dance: The Story of American Vernacular Dance* (New York: Macmillan, 1968; reprint ed., New York: Da Capo, 1994), 144; Liza Gennaro, *Making Broadway Dance* (New York: Oxford University Press, 2022), 14.

[22] James Weldon Johnson, *Black Manhattan* (New York: Knopf, 1940 (first published 1930); reprint ed., New York: Arno Press and The New York Times, 1968), 190.

[23] Hylton, *Dancing in Time*, 112.   [24] Hylton, *Dancing in Time*, 119.

Figure 1.2 Elisabeth Welch and chorus in *Runnin' Wild*. Photo by White Studio. ©Billy Rose Theatre Division, The New York Public Library for the Performing Arts.

African American roots.[25] The Charleston, with its flamboyant limb crossing, could be danced as a solo dance or with a partner. Fundamentally, it represented a new, modern world filled with energy and possibilities.

For the white flappers – with their bobbed hair, headbands and knee-length dresses – the Charleston was a vibrant symbol of new opportunities and new roles in a rapidly changing world. The flapper, as Gerald Leinwand describes her, was 'radiant, energetic, volatile, voluble, brazen.'[26] The Charleston, therefore, held strong cultural capital in 1920s' white popular culture.

[25] See Ksenia Parkhatskaya, 'The History of the Charleston Dance', 23 August 2020, Ksenia's Secrets of Solo, https:secretsofsolo.com/2020/08/the-history-of-the-charleston-dance/, accessed 6 July 2021.

[26] Leinwand, *1927*, 173.

When the dance appeared in *Runnin' Wild*, the accompanying chorus, 'The Dancing Redcaps', clapped their hands and stamped their feet to create a series of complex layered rhythms that Johnson described as 'electrical'.[27] This use of the Black body brought to the fore aspects of buck dancing, which Hylton describes as 'a rhythmic stomping of the feet danced by slaves.'[28] It also pays homage to the Charleston's ancestor, the juba, with its stomping and slapping of the limbs and torso.[29] When the Charleston migrated to white dance floors, these defining visceral aspects of the dance, ones tightly intertwined with the legacies of enslaved peoples, were excised.

The Charleston's closest rival in popularity as a dance in the 1920s was the Black Bottom, another dance with African American roots. Like the Charleston, the exact origins of the Black Bottom are somewhat nebulous, though it is thought that the name comes from an area in Detroit, Michigan.[30] Similar to the Charleston, it can be danced as either a solo or a partner dance. The Black Bottom, with its side-to-side rocking motion, joined the Charleston on white ballroom floors as an emblematic step of the decade.

The Black Bottom, not surprisingly, was also featured in a musical that opened in 1923 and continued into 1924, but not one that played in the greater Times Square area. *Dinah*, the show that introduced the Black Bottom, opened at the Lafayette Theatre in Harlem on 2 December. In 1913, the Lafayette had become the first major theatre to desegregate.

The Black newspaper *The New York Age* called *Dinah* a 'typical Irvin C. Miller show', referring to its producer. Irvin C. Miller (1884–1967) was an actor who, after appearing in his brother's Flournoy's shows – the same Flournoy Miller of *Shuffle Along* and *Runnin' Wild* fame – toured on the vaudeville circuit. When it came to producing Black musicals, according to Bernard L. Peterson, Jr, Miller 'gave Black audiences exactly what they wanted when they came to the theatre.'[31] According to a writer for *The New York Age*, this meant 'a large and beautiful chorus, a waltz number and a lot of jazz, and the ghost scene'[32] – the last recalling the popularity of spiritualism at the time.

Miller came up with *Dinah*'s slight plot along with its requisite improbable twist. Dinah is set to receive an inheritance, which she plans to invest

---

[27] Johnson, *Black Manhattan*, 190.   [28] Hylton, *Dancing in Time*, 40.
[29] Hylton, *Dancing in Time*, 44.   [30] Hylton, *Dancing in Time*, 114.
[31] Bernard L. Peterson, Jr., *Profiles of African American Stage Performers and Theatre People, 1816–1960* (Westport: Greenwood, 2001), 181.
[32] 'At the Lafayette Theatre', *New York Age*, 8 December 1923, newspapers.com.

in a dance hall, but it gets lost in a haunted house (hence the chance to include one of Miller's popular ghost scenes). Because of the centrality of a dance hall to the plot, the show offered plenty of opportunities to showcase the latest moves, including the Black Bottom. Ethel Ridley, playing Corine, led the sixty-member cast in the new dance. Lt. Tim Brymn (1881–1946) and Sidney Bechet (1897–1959) crafted the songs for the show, which included the evocative 'Ghost of the Blues'. The song quickly found its way into the recording studio and likewise to turntables. Prion's New Orleans Orchestra recorded it in February 1924,[33] as did Fletcher Henderson with his orchestra in March[34] and Eva Taylor, accompanied by Clarence Williams's Harmonizers, in May.[35] It is the only song from the show to have achieved renown outside the theatre.

It was not just Ridley leading the Black Bottom that is a reason to remember this notable show. Playing the title role was Gertrude Saunders (1903–1991), who originated the role of Ruth Little, the romantic lead, in *Shuffle Along*. If Saunders's performances of songs in *Dinah* were anything like her recordings, audiences would have been in the presence of a remarkable female talent.[36] Her distinctive timbre, at once piercing and resonant, and especially her gifts at vocal improvisation and her uncanny ability to utter unique vocal tones, would have given her performances an unmistakably personal imprint.

The plots of *Dinah* and *Runnin' Wild*, as well as that of *Shuffle Along*, were necessarily thin. In many ways, the plot's purpose was less to tell a story than to hold together an entertaining array of skits, songs and dance spectacles. If such plots are minimized or even suppressed, one could say that we have crossed a soft boundary into the glamorous world of the revue.

The Glamour of the Revue

Among the most popular and most prolific types of musical theatre to appear on Broadway in the 1920s was the revue. With a spelling borrowed from the French, these lavishly staged productions – which included the likes of *Follies*, produced by Florenz Ziegfeld; *The Passing Show*, produced

---

[33] Columbia 99 D.   [34] Emerson 10744.
[35] OKeh 8145, recorded 16 May 1924, released July 1924.
[36] Saunders recorded two songs from *Shuffle Along* in April 1921: 'I'm Carving for that Kind of Love' and 'Daddy Won't You Please Come Home', released on OKeh 8004. Other recordings include 'Potomac River Blues', which she recorded in 1923 and which was released on Victor 19159.

by the brothers J. J. and Lee Shubert; and *Scandals*, produced by George White (the producer of *Runnin' Wild*) – were known for their large choruses of physically 'idealized' women who paraded around an expansive stage in revealing costumes amidst glamourous sets. Many provided a review of the current theatrical season, hence the title of the genre, but they became especially famous for their star performers and problematic commodification of female bodies. New material appeared every year, so many revues included the year in their titles (e.g., *The Passing Show of 1923*, *The Passing Show of 1924*). These annual versions were referred to as editions, a term that continues to be used when discussing revues. Changes also took place during the run of a particular edition as various stars left or joined the production.

Several important revues opened in 1923 and continued into 1924, including the 1923 edition of Ziegfeld's *Follies*. It opened at the New Amsterdam Theatre on 20 October and played until May 1924, when it went on tour.[37] (Pre- and post-Broadway tours were typical of musical theatre at the time, including revues.) Central to the *Follies* were the glorious costumes that adorned the female chorus. The story of this dimension of Ziegfeld's brand can be traced back to the influential British fashion designer Lucile (1862–1965), whose reputation was such that she would be recognized by only a single first name. Born Lucy Christiana Sutherland, she became Lady Duff-Gordon after marrying Cosmo Duff-Gordon in 1900. Lucile added theatrical flair to her London showroom when she installed rich carpets, curtains and a limelight-lit stage. She became even more renowned when she hired six women, whom she called 'mannequins', to wear her creations.[38] Lucile began working with Ziegfeld in 1915, and her 'fashion show' approach to not only the gowns themselves but also to how the women moved while wearing them remained a constituent part of the *Follies* brand long after her departure in 1921. Ned Weyburn's slow-moving choreography and Joseph Urban's iconic stair-centred sets, defining features of the *Follies*, were in many ways extensions of Lucile's fashion-show aesthetic.

The *Follies of 1923* opened with a number that showcased these trade-mark Ziegfeld features. Called 'Glorifying the Girls', even its title was a reminder of Ziegfeld's marketing tagline: 'Glorifying the American Girl'. What followed was a series of songs and sketches that featured five

---

[37] Ziegfeld chose the name *Follies* for his series after the Folies-Bergère in Paris.

[38] Marliss Schweitzer, *When Broadway Was the Runway: Theatre, Fashion, and American Culture* (Philadelphia: University of Pennsylvania Press, 2009), 195.

Ziegfeld stars: Fanny Brice (1891–1951), whose sense of physical comedy was unequalled and who delighted audiences with her Yiddish accent and general zaniness; Eddie Cantor (1892–1964), known for his racist blackface antics; Roy Cropper (1896–1954), a singer who would eventually make his career in operetta; Brooke Johns (1893–1987), a singer known for his ragtime-style songs; and Ann Pennington (1893–1971), an exquisite dancer and singer. The quintet, along with the chorus, offered a standard mix of songs, skits and dances.

This is exactly what critics then and commentators now agree was wrong with the show: a lack of originality and a stifling reliance on its past.[39] The spectacle of the series had become, in some ways, a victim of its own success. One aspect was novel, however. A special 'shadowgraph', which required audience members to wear special 'Follies-Scope' glasses, produced a 3-D effect in which shadows seemed to leap over the footlights into the audience. Laurens Hammond, the same person who invented the Hammond Organ, designed and patented the unusual visual apparatus.

As was typical for the *Follies*, a variety of composers and lyricists appeared on the bill. Among the contributors to the 1923 edition was the team of Harry Tierney and Joseph McCarthy, known for their gently syncopated songs such as the foxtrot 'Take, Oh, Take Those Lips Away', to which Johns sang and Pennington danced. Cropper showed his vocal prowess in lyrical numbers by operetta-leaning composers Rudolf Friml and Victor Herbert.[40]

While *Follies* was treading the all-too-familiar, other revues were forging new directions. Among these was the Shubert-produced *Artists and Models*, the first edition of which appeared in 1923 and continued, like Ziegfeld's *Follies*, into 1924 (see Plate 2). This series in particular very much emphasized the visual, as its title suggests, but in a different way than the *Follies*. The goal of *Artists and Models*, according to one reviewer, was 'to blaze a new trail in the matter of undraping the feminine form'.[41] *Artists and Models* also represented a different approach to the genesis of a revue. Rather than a theatrical producer (e.g., Ziegfeld) assembling a team of

---

[39] Ann Ommen van der Merwe, *The Ziegfeld Follies: A History in Song* (Lanham: Scarecrow, 2009), 172.

[40] Friml's contribution was 'My Lady Fair', a texted version of his 'Chanson' from 1920 that surged in popularity in various guises throughout the next two decades, including 'Donkey Serenade' in the 1937 film *The Firefly*. Victor Herbert's 'I'd Love to Waltz through Life with You' is as sweeping as its title suggests.

[41] '"Artists and Models" Has Much Beauty', *New York Times*, 16 October 1924.

creators and performers to realize their vision, *Artists and Models* originated not in the theatre industry but instead in the visual arts.

In 1901, the Society of Illustrators was founded in New York. Its mission, according to itself, was to 'promote generally the art of illustration and to hold exhibitions from time to time'.[42] In addition to curating displays in prominent New York galleries, the society also produced a series of what it called Illustrators Shows, otherwise known as 'Girlie Shows'. Society members – that is, the artists themselves – wrote the skits and songs and performed their own material, often with the assistance of their models: hence, 'artists and models'. The society also designed and built their own sets. One of its members, Watson Barrett, was the principal set designer for the Shuberts, and it was through him, in May 1923, that the group was able to secure the Century Roof Theatre for their show. (Roof theatres – which, as the name implies, were located above Broadway theatres – were extremely popular in the hot and humid New York summer evenings.) The Shuberts saw the production, liked it, secured the rights for the skits and used the rooftop production as the basis for what would become their latest series of revues: *Artists and Models*.[43]

The new revue had its much-anticipated Broadway opening at the Shubert Theatre on 20 August 1923. Shubert staff writers such as playwright and lyricist Harold Atteridge (1886–1938) and composer Jean Schwartz (1878–1956) were credited on the playbill, along with a long list of 'Contributing artists, authors and composers'. These were the members of the Society of Illustrators whose material appeared in the show. As was typical for a Shubert revue, the production carried the line 'Entire production under the personal supervision of J. J. Shubert'. In March 1924, the production moved to the Winter Garden Theatre, the Shuberts' principal venue for revues, where it closed in May before embarking on a highly successful tour.

The opening night audience, according to *The New York Times*, gave 'appropriate gasps' when they realized that the models who were moving slowly across the stage were unclothed from the waist up. As one critic noted, 'the absence of what has hitherto been regarded as the minimum in adornment for stage models was decidedly conspicuous'.[44] Among the most memorable sketches was 'All Wet',[45] a burlesque, or comic reworking,

[42] Society of Illustrators – History of the Society. https://societyillustrators.org/about/history-of-the-society/. Accessed 22 November 2021.

[43] Society of Illustrators – History of the Society.

[44] '"Artists and Models" in Scant Adornment', *New York Times*, 21 August 1923.

[45] By Harold Atteridge and Harry Wagstaff Gribble.

of Somerset Maugham's short story 'Rain' and its popular theatrical adaptation by John Colton and Clemence Randolph, which was playing on Broadway at the time. 'Rain' concerns a missionary on a South Pacific island who tries to reform a prostitute and, according to the playbill, 'soon succumbs to the lure of her easy virtues'. During the revue's post-Broadway tour, the sketch often drew the ire of local censors, some of whom demanded its removal. Famously playing the prostitute, in drag, was the middle-aged George Rosener (1879–1945), who became a prolific film actor and screenwriter in the 1930s.

Another Shubert-produced revue that opened in 1923 and continued into 1924 was *Topics of 1923*. *Topics* was almost a polar opposite to *Artists and Models*, for dress rather than undress defined its visual aesthetic. Though critics noted its lack of real humour, the production was redeemed by its leading lady, Alice Delysia (1889–1979), a French actress and London revue star. Delysia captivated audiences with her brilliant and dazzling gowns. She shared accolades with the acrobatic dancing of Nat Nazarro and a spectacular diamond-studded Act 1 finale.[46] The revue opened on 20 November 1923 at the Broadhurst Theatre and transferred to the Winter Garden Theatre, where it played until March, when *Artists and Models* moved in.

Revues were also popular in London. Rather than relying on the sensuality and splash of their Broadway cousins, British revues focused on satire, modesty and intimacy. David Linton aptly describes what made the revues that played in London's West End in particular so distinctive:

Often politically conservative, protective of the status quo and concerned with appealing to a mainstream audience, revue was highly sensitive to the status and position of Britain and London and cultivated a sense of itself as the defender of a colonial empire and, at the same time, the centre of a cosmopolitan culture competing with other metropolitan centres such as Paris, Berlin and New York.[47]

This aesthetic is readily apparent in *London Calling!*, which opened at the Duke of York's Theatre on 4 September 1923 and played well into 1924. The show's title, a call sign for BBC radio, connected the revue directly to the British capital and to technology. The revue opened with a scene that featured the same Shadowgraph technology that Ziegfeld included in his 1923 *Follies*. *London Calling!*, though, was much more than a display of theatrical technology. Produced by the French-born impresario André

---

[46] 'Triumph of Gowns in "Topics of 1923"', *New York Times*, 21 November 1923.
[47] David Linton, *Nation and Race in West End Revue, 1910–1930* (London: Palgrave Macmillan, 2021), 10–11.

Charlot (1882–1956), the show included among its stars Noël Coward (1899–1973) and Gertrude Lawrence (1898–1952), who were appearing together on stage for the first time. Theirs would become one of the most celebrated theatrical partnerships of all time. Coward contributed nearly all the songs to the show, with one notable exception. That was the final duet for himself and Lawrence, 'You Were Meant for Me', which was by none other than the musical creators of *Shuffle Along*, Sissle and Blake. While one might expect the song to be along the lines of *Shuffle Along*, or at least to emulate the various syncopated songs in vogue, 'You Were Meant for Me' is a moderately paced, basically diatonic tune, virtually void of syncopation, that exudes a sense of stasis and repose. Coward's songs which Lawrence brought to life in the show included 'Russian Blues' and 'Parisian Pierrot', the latter of which became one of the singer's standards. Lawrence left the show at the end of November 1923, and a second edition opened on 1 December. Lawrence departed for a very good reason: she was going to New York to star in *André Charlot's Revue of 1924*. A third edition of *London Calling!* opened on 19 February 1924, by which time Maisie Gay was the only star of the original cast still with the production.

2 | Transnational Connections

The transnational nature of the musical theatre business in the 1920s operated within a complex web of producers, stars, agents, creators, publishers, recording companies, film studios and more that criss-crossed domains, both geographic and medial.[1] In addition to commercial aspects, many musicals afforded representations of other countries and cultures. While such depictions could easily move into realms of exoticism and include highly racist aspects, many imagined other white, European locales.

American Musical Comedies in London

The line between revue (see Chapter 1) and musical comedy can be extremely porous. Some revues have a semblance of a unifying plot, while many musical comedies offer only minimal storylines. An unnamed critic writing in September 1924, however, noted a particular distinction: 'The difference between a "revue" and a "musical comedy" is considerable. A normal week's gross receipts for the "Follies" is $42,000. The average weekly box office receipts of an ordinary musical comedy is $10,000.'[2] This keen observation helps account for why revues were so popular, and also why producers were eager to mount musical comedies that would be far from 'ordinary'. British and American producers especially kept their eyes on what was happening 'across the pond', hoping to spot something that would attract audiences to their theatres.

---

[1] For more on the topic, see Christopher B. Balme, *The Globalization of Theatre 1870–1930: The Theatrical Networks of Maurice E. Bandmann* (Cambridge: Cambridge University Press, 2019); Nic Leonhardt, *Theatre Across Oceans: Mediators of Transatlantic Exchange, 1890–1925* (Cham: Springer Nature Switzerland/Palgrave Macmillan, 2021); and Matteo Paoletti, *A Huge Revolution of Theatrical Commerce: Walter Mocchi and the Italian Musical Theatre Business in South America* (Cambridge: Cambridge University Press, 2020).

[2] The NEA Play Jury, 'It Is a Gay Time for the Bald-Headed Business Man', syndicated column, *Muncie Evening Post* (Indiana, USA), 23 September 1924, newspapers.com.

One case in point is *Stop Flirting*, which when it played on Broadway in 1922 was called *For Goodness Sake*. With a book by Fred Jackson, lyrics by Arthur Jackson and music by William Daly and Paul Lannin, the show became famous because of its secondary leads: the Nebraska-born dancing and singing siblings Adele (1896–1981) and Fred Astaire (1889–1987). Beyond the songs of the principal creators, the score also featured two songs, 'Someone' and 'Tra-la-la', by another pair of siblings, George and Ira Gershwin (Ira writing under the pseudonym Arthur Francis). *For Goodness Sake* was a modest success, but when it crossed the Atlantic and opened at the Shaftesbury Theatre on 30 May 1923 with a new title and Fred Thompson's anglicized book, the musical became a runaway hit and the Astaires were catapulted to stardom.

When *Stop Flirting* arrived in London, its setting was moved from Long Island to a glamorous English country estate. The Astaires played Teddy Lawrence and Susan Hayden (see Plate 3), an American couple (yes, as odd as it seems, the siblings played a romantic couple) who are guests at a weekend fête hosted by Perry Reynolds (played by the comically entrancing Jack Melford) and his fiancée, Vivian Marden (played by Marjorie Gordon). Vivian likes to flirt – it seems to be her favourite pastime – and she begins to do so unashamedly with Teddy. To test Vivian's fidelity, Perry fakes his own death in a plane crash. Vivian, keenly aware that Perry is alive and intent on spying on her, only increases her flirtations.

The most significant change to the show was the addition of another sparkling song by George Gershwin, this one with lyrics by Ira Gershwin and Buddy De Sylva: 'I'll Build a Stairway to Paradise'. As Fred Astaire recalled about the suave number with its bluesy harmonies, 'This pepped up our show'.[3] The song had been featured in George White's *Scandals of 1922*, and its presence in *Stop Flirting* is another example of the permeability between revues and musical comedies.

But it was the performances of the Astaires, especially Adele, that made the show shine. The noted critic St John Ervine opined, 'Miss Astaire has a tiny little American voice which first of all vaguely irritates you and then becomes irresistible. I could willingly have watched Miss Astaire dancing for the whole evening.'[4] Because of theatres being already booked and not anticipating the show's immense popularity, the production had to move twice: first to the Queen's Theatre, and then to the Strand Theatre. Its London run ended on 15 December only because the Strand was already

---

[3] Fred Astaire, *Steps in Time: An Autobiography* (New York: Harper & Brothers, 1959), 106.

[4] Astaire, *Steps in Time*, 112.

booked – London's popular panto season was about to begin – and no other theatre was available. Nonetheless, *Stop Flirting* lasted more than twice as long as *For Goodness Sake*. Not allowing itself to be shuttered, *Stop Flirting* packed up and went to Birmingham, where it played for five highly successful weeks at the Prince of Wales's Theatre. There was every hope that it would return to London the following spring, which it indeed did.

On 18 October 1923, the Astaires travelled to the HMV Studios in Hayes, Middlesex, where they recorded two songs from *Stop Flirting*: 'The Whichness of the Whatness' and 'Oh, Gee! Oh, Gosh!'[5] These recordings offer aural glimpses into the brilliance of their performance and why London audiences flocked to see these two Americans. The fast-paced patter of 'The Whichness of the Whatness', which continually shifts between rhythmic speech and song, bubbles with sheer joy, as does the orchestra (conducted by George W. Byng) in the dance sequence that concludes the number. By contrast, the lilting lyricism inherent in 'Oh, Gee! Oh, Gosh!' reveals the innate sense of musical line and rounded vocal timbres that made the siblings such successes on the musical stage.

Another show that played on Broadway in 1922 and transferred to London the next year was *Little Nellie Kelly*. The legendary George M. Cohan (1878–1942) wrote the book, music and lyrics, as well as directing and producing it on Broadway. The English producer Charles B. Cochran brought the show to London, hoping to make it a hit there. He succeeded in this regard, for *Little Nellie Kelly* played an impressive 263 performances at the New Oxford Theatre (2 July 1923 to 16 February 1924) before going on tour. The story concerned Nellie (played by the single-named June), a young shopgirl at a New York department store who has two suitors: the wealthy but womanizing Jack Lloyd (played by Roy Royston), and the working-class and good-hearted Jerry Conroy (played by Ralph Whitehead). Since Nellie and Jerry are both of Irish descent, it becomes inevitable that, after a series of comic misadventures and Jerry being falsely accused of stealing a string of pearls, they are united at the end.

The plot played on the notion of the so-called 'American Cinderella' musicals that had become popular in the previous decade, themselves a legacy of the 'girl' musicals that had been especially popular (and populous)

---

[5] 'The Whichness of the Whatness' on HMV BB 3618–3, and 'Oh, Gee! Oh, Gosh!' on HMV BB 3619–2.

on London musical stages since the 1890s. In both scenarios, young employed women find love and oftentimes wealth in a respectable suitor. In British musical comedies such as *The Shop Girl* (1894), social-class distinctions would be at the fore, since these shows often satirized aspects of the British class system. In the American shows, they secure husbands not through gold-digging but rather because of their own professional work ethic. As young professionals, their participation in the American dictum of hard work bears direct results. Theatre scholar Maya Cantu astutely asserts that these sorts of stories 'valorized the working girl'[6] and made their title characters role models of sorts for many young women in the audience. Often, these American Cinderella stories featured women of Irish descent who pair up with WASP (white Anglo-Saxon Protestant) men. According to Cantu, such plotlines reflect assimilation patterns among Irish Americans.[7] When such stories become so commonplace as to be predictable, they need to be undermined. This is what happens in *Little Nellie Kelly*, where although the title character *could* be with the wealthy WASP playboy, she instead chooses the modest Irishman. True love can be more powerful than monetary riches or upward social mobility. Importantly, Nellie is one who chooses her husband; her agency as a working woman allows her to do this.

A surviving playbill for 25 September 1923 includes a note on how at least one audience member responded to the American import: 'Most exhilarating and delightful, if somewhat overwhelmingly hustled and rowdy.'[8] This description seems to capture the reception of so many American musical comedies in Britain: lively and fun, and a bit brash. Musical highlights included the title character's foxtrot song 'The Name of Kelly', the comic dance number 'The Flirting Salesman' and Jerry and Nellie's sentimental duet 'You Remind Me of My Mother'.

It was not just American shows that were playing in London as 1923 turned to 1924. American creators of musicals also travelled across the Atlantic to create new works expressly for the UK market. Among these individuals was someone who was no stranger to the world of British musical theatre: Jerome Kern (1885–1945).

---

[6] Maya Cantu, *American Cinderellas on the Broadway Musical Stage: Imagining the Working Girl from 'Irene' to 'Gypsy'* (Houndmills: Palgrave Macmillan, 2015), 13.
[7] Cantu, *American Cinderellas*, 15.
[8] Playbill for *Little Nellie Kelly*, 25 September 1923, MM/REF/TH/GR/OXF/3/2, M&M.

Jerome Kern: Transatlantic Successes

In 1923, Jerome Kern was already a familiar name in London's West End. He had visited the British capital almost every year between 1905 and 1910 (1907 being the exception), and many of his individual songs were being added to shows with scores by other composers. This process of interpolating songs by one composer into someone else's work had been common practice for decades. While in the United Kingdom, Kern not only met his wife, Eva, but also made useful contacts in the London theatrical sphere.[9] These led to his hit Broadway musical comedy *Sally*, which opened in 1920, transferring to London's Winter Garden Theatre the following year. Its success resulted in Kern writing two musical comedies expressly for the Winter Garden: *The Cabaret Girl* (1922) and *The Beauty Prize* (1923), the latter of which played into 1924.

This London trio of works featured not just the same trio of lead performers but, for the ones created for the Winter Garden, the same creative team. Three of the era's most beloved stars led the casts: George Grossmith, Jr (1874–1935), Dorothy Dickson (1893–1995) and Leslie Henson (1891–1957). All were audience draws who played off each other to create a dynamism that transcended their formidable individual talents. Crafting the book and lyrics were two of the most celebrated British theatrical writers: the aforementioned Grossmith, and P. G. Wodehouse, who became especially well known for his Jeeves and Wooster tales.

George Grossmith, Jr came from an established theatrical and literary family. He followed in his father George Grossmith's footsteps by performing his own material and later began producing and directing shows. When it came to *The Beauty Prize*, he was credited as writer, actor, producer and director.

Born in Kansas City, Missouri, Dorothy Dickson began her career in a ballroom dance duo with her husband, Carl Hyson. The graceful pair danced on Broadway before travelling to London in 1921 at the invitation of Charles B. Cochran, who invited them to join his revue *London, Paris and New York*. Dickson was soon cast as *Sally* for its London production. She charmed audiences with 'Look for the Silver Lining' and its subsequent dance.

Leslie Henson was especially famous for his raspy voice and distinctively droll facial expressions. Typical of his well-known physical comedy is

---

[9] Andrew Lamb, *Jerome Kern in Edwardian London*, I.S.A.M. Monographs 22 (Brooklyn: Institute for Studies in American Music, Brooklyn College, 1985), 36.

a scene in *The Beauty Prize* that takes place on the deck of a transatlantic liner, thankfully preserved in a Pathé film from the time.[10] A heavily clad Henson enters the stage and begins to shed layer after layer of sporting costumes, dumping each in turn onto an unsuspecting crew member.

On 5 September 1923, *The Beauty Prize* opened at the Winter Garden Theatre. Grossmith and Wodehouse's libretto tells the frothy tale of American heiress Carol Stuart (Dickson) who goes to England to find a husband. In doing so, she is following in her American father's footsteps, for Carol's mother is English. Carol meets the wealthy John Brooke at what she calls 'an awful charity ball', and the two, both choosing not to mention their respective fortunes to the other, agree to marry in a week's time. Meanwhile, Lovey Toots, who works at Carol's favourite hat shop, tells her American friend that she's entered her in a newspaper beauty competition, the prize for which is . . . a husband! As Carol is preparing a surprise lavish wedding for John, news arrives that Carol has won the competition and that her 'prize', the eccentric millionaire Odo Philpotts (Henson), is on his way. Meanwhile, the vexing Mrs Hexal, Carol's chaperone, informs John that her charge is in fact extremely rich and goes around buying anything and everything she wants, including an Italian villa and, most recently, a husband. Carol and John confront each other about not being honest – neither knew the other was anything but an ordinary working person – and call off their nuptials. The miffed Carol, in revenge, decides to take her quirky new fiancé, Odo, to America to meet her father. Lovey, meanwhile, has taken a liking to Odo, and she and John, who of course truly loves Carol and wants to be with her, decide to follow the mismatched pair across the Atlantic.

As Act 2 begins aboard the ocean liner, Lovey and John feign a romance to make Odo and Carol jealous. Flutey Warboy (Grossmith), John's secretary, notices just how much Carol and John are putting on with their 'new' romantic partners and suggests to each of them, separately, that they each send themselves a telegram, supposedly from their families, telling them that their fortunes have vanished. Thus, their self-imposed impediment to romance will disappear. Carol and John follow Flutey's suggestion, but things of course go awry, for Odo and Lovey become so concerned about their 'new' partners' misfortune that they feel they must provide even more emotional support than before. Everyone gathers at Carol's father's Florida estate. Odo realizes that Carol in fact has *not* lost her money and, more

---

[10] 'Beams From – "The Beauty Prize" at the Winter Garden Theatre, London (1923)', www .youtube.com/watch?v=zDV1fP-SwVQ.

importantly, that she is much too independent for his traditional views. He breaks his prize contract, which allows him to be with Lovey and Carol with John.

In quintessential British musical comedy fashion, the plot was filled with satire, here on the omnipresence of class as well as on transatlantic relations. Carol and John can only be together if they are financial equals, whether rich or poor. Being an eccentric, though, Odo can become the conduit for Lovey and her Cinderella story, as she goes from being a milliner's assistant to a wealthy wife. This secondary plot aligns with the various rags-to-riches scenarios in vogue at the time. Carol, as an American from 'new money' – not from generations of inheritances – is considered somewhat suspicious in her motives to garner a British husband. Mrs Hexel personifies a malicious disdain for money- and title-seeking Americans.

Kern's score was intended more to be hung onto the story than to illuminate it. Reviewers then and writers now remark that it is not one of his best efforts. Kern's songs for *The Beauty Prize* are perhaps more intriguing because of their pasts and their futures than their presents in 1923 and 1924. Looking to the past, Lovey and Odo's comic duet 'A Cottage in Kent' is a revised version of an earlier Kern and Wodehouse song, 'Bungalow in Quogue',[11] an interpolation for *The Riviera Girl*, which opened on Broadway in 1917. Rural English place names replace the Long Island ones of the original, just as happened when *For Goodness Sake* became *Stop Flirting*. Looking to the future, parts of *The Beauty Prize* ended up in other Kern scores. As Stephen Banfield has noted, a version of the ballad 'Moon Love' resurfaced as 'Sunshine' in *Sunny* (1925), and Carol and Flutely's comic duet 'You Can't Make Love by Wireless' morphed into 'Bow Belles' for *Blue Eyes* (1928).[12]

The Beauty Prize was not Kern's only show to open in 1923 and play into 1924. *Stepping Stones*, which debuted on Broadway on 6 November at the Globe Theatre, was the seventh star vehicle Charles B. Dillingham (1868–1934) produced specifically for the evergreen song-and-dance comedian Fred Stone (1873–1959). Stone had achieved tremendous fame after the turn of the twentieth century as one half of the vaudevillian and musical comedy duo Montgomery and Stone (with David C. Montgomery, 1870–1917). The pair had starred in such shows as *The Wizard of Oz* (1902), *The Red Mill* (1905) and *Chin-Chin* (1914).

---

[11] Quogue is a village on Long Island, New York.
[12] Stephen Banfield, *Jerome Kern* (New Haven, CT: Yale University Press, 2006), 127.

Stone continued to milk the team's penchant for creative retellings of fairy or fantasy tales after Montgomery's death. In *Stepping Stones*, Fred played a plumber called Peter Plug who helps Prince Silvio (whose name comes from the Latin for woods) be with his true love, the shop girl Rougette (French for 'little red'). To do this, Plug must defeat the villainous Otto de Wolfe (wolf), who wants his own daughter, Lupina (her name from the Latin for wolf), to marry the prince. As the characters' names cleverly reveal, the librettists Anne Caldwell and R. H. Burnside imprinted their farcical plot onto the tale of Little Red Riding Hood. The show was a massive success, and Kern's songs, with Caldwell's lyrics, included the enchanting lullaby 'Once in a Blue Moon'. Adding to *Stepping Stones*' sense of spectacle was a troupe of Tiller Girls, the Tiller Sunshine Girls, who performed several routines in the show. The Tiller Girls (see Figure 2.1) were troupes of precision dance teams trained by the British director and presenter John Tiller (1854–1925). Tiller assembled his companies to create uniformity in terms of height and weight, and hence in how the bodies moved on stage. Tiller Girls became immensely popular on both sides of the Atlantic. Stone was impressed with the wholesome reputation of Tiller Girls, who helped project the family-friendly image he was keen to promote.[13]

In *Stepping Stones*, Stone shared star billing with his seventeen-year-old daughter Dorothy, who was making her stage debut as Rougette (see Plate 4). Critics adored Dorothy, one of whom called her 'a chip off the old Stone'.[14] After father and daughter performed the duet 'Wonderful Dad' in Act 1, there was thunderous applause. This was partly due to what could be called the song's metatheatricality, for it was not just the characters in the show singing the song to each other but also the actors themselves doing the same. The line between character and performer evaporated; Dorothy Stone was singing to her beloved father every bit as much as her character, Rougette, was singing to hers.

Italian Connections: An American View of Italy and an Italian View of the Netherlands

In 1923, two very popular musicals whose legacies continued into 1924 and beyond, both with connections to Italy, had their premieres. The Broadway musical *Wildflower* was set in Italy, while the Italian operetta (literally,

---

[13] Doremy Vernon, *Tiller's Girls: The Colourful Story of the Legendary Dancing Troupe* (London: Robson, 1988), 96.

[14] 'Dorothy Stone a Hit in Father's Play', *New York Times*, 7 November 1923.

Figure 2.1 A troupe of Tiller Girls.

a little opera) *Il paese dei campanelli* (The Land of the Bells) took place in an imaginary town on the Dutch coast. Both feature humour and romance, sumptuous music and highly memorable characters.

In *Wildflower*, the wondrous Edith Day (1896–1971) delighted audiences for more than a year playing the fiery Italian farmgirl Nina. Nina stands to inherit a fortune, but only if she can keep her temper under control for six months while living with her unpleasant relatives in a villa on Lake Como. If she does not succeed, the money will go to her envy-filled cousin Bianca. Bianca, not surprisingly, comes up with plan after plan to antagonize Nina. Among her nefarious schemes is trying to convince Nina that her gentle lover, Guido (played by Guy Robertson), has been unfaithful. As it is a musical comedy, Nina of course wins in the end. Filled with entrancing music by Vincent Youmans and Herbert Stothart that complemented the delight-filled book and lyrics by Otto Harbach and Oscar Hammerstein II, *Wildflower* played 477 performances at the Casino Theatre in New York (7 February 1923 to 29 March 1924), making it the biggest hit of the 1922–1923 season. Day's effervescent stage presence and glorious singing were featured in numbers such as the title song, with its smoothly descending chromatic melody, and the wistful waltz 'You Never Can Blame a Girl for Dreaming'. The show's big hit, though, was the celebratory pseudo-folk dance 'Bambalina', with its stomping downbeats.

At the same time that *Wildflower* was delighting its New York audiences with a romanticized view of northern Italy, *Il paese dei campanelli* was regaling its Italian audiences with a fanciful imagining of a sexually repressed Dutch fishing village. The satirical delight opened at the Teatro Lirico in Milan on 23 November 1923, after which its fame spread quickly across the peninsula. With a libretto by the famed manager–author–impresario Carlo Lombardo[15] (1869–1959) and music co-written by Lombardo and the violinist–conductor–composer Virgilio Ranzato (1882–1937), *Il paese dei campanelli* became one of the most famous Italian musical theatre works of the twentieth century. Operatic leanings are characteristic of Italian operetta, and this aesthetic sets *Il paese* apart, in many ways, from its continental and American siblings. Part of this almost certainly had to do with Ranzato's career as a violinist, which included serving as concertmaster at La Scala under Arturo Toscanini. The original production by the Compagnia Regini Lombardo starred one of the company's owners, Nella Regini (with two l's), as Nela (with one l), and was conducted by the other, the same Carlo Lombardo who was central to its creation. Regini often played the romantic lead in Lombardo's operettas (see Plate 5).

The unnamed Dutch seaside locale where the action takes place is cursed. Every house has a bell on its roof, and if any adulterous affair takes place inside, the bell rings. Three women, all of whom are married, take centre stage in the story. First is Nela, the sweetest girl in the village. She does everything she can to please her all-too-often-distracted husband. Second is Bombon, Nela's self-possessed polar opposite. Bombon dresses seductively in order to attract men and whiles away her time posing for

---

[15] Lombardo's full name was the impressive Carlo Lombardo dei Baroni Lombardo di San Chirico.

picture postcards and organizing parties. Finally, there is Pomerania, the boorish wife of the mayor. None of the village husbands seem to show much affection toward their wives. Since no one wants to hear the bells ring, everyone, especially these three principal couples, maintains a status quo of quiet abstinence.

This all changes when a British naval vessel returning home from Japan experiences engine trouble and must stop for repairs. The ship's captain, Hans, falls for the charming Nela, while his attaché, the appropriately called La Gaffe, since he constantly makes mistakes and gets things wrong, is entranced by Bombon's allure. The sea-weary sailors want to enjoy some female companionship before going home to their wives, so when La Gaffe offers to send a telegram to the Olympia Theatre inviting its female chorus to come to the Dutch village, the crew is elated. Since La Gaffe is going to the telegraph office anyway, Hans asks him to send a telegram to his wife, Ethel, telling her that their homecoming will be delayed due to the ship needing repairs and asking her to let the other wives know. That evening, Hans, with his sweet words – and his lyrical tenor voice – succeeds in seducing the somewhat reluctant Nela. Bombon, too, eventually succumbs to La Gaffe's advances and invites him to come visit her. Poor La Gaffe, though, doesn't know which house is hers and ends up making a nocturnal visit to a very surprised – and delighted – Pomerania. The other sailors similarly flirt with village women, who feign resistance, though none of them completely closes her door as she enters her house. The men of the village return home late from the pub. They are convinced that it is now safe to sneak into their homes, since by now their wives must surely be asleep. Just then, a bell begins to ring. Trying to figure out who has committed an indiscretion, everyone except Nela's husband realizes it is coming from his house. Soon, all the bells begin to ring as the women of the village and their English Romeos join the confused husbands on stage.

As Act 2 begins, the British sailors make a deal with the Dutch husbands. As recompense for the previous evening, when the troupe from the Olympia Theatre arrive, the husbands may go and enjoy the actresses' company. A group of women enter, and the Dutch husbands are elated – unlike the British sailors, who realize that these are not the chorus girls from the Olympia but their own wives! The gaff-prone La Gaffe has done it again: he reversed the telegrams. The British officers are none too keen to have the Dutch husbands cavorting with their wives. Act 3 begins with Hans trying to reconcile with his wife, while Nela, in an especially tender scene, realizes that Hans was just playing with her affections. She has finally received the attention she wishes her husband would give her, but it was all a lie. Meanwhile, what is to be done about the lingering curse? It is revealed that if everyone can remain chaste for twelve hours on a particular day, from 6 a.m. to 6 p.m., then the curse will be lifted. In true operetta fashion, this happens to be that very day. The sailors are planning to leave at 6 p.m., and La Gaffe, desperately wanting to rendezvous with Bombon before his departure, moves the town's clock ahead by one hour so that he can steal some time with her. His trick of course backfires, since when he comes to her, it is in reality only 5 p.m., and the bell begins to ring. The sailors finally depart with their wives. The Dutch husbands and wives reconcile; the husbands show new affection and appreciation for their spouses. While some directors amend the ending, the original shows a heartbroken Nela sobbing on stage as she realizes that Hans will probably forget all about her, while the power of their encounter will always remain for her a poignant memory.

As is the case in so many operettas, the true star here is the musical score. When *Il paese* played briefly in New York in 1935, the critic Arthur Pollock noted, 'It makes you want to live longer, that music.'[16] Among the many highlights is 'Luna tu' (You moon), a trio for Nela, Hans and Bombon. Following languid verses in which Nela and Hans sing of the nocturnal mysteries of love, Bombon offers a wistful paeon to the moon about its effect on lovers. The gentle foxtrot features such contemplative lines as 'Without you / Is it not possible to love? / Without you / Is it not possible to kiss?'[17]

'Luna tu' reflects a fundamental musical precept of the score. Nela, as the romantic female lead, sings in a lyrical, flowing, nearly operatic style, while Bombon, as the sexualized comic, performs songs with a narrower range and rhythmic dance underpinnings. Therefore, in order to communicate, the sailors who show interest in these two women must accommodate their respective styles. Hans must complement Nela's soprano by being a lyric tenor, while La Gaffe flirts with Bombon through his comic baritone.

Nela's vocal grace infuses her first number in the operetta, 'La canzone del latte' (The Milk Song), which she sings as she pours milk for the three principal husbands. The final refrain even includes a dash of coloratura obligato, the aural calling card of an operetta soprano. When he arrives, Hans joins her in this vaulting style of singing for 'Duetto del ricamo' (The Embroidery Duet). The two exchange lyrical niceties before Nela, through

---

[16] Arthur Pollock, 'The Theatre', *Brooklyn Daily Eagle*, 10 May 1935, newspapers.com.

[17] 'Senza te / Non si può forse amar? / Senza te / Non si può baciar?' Translation via Google Translate and by the author.

a flowing waltz melody, confesses her elation at meeting him, 'even if the golden dream goes away'.[18] Her joy becomes complete when Hans joins her at the end of the refrain for a series of vocally impassioned sustained high notes. Such intensity is also central to their 'separation' duet at the beginning of Act 3, which ends with a return of the final emotive lines of the Embroidery Duet, an aural reminder of that first meeting.

By contrast, Bombon lives in the syncopated world of the foxtrot. In addition to the refrain of 'Luna tu', she leads the ensemble in two other foxtrots: the 'Foxtrot dei fiori' (Foxtrot of the Flowers) and the 'Foxtrot dei campanelli' (Foxtrot of the Bells). Additionally, Bombon and La Gaffe, as the comic leads, enjoy a light-hearted duet in each of the three acts. It was up to them and their music to keep *Il paese* from becoming too serious and sentimental and instead to ground it firmly within the light-hearted spirit of 'operetta giocosa' (comic operetta).

Il paese dei campanelli was an immediate success. A second production opened in Venice at the famed Teatro La Fenice on 16 February 1924, and a third began performances at the Petruzzelli Theatre in Bari on 30 October 1924 before moving to the Politeama Alhambra in Taranto on 5 November. Its captivating music, especially the foxtrot 'Luna tu', and Lombardo's witty characterizations have kept the classic work in the public's eyes and ears for more than a century. Luisa Longobucco, in her study of the operetta, explains what makes Lombardo's style so effective: 'Lombardo writes in a simple language that everyone can understand, but he also manages to insert poetry when necessary.'[19] This blend of directness with stylized glamour is a key component of successful musical theatre writing, no matter the language or style.

From Paris to New York

In the 1920s, adaptations of popular works for transnational markets formed a major part of the theatrical ecosystem. The phenomenal success of *Die lustige Witwe* (1905) becoming *The Merry Widow* in London and New York in 1907 inspired a string of similar adaptations from German-language works into English (and other languages). Works originally in other languages proved more elusive for Anglophone audiences. For

---

[18] 'Contenta pur se il sogno d'or s'en va!'.

[19] Luisa Longobucco, *Carolo Lombardo e 'Il paese dei campanelli': breve storia dell'operetta* (Cosenza: Luigi Pellegrini Editore, 2013), 89. ('Lombardo scrive in una linguaggio semplice e comprensibile da tutti, ma riesce ad inserire anche la poesia quando e necessario'.)

example, in 1923, New York impresario Charles B. Dillingham, the producer of *Stepping Stones*, decided to bring an English-language version of
a popular French work to New York. This was *One Kiss*, an adaptation of
Maurice Yvain's highly popular French *opérette Ta bouche* (literally, Your
Mouth), which had been delighting Parisian audiences since 1922. The
story of the son of a fortune-hunting father who falls in love with the
daughter of a fortune-hunting mother was told in such a sexualized way
that, according to the New York critic Alexander Woollcott, 'even Paris
blushed faintly'.[20] When audiences came to see *One Kiss* at the Fulton
Theatre, where it played from 27 November 1923 to 16 February 1924, they
saw something very different from the original. To accommodate the more
conservative theatrical tastes in the USA, Yves Mirandeis and Albert
Willemetz's book had undergone what one reviewer called 'a good
Puritan scrubbing'.[21]

The person responsible for the scrubbing was the composer, author
and playwright Clare Kummer (1873–1958). Indeed, playbills called
One Kiss 'A New CLARE KUMMER Comedy with Music' (emphasis
in original). Kummer was among several women at the time who were
adapting European works for the Broadway stage. She had established
herself after the turn of the twentieth century as a composer of
popular songs, crafting both words and music. Several of these made
their way into stage musicals. During the teens, Kummer became
known as a playwright, and several of her plays were produced on
Broadway. Then, in 1921, she wrote the book, music and lyrics for two
one-act musicals that for a time ended up playing simultaneously: *The
Choir Rehearsal* and *Chinese Love*. It was – and remains – exceptional
for one individual to take on the roles of composer, librettist and
lyricist. One can think of Kummer's contemporary George M. Cohan,
as well as later figures such as Frank Loesser (*The Most Happy Fella*,
1956; *Greenwillow,* 1960), Lin-Manuel Miranda (*Hamilton*, 2015) and
Michael R. Jackson (*A Strange Loop*, 2019) in this regard. Kummer
was also active as a producer, with her own *Chinese Love* being among
the works she produced. For *One Kiss*, Kummer preserved Yvain's
score and added interpolations from another of his *operettes*, *La-Haut*
(Up There), which had recently opened in Paris.

---

[20] Alexander Woollcott, 'The Stage', *New York Herald*, 28 November 1923.
[21] Uncited review, '"One Kiss" Starts Colorful Affair at the Fulton', *One Kiss* Clipping Folder, Billy
Rose Theatre Collection, NYPL.

Transnational connections such as those surveyed here in terms of performers, creators and subject matter formed a significant part of the Atlantic theatrical infrastructure of the time. What Clare Kummer and Charles B. Dillingham were trying to accomplish by translating and adapting *One Kiss* was by no means a one-off. The translation and adaptation of continental works for English-speaking audiences had the potential for big business, new opportunities for singers and creators and immense audience satisfaction.

3 | Playing on the Past

Alongside the many shows that celebrated the present as 1923 moved into 1924 were many that looked to the past. These works hearkened back, somewhat nostalgically, to simpler times, though the stories were often fraught with deceit and sometimes could be a bit salacious. The lead female characters in such works ranged from a young circus waif to a Russian empress, a royal mistress and a young Spanish woman who finds herself in a complex labyrinth of romantic entailments.

A Con Man and a Circus Waif

While the idea of a travelling con man taking advantage of a young inno-cent to help him in his illicit schemes is far from model behaviour, it provided the basis for a highly successful musical comedy that opened on Broadway in 1923 and transferred to London the following year. The show was *Poppy*, and it starred W. C. Fields (1880–1946) as the con man and Madge Kennedy (1891–1987) as the young waif.

Poppy was the result of a collaboration between actress-turned-lyricist and librettist Dorothy Donnelly (1876–1928) and composers Stephen Jones and Arthur Samuels. Donnelly also served as co-director for the musical comedy, which opened at the Apollo Theatre on 3 September 1923 and ran until late June 1924. Fields, a former *Follies* headliner, was known for his physical antics and expert juggling, but perhaps more for his highly dis-tinctive voice and humorous delivery. Kennedy (1891–1987) was con-sidered one of the best farce actors on Broadway, and several critics were surprised to see her starring in a musical. Her voice was described as 'one of those pretty parlor sopranos',[1] and she sang with notable precision and clarity.

Donnelly set her story in 1874. Poppy's mother ran away to join the circus and died soon after Poppy (Kennedy) was born. Professor Eustace

---

[1] Burns Mantle, 'Madge Kennedy Tries Her Voice in Musical Show', *New York Daily News*, 4 September 1923, newspapers.com.

McGargle (Fields), a member of the circus troupe and a slick con artist, adopted Poppy and brought her up to be his assistant. When the circus visits Poppy's mother's home town, McGargle tries to pass off Poppy as a long-lost heiress. She not only meets a rich man and falls in love with him, but also discovers that she truly is the heiress she was impersonating.

The comic antics of Kennedy and Fields carried the show. Although they both had songs, the score's two outstanding numbers, 'Mary' and 'Alibi Baby', were performed by the character actor Luella Gear (1897–1980) in the role of Mary Delafield. Although *Poppy* was billed as a musical comedy, in reality it was a vehicle to showcase the marvellous non-singing talents of its two lead performers.

Regal Operettas Delight London

A British cousin to American rags-to-riches tales such as *Poppy* were fictionalized tales of historical women who rose to the highest levels of society, often set to sweeping musical finery. Two of these captivated audiences in London in late 1923. First was *Catherine*, which tells the story of Marta, a fiery-tempered village girl who eventually becomes the wife of Russian Czar Peter the Great and Empress of Russia. Second was *Madame Pompadour*, which related a concocted episode in the life of Jeanne Antoinette Poisson, Marquise de Pompadour (1721–1764), the official chief mistress of King Lous XV of France (1710–1774; ruled 1715–1774). The actors who played the title roles in these glamourous productions, José Collins (1887–1958) and Evelyn Laye (1900–1996), reigned not just on stage in their respective shows but also off stage as two of the leading luminaries of their generation.

Both works, especially *Madame Pompadour*, are sometimes referred to as operettas. 'Operetta' is an umbrella term for a variety of works, originally of continental European origin, that combine music, often with an operatic aesthetic, and spoken dialogue. Typically, operettas include an array of musical styles, particularly expansive waltzes (especially in the Viennese variety). Operettas are generally set in a time and place other than that of their creation, though this is not always the case. Librettos are often satirical or include some sort of socio-cultural commentary. One could say that operettas offer commentary on real-life situations set in faraway places while musical comedies feature highly improbable situations in familiar surroundings.

'A Jose Collins first night is always an event in the theatre', quipped one London critic, and on 22 September 1923, when Collins opened in the title role of *Catherine* at the Gaiety Theatre, 'the enthusiasm of the house knew no bounds'[2] (see Figure 3.1). In this lavish spectacle based on the historical figure of Marta Helena Skowrońska (1684–1727; Empress Consort of Russia, 1721–1725; Empress of Russia, 1725–1727), Collins yet again proved herself as Empress of the West End. She recalled that it was 'the most spectacular and exhausting role' of her entire career.[3]

In the operetta, though not in reality, Marta single-handedly wards off the Russian army and captures the heart of 'Field Marshal Menshikoff', a conflation of two historic figures: Field Marshal Boris Sheremetev and Prince Alexander Menshikov. She then meets Peter the Great (1672–1725; ruled 1682–1725), and, following history, they are married and she is crowned Empress Consort. *Catherine* was an adaptation of the German

Figure 3.1 José Collins in *Catherine*.

---

[2] 'Dazzling Scenes in "Catherine"', *The People* (London), 23 September 1923, newspapers.com.
[3] José Collins , *The Maid of the Mountains, Her Story: The Reminiscences of José Collins* (London: Hutchinson & Co., 1932), 222.

musical comedy *Die Siegerin* (The Winner), with libretto and lyrics by Béla Jenbach and Oscar Friedmann and music by Joseph Klein adapted from melodies by the quintessential Russian composer Pet'r Ilyich Tchaikovsky (1840–1893). When Robert Evett produced the English-language version in London, he added more of Tchaikovsky's music to go with Reginald Arkell and Madame Frédérique de Grésac's reworking of the libretto.

José Collins's huge success in *The Maid of the Mountains* five years earlier had made her a star, and her glory had remained undiminished in *The Last Waltz*, also produced by Evett at the Gaiety. Collins continued to shine, literally, in *Catherine*, for the dress she wore in the coronation scene was embroidered with more than 60,000 diamond beads. Collins recalled this 'most magnificent' of dresses:

It was made of heavy white satin with a berther of fine antique lace, and embroidered all over in a design depicting the double-headed Russian eagle. . . . With this robe I wore a train of old-rose velvet, on which the same design was worked, lined and bordered with velvet. The colouring of this Coronation robe was almost of Arabian Nights splendour, and fitted into its gorgeous stage setting like a gigantic, dazzling ruby.[4]

Glamour infused *Catherine* not only in Collins's exquisite gowns but also in the production's lavish sets and Tchaikovsky's highly romanticized music. Collins sang two big numbers in the show: 'I Am But a Simple Maid' in Act 1, performed to 'Chanson Triste', and 'Star of Fate' in Act 2, sung to 'Chanson sans Paroles'. Also popular was a duet for Marta and Menshikov (played by the noted operetta star Robert Michaelis) called 'Love Letters' and sung to the Mazurka, op. 39.[5] But the highlight of the score was the reworking of the *1812 Overture* that appeared in the culminating coronation scene. Evett imagined that 'all the bells of London will join in, and guns will be fired at the Tower of London, all along the Mall, and even at the Powder Magazine in Hyde Park'.[6] Of course cannons and bells are often used in live performances of the *1812 Overture*, but for *Catherine* the sounds were limited to the theatre and, to provide the additional aural ballast, an organ was added to the orchestra. The show played a solid 217 performances and closed in late March 1924.

Outshining the Russian court of Peter the Great was the international hit *Madame Pompadour*, in which the French court of Louis XV blossomed into life. Leo Fall's German operetta was an overwhelming success when it

---

[4] Collins, *The Maid of the Mountains*, 222.   [5] Collins, *The Maid of the Mountains*, 223.
[6] Collins, *The Maid of the Mountains*, 224.

opened at the Berliner Theater in Berlin on 9 September 1922, conducted
by the composer. Just under six months later, on 2 March 1923, a second
production opened at Vienna's prestigious operetta venue, the Theater an
der Wien, that was every bit as popular as the Berlin original. *Madame
Pompadour*'s English-language adaptation, however, was the one that
cemented its reputation on the international stage. When it opened at
Daly's Theatre in London on 20 December 1923, it continued to draw
adoring audiences, running for an astonishing 469 performances before it
closed in late January 1925. Fall's biographer Stefan Frey declared it 'the
most successful of all Pompadours'.[7]

Daly's Theatre, located just off Leicester Square in the heart of London's
theatre district, was already known for its long runs of English-language
versions of continental operettas. The legendary impresario George
Edwardes brought *The Merry Widow* there in 1907 when he realized that
there was a massive market for this sort of entertainment. From then on,
one long-running adaptation followed another. After Edwardes's death in
1915, James White (1877–1972), better known as Jimmy, purchased the
venerable venue from Edwardes's estate. White wanted to continue
Edwardes's lucrative operetta legacy, something he achieved with tremendous flair and élan.

What London audiences saw basically followed the original plot as
devised by Rudolph Schanzer and Ernst Wellsch, and adapted by
Frederick Lonsdale and Harry Graham. It is carnival season, and the
flirtatious Count René is enjoying time away from his wife, Madeleine.
He frequents the Tavern of the Nine Muses along with his friend Joseph
(Josef in the original) Calicot, a poet known for his satiric and oftentimes
bawdy ballads. The count ends up in an amorous situation with a beautiful
masked woman, who turns out to be none other than Madame
Pompadour, the mistress/confidante of King Louis XV. The Minister of
Police, who is out to destroy Madame's reputation and influence, recognizes Pompadour and forces her to reveal her true identity. Joseph and
René are both arrested for their inappropriate behaviour – Joseph for his
poems and René for his flirtations – and, as 'punishment', Madame insists
that they both must take positions at court: René will become her bodyguard and Joseph must write a new play for her birthday. René's wife, on
the advice of her father, comes to Madame to seek assistance in dealing
with her wayward husband. It transpires that Madeleine and Madame are

---

[7] Stefan Frey, with Christine Stemprok and Wolfgang Dosch. *Leo Fall: Spöttischer Rebell der
   Operette* (Vienna: Edition Steinbauer, 2010), 195 ('die erfolgreischste aller Pompadours').

half-sisters – they share the same father – and Madame pledges to help her sibling. Meanwhile, the king learns that both men have been in his mistress's rooms. Madame easily convinces the monarch that Joseph is no rival; as for René, she asks the king to hide behind a screen while she cleverly has a 'private' talk with the count about his inappropriate behaviour toward her and pleads with him for Madeleine's happiness. Of course, this is all intended for the king to hear. Louis XV, it turns out, slept through the whole thing but is so moved by Madame's initiative and René's repentance that he rewards the count with a place in his bodyguard and elevates Madame to the rank of duchess.

Madame Pompadour's fictional plot displays several distinctive qualities. First, it brims with marital infidelity and the overt sexuality associated with Berlin operetta in the 1920s (problematic plot points it shares with *Il paese dei campanelli* that cautions revivals of both works in the English-speaking world). Second, the primary 'romantic' couple, the one that gets to revel in waltzes, consists of the king's mistress and, unbeknownst to her at the time, her brother-in-law. They are not together at the end, for both return to their respective partners.

Fall wrote two exquisite solo waltzes for *Madame Pompadour*: one associated with each of the 'romantic' leads, the title character and René. The waltz, with its origins in Central Europe in the seventeenth century, came to represent a sense of elegance through its couples rotating clockwise while flowing in a counter-clockwise circle. Because of its close hold, its early history includes many who saw it as obscene, and likewise, as Robert Hylton asserts, it gained a reputation as a dance for prostitutes and mistresses.[8] It thus fit perfectly into *Madame Pompadour* from a historical point of view, though this almost certainly was not a consideration for Fall and his librettists. By the mid-nineteenth century, the waltz had become a ballroom favourite and came in two modes, fast and slow, which allowed for variety on the dance floor. Hylton goes on to describe the importance of dance in European court culture, the world that is evoked in so many operettas: 'In dance, style is everything. Your posture, clothes and the way you stand or sit are carefully structured gestures that project your place and ambition. ... When, where and with whom you danced signalled who you were or aimed to be.'[9] It is within these very theatrical contexts that Fall's waltzes for *Madame Pompadour* fit so perfectly.

---

[8] Hylton, *Dancing in Time*, 25.   [9] Hylton, *Dancing in Time*, 34.

First is 'Love Me Now', which Madame Pompadour introduces in Act 1 as she tells her maid, Mariette, about wanting to find a momentary lover who will 'love me now, for the night is so fleeting'. This waltz of desire, with its gliding descents and skipping ascents, gains momentum in the final lines as the title character realizes the precious fragility of the moment.

Second is the title song, introduced by René with the male chorus in Act 2 and marked 'valse lente' in the published vocal score. In terms of music, 'lente' is usually translated as 'slow', though here its literal meaning – 'lens' – might also be appropriate, since it allows us to see – and hear – René's admiration for his royal benefactor. By contrast, the male chorus, through its own collective lens, seems more interested in her sexual prowess as they sing lines such as 'kitting your skirt up to the knee!' René, though, sees Madame Pompadour as being much more than the king's mistress. When he begins the reprise of the glowingly seductive refrain, which spans nearly two octaves, it is marked *pppp*: literally twice as soft as *pp*, truly as soft as possible. This indication is not for volume, but for sentiment. His imploring words come from the depths of his own secret and idealized devotion.

To contrast with the sumptuousness of the waltzes, Fall created a different sort of music for Joseph, the salacious poet. His music is more in the style of what one would expect in inter-war cabaret, with shorter phrases, a narrower range and a more raucous aesthetic. These features infuse the opening scene, during which Calicot performs his song about Madame to an attentive and appreciative tavern audience. The first words uttered – or, more precisely, sung – from the stage are Calicot's purposefully punctuated plosives 'Pom, Pom, Pom, Pompadour'. Carnival laughter, simultaneously celebratory and deriding, infuses this opening number.[10] Calicot tells us, somewhat satirically and knowing full well what cannot be said, that:

She's such a famous Ha! Ha! Ha!
She's such a famous lady!
Her reputation's Ha! Ha! Ha!
Well, anything but shady.[11]

The distinctive 'pom' plosives followed by an arpeggiated descent to complete the royal mistress's name become a recurring motif throughout the

---

[10] On carnival laughter, see Camille Crittenden, *Johann Strauss and Vienna: Operetta and the Politics of Popular Culture* (Cambridge: Cambridge University Press, 2000), 142–143.

[11] Harry Graham and Leo Fall, *Madame Pompadour* [vocal score] (London: Ascherberg, Hopwood & Crew, n.d.), 9.

score, an earworm of sorts that remains in one's memory long after the curtain falls.

Operetta requires a multitude of performance styles from its stars. In the effusive 'Joseph', Madame Pompadour feigns an interest in Calicot, and to do so effectively she must embrace his performance style – that of the cabaret. The duet features fast-paced patter for both characters, with Pompadour confessing that 'Mine's a mad infatuation!', a remark that prompts Calicot to exclaim 'I shall lose my head, I know it!'[12] In the jocular foxtrot refrain, Pompadour responds to Calicot's plosives in the song about her by repeating the first syllable of his name, 'Jo-jo-jo-jo-Joseph', adding one more iteration than he did for her in his opening number. She, as the one in authority, is not to be outdone. Fall incorporates the fate motive from Bizet's *Carmen*, along with various chromatic countermelodies, into the duet to add a sense of foreboding to the otherwise jubilant number. They are playing a potentially dangerous game. 'Joseph' took on a life of its own outside the theatre as a popular number for dance bands and café orchestras. Of particular appeal are the spritely and vivacious recordings made by the Savoy Orpheans in January 1924 and Paul Whiteman and His Orchestra in December 1924.[13]

To make an operetta succeed, a cast of dedicated performers well versed in its stylistic conventions is essential. Bringing the title character to life was the enchanting Evelyn Laye. Before 1923, Laye was known largely for her work in musical comedy, with its songs in a decidedly popular vein. On 19 May 1923, she delighted audiences and surprised critics with her performance in the title role of *The Merry Widow* at Daly's Theatre.

Jimmy White wanted to make *Madame Pompadour* the latest in his series of long-running operetta adaptations at Daly's Theatre. After Laye's success in *The Merry Widow*, he decided that she should play the royal mistress. According to Laye, White had a novel way of piquing her interest in the dramatically and musically challenging role. He sent her, accompanied by her father, to Berlin to see *Madame Pompadour*, where the quintessential operetta soprano Fritzi Massary (1882–1969) was still performing in the title role she created. Laye wrote of Massary, 'She was gay, she was polished, she had joy in her; and she played the stupendous part of Madame

[12] Graham and Fall, *Madame Pompadour*, 104.

[13] Derek B. Scott, *German Operetta on Broadway and in the West End, 1900–1940* (Cambridge: Cambridge University Press, 2019), 193. Columbia 3373, A560-1, recording c. 16 January 1924; on *Madame Pompadour Paleophonics* 109 (2013). Paul Whiteman and His Orchestra recorded their version, most likely arranged by Whiteman's staff arranger Ferde Grofé, on 16 December 1924. It was released as Victor 19546-B.

Pompadour quite flawlessly.'[14] Laye recalled seeing the show twice before summoning the courage to send a telegram to White: 'I long to play it, and will work terribly hard not to let you down.'[15] White's clever ploy had succeeded.

Laye knew the stakes were high. This was an expensive show to put on, plus White had a reputation for producing lasting hits. She continued taking voice lessons so that she could confidently conquer Fall's demanding vocal lines night after night. As Laye recalled,

[N]o one believed I was capable of such an exhausting and demanding role, except Jimmy White. And, because I was well known, this First Night could do one of two things – it could show me as a nice, blonde, little musical comedy actress trying to outplay her limitations – or it could make me a star.[16]

It did the latter. The critic Davis Edwards was by no means alone in his praise: 'Miss Evelyn Laye, not absolutely unknown previously, but not regarded as of importance of great promise, has swept the theatregoers of this metropolis off their feet. This is an achievement. Stodgy old London is not easily moved.'[17] Laye had become a true West End star (see Plate 6). A surviving recording of her performing the ebullient waltz 'Love Me Now' reveals her clarion high notes, expressive ever-so-slight fluctuations of tempo and impeccable diction, all of which contribute to the glamour and radiance of Madame Pompadour.[18] Laye's experience in musical comedy and its requisite comic timing is likewise evident in her recording with Huntley Wright of 'Joseph', with its sprightly sense of perky flirtation.

Appearing alongside Laye were two notable male stars: the famed tenor Derek Oldham (1887–1986) as René and the veteran comic singer Huntley Wright (1868–1941) as Joseph. These two actors brought vividly contrasting singing styles to their roles that aptly reflected their character's fundamental yet complementary differences. René (Oldham) is a sentimental romantic, Joseph (Wright) a genial comic. After serving in the Great War, Oldham joined the D'Oyly Carte Opera Company, with whom he sang the leading tenor roles in its productions of Gilbert and Sullivan. In 1925, Oldham played Jim opposite Edith Day in the London premiere of *Rose-Marie*, which opened on Broadway while he was singing René in London.

[14] Evelyn Laye, *Boo, to My Friends* (London: Hurst & Blackett, 1958), 68.
[15] Laye, *Boo, to My Friends*, 68. [16] Laye, *Boo, to My Friends*, 69.
[17] Davis Edwards, 'Pompadour' is hit, thanks to Evelyn Laye', dateline London, 19 January 1924; appeared in *Detroit Free Press*, 20 January 1924, newspapers.com.
[18] Recorded with the Daly's Theatre Orchestra, conducted by Arthur Wood (Columbia 966 AX 284–2, recorded on 10 January 1924), available on *Evelyn Laye: 'Queen of Musical Comedy'* (Avid Entertainment AMSC 977, 2009).

Wright was no stranger to the Daly's Theatre stage, for he had been one of its major stars in the 1890s. There, he originated the primary comic roles in works such as *The Geisha* (1896) and *San Toy* (1899), with songs that were closer in style to music hall than operetta.

Zarzuela: 1920s Style

The English-language musical was by no means alone in its complex web of various sub-genres and their often ambiguous descriptors. The Spanish-language musical shows similar traits. This is evident in the genre of zarzuela and the various types that can be placed under its umbrella, such as *sainete*, *revista*, *género chico* and *zarzuela grande*, amongst others. Zarzuela scholar Janet L. Sturman's phrase 'in and out of the shadow of opera' is a wholly apt way to think about the genre.[19] With roots in the seventeenth century, zarzuela's focus on well-crafted verse, spoken or sung, and debates over how much these works should emulate Italian models continued into the early twentieth century. Furthermore, as Eva Moreda Rodríguez has shown, zarzuela singers were expected first and foremost to communicate texts expressively, and many singers combined aspects of an operatic mode of vocal production with a more speech-like one in order to accomplish this goal. Their specific approach to performance often included portamento effects (sliding into notes) or making slight adjustments to the tempo.[20]

An important composer of zarzuela, Amadeo Vives (1871–1932), from Catalonia, began his career writing sung-through operas based on the ideas of his teacher, the Catalan composer and musicologist Filipe Pedrell (1841–1922), who believed that Spanish opera should exhibit a combination of popular and formal traditions.[21] Vives achieved moderate success with his pastoral opera *Maruxa* (1914), though his two most popular works were both in the zarzuela vein: *Bohemios* (1904, based on Henri Murger's *Scènes de la Vie de Bohème* (Scenes of Bohemian Life), the same inspiration for Giacomo Puccini's *La bohème*) and *Doña Francisquita* (1923), probably his greatest work.

---

[19] Janet L. Sturman uses this phrase for a sub-heading in the first chapter of her book, *Zarzuela: Spanish Operetta, American Stage* (Urbana: University of Illinois Press, 2000), 17.

[20] Eva Moreda Rodríguez, 'Singing and Speaking in Early Twentieth-Century *Zarzuela*: The Evidence from Early Recordings', *Journal of Musicological Research* 41, no. 1 (2022): 42.

[21] Sturman, *Zarzuela*, 23.

On 13 September 1923, just over a month before *Doña Francisquita* opened, Miguel Primo de Rivera (1870–1930) led a Mussolini-inspired military coup against Spain's parliamentary government. His supporter, King Alfonso XIII, appointed Primo de Rivera prime minister, and a period of authoritarian dictatorship began. In the world of the zarzuela, composers and librettists retreated into the past, looking especially to Spain's Golden Age of the seventeenth century, in order to distance themselves from the dire realities of the present day.[22] Musical glamour infused their scores, which often would include evocations of Spanish dances. Zarzuela itself became institutionalized in the new regime. As historian Clinton D. Young argues, although zarzuela sold tickets, it could no longer be considered a purely popular art form, for 'it had acquired an official status and as such had to aim its ambitions higher than mere popular entertainment'.[23] The genre's official links with Primo de Rivera's dictatorship meant that zarzuela 'could not now claim to be a representation of the national identity of the Spanish people'.[24] The genre had become a means for the Spanish government to influence what it meant to be Spanish.

It was in such an environment that *Doña Francisquita* opened at the Teatro Apolo in Madrid on 17 October 1923. The zarzuela immediately found an audience and its popularity quickly spread throughout Spain and, indeed, overseas. It remains a standard part of the zarzuela repertory and is one of the most frequently recorded of any Spanish work for the musical stage (see Plate 7).[25]

The creation of *Doña Francisquita* can be traced back to December 1922, about nine months before the military coup. As the story goes, Vives met up with his eventual librettists Federico Romero and Guillermo Fernández-Shaw and gave them each a copy of the classic play *La discreta enamorada* (The Ingenious Lover, *c.*1604) by the Golden Age playwright Lope de Vega (Félix Lope de Vega y Carpio, 1562–1635). The librettists ended up adapting this hallmark of Spanish literature into what critics called something more than a popular zarzuela and, indeed, 'a true work of art'.[26] This was a true adaptation, for it consisted of more than just adding musical numbers to a pre-existing play. The new libretto is set not in the early

[22] Clinton D. Young, *Musical Theatre and Popular Nationalism in Spain, 1880–1930* (Baton Rouge: Louisiana State University Press, 2016), 146.

[23] Young, *Musical Theatre and Popular Nationalism in Spain*, 149.

[24] Young, *Musical Theatre and Popular Nationalism in Spain*, 150.

[25] Christopher Webber, *The Zarzuela Companion* (Lanham: Scarecrow, 2002), 256

[26] Young, *Musical Theatre and Popular Nationalism in Spain*, 151.

modern period (like the original), but in the 1840s, and it thus facilitates a romanticized imagining of Spanish culture and history.

The plot is essentially a love polygon, far more complex than a love triangle – or even two love triangles. Set in Madrid during carnival season, Francisquita is in love with Fernando, who is infatuated with Aurora, who is the lover of Lorenzo. Doña Francisca, Francisquita's mother, thinks Don Mathias, Fernando's father, is romantically interested in her when he actually has amorous feelings for Francisquita. In other words, the father of the man who Francisquita wants to pursue wants to pursue her. All works out at the end, with Francisquita and Fernando being together. Critics noted the fast-paced clarity of Romero and Fernández-Shaw's storytelling in the complex plot.

Vives's score looks back to the mid-nineteenth-century grandeur of *zarzuela grande* (big zarzuela).[27] Rather than syncopated dances or Viennese waltzes, Vives focuses on Spanish dance styles such as bolero, seguidilla and fandango. He also emphasizes the narrative role of the chorus, which represents the social community in which the action takes place. This happens perhaps most vividly in the seguidilla 'Canción de la juventud' (Song of Youth), a celebration of the youthfulness of Madrid introduced in Act 1 and reprised in the show's finale. A spirited choreographed fandango that features prominently in the final scene has also enjoyed a life and popularity of its own in the concert hall and on recordings. This is due in no small part to its vibrant brass writing and pervasive rhythmic vitality. Two romanzas (solo songs) from *Doña Francisquita* have entered the standard vocal repertory (mostly among Spanish-language singers), and with good reason: Francisquita's 'Canción del ruiseñor' (The Song of the Nightingale), with its bird-like trills and warbles, and Fernando's verismo-inspired 'Por el humo se sabe donde está el fuego' (By Smoke We Know Where There is Fire).

---

[27] Young, *Musical Theatre and Popular Nationalism in Spain*, 153.

4 | Getting Ready for 1924

Holidays are associated with presents, and this was certainly the case in late 1923. Several musical gifts opened during the winter holidays, though only one of them enjoyed success beyond a few months. What was significant, though, was that these works whetted audience appetites for what was to come in 1924.

Christmas and Boxing Day Treats

Two musical comedies, both featuring title characters of Irish descent, opened in New York on Christmas Day. The next day, an Orientalist fantasy opened in London. None lasted long, in part because the theatrical marketplace had reached its saturation point with so many works in similar veins.

On Broadway, *The Rise of Rosie O'Reilly*, with book, music and lyrics by George M. Cohan (1878–1942), greeted audiences at the Liberty Theatre. Presented by George M. Cohan's Comedians, it carried the subtitle *Poking Fun at Cinderella* and concerned a wealthy young suitor who is cut off from his family money after falling in love with the young Irish immigrant of the show's title. Without access to his fortune, he must become a song-and-dance man. Rather than a woman going from rags to riches, here a man goes from riches to rags. 'Rags' refers not only to his financial status but also to the style of his music: ragtime. The show had plenty of vaudeville-style turns and an abundance of dancing. Its relative lack of a plot is comically and knowingly acknowledged in the opening number, 'The Arrival of the Plot', and then again very late in Act 2, 'The Plot Again'. *The New York Times* critic called it '[a]nother of Mr. Cohan's speedy musical entertainments', formulaic and 'a workmanlike and brisk entertainment'.[1] Its innovative take on the all-too-familiar Irish immigrant trope wasn't enough to keep it going beyond March.

---

[1] 'Cohan's New Show a Dancing Success', *New York Times*, 26 December 1923.

Rosie's tale was complemented by that of *Mary Jane McKane*, which opened at the Imperial Theatre. Just as *The Rise of Rosie O'Reilly* had a recognizable figure in the person of Cohan, *Mary Jane McKane* featured some of the same creative team behind the success of that year's *Wildflower* (see Chapter 2): Herbert Stothart, Vincent Youmans and Oscar Hammerstein II, now joined by librettist William Cary Duncan. Produced by Arthur Hammerstein, also reprising his *Wildflower* role, this was another take on the familiar 'poor Irish immigrant' trope. When Mary Jane enquires about a job, she shares fleeting glances with the boss's son, Andrew Jr. She doesn't get the job because, as she is told, the office manager thinks she is too attractive. The office manager has promised Andrew Sr's wife that she will not hire any woman that the boss may find physically tempting. So, Mary Jane dresses down, puts on large-rimmed glasses and tries again. This time she gets the job. She's delighted to be spending time with Andrew Jr and saves him from the dastardly deeds of a business rival. He gives her only a quick verbal thank you, confessing to her that's he's in love with a woman he only saw for a few seconds. Everyone – except, of course, Mary Jane – realizes that she is that woman. By the final curtain, Andrew Jr has started his own business and he and Mary Jane are together.

Youman's contributions included the songs 'Flannel Petticoat Gal' and 'My Boy and I'. The first was recycled from *Hammerstein's 9 O'Clock Revue*, a short-lived production that played a week and a half in October. What Gerald Bordman calls 'its music-box sugariness'[2] was balanced with unexpected slinky chromaticism to create a version of the sweet past inserted musically into the murky present. 'My Boy and I' reflected a similar blend, for to the classic waltz paradigm, Youmans added metric misalignment and evocative, modernist harmonies to create, like he did with 'Flannel Petticoat Gal', something that sounded both old and new. Youmans subsequently reset 'My Boy and I' as a fast-paced, duple-metre syncopated tune, and when Otto Harbach gave it new lyrics, the result was the snappy title song to *No, No, Nanette*, which would have its pre-Broadway tryout in 1924 and open on Broadway in 1925.[3]

What was especially novel, however, about *Mary Jane McKane* was its 'Scenic Overture'. In a series of silhouette images, we learn how Mary Jane came from Slab City, Massachusetts, to New York City. This notion of

[2] Gerald Bordman, *Days to Be Happy, Years to Be Sad: The Life and Music of Vincent Youmans* (New York: Oxford University Press, 1982), 65.
[3] Larry Stempel, *Showtime: A History of the Broadway Musical Theater* (New York: W. W. Norton & Co., 2010), 229–230.

integrating the overture into a musical's storyline was something unusual at the time.

Moving from Irish immigrants to Asian caricatures, *Almond Eye* opened at the New Scala Theatre in the King's Cross area, away from the heart of the West End, on 26 December. It lasted for twenty-four performances. While *Almond Eye* could be assumed to be some sort of pantomime offering, and hence a holiday special event, this was not the case, even though its exoticism, costumes and many of its plot elements certainly evoked British pantomime.[4] Instead, *Almond Eye* was an Orientalist amalgamation of the story of Aladdin, the World War I hit *Chu Chin Chow* and Gilbert and Sullivan's *The Mikado*. Perhaps this intermingling of references was just too confusing for audiences. The plot is filled with twists and turns, including a hidden stash of jewels, a magic lamp and a mother who is continually disappointed in her son. But at its heart is the story of the financially and emotionally impoverished Ya-Mao, who falls in love with the Princess Ai-Lien. Their first-act duet, during which they fall in love at first sight, is prescient of 'Twin Soliloquies' in Rodgers and Hammerstein's *South Pacific* (1949), with Ya-Mao singing lines such as 'All alone in a world of her own' and Ai-Lien responding to herself, 'She may be just longing you know'.[5] They are from two different worlds (her name reflects this: Ai-Lien/Alien), and, of course, they ultimately end up together. The book and lyrics were by Joe Farren Scoutar, who played the Moorish peddler Amarak, and Arthur Veasey, with music by Frederick Rosse.

New Year's Eve Treats

As happened on Christmas Day, two new shows opened on New Year's Eve. Here, however, both featured famous stars. One was a comic play, not a musical, while the other was a full-fledged musical comedy with a *Follies*-style revue integrated into the plot.

First, George M. Cohan (1878–1942) opened as the title character in his own spoken-word comedy, *The Song and Dance Man*, at the Hudson Theatre. Cohan did not sing and dance in the role, but rather played someone who once did. At a theatrical boarding house, John 'Hap' Farrell, of the former vaudeville team Farrell and Carrol, meets a woman

---

[4] Pantomime, or panto, is a British tradition of retelling familiar tales, including fairy tales, in a particular stylized fashion. They are usually performed around the Christmas holiday season.

[5] Joe Farren Scoutar and Arthur Veasey, 'Almond Eye', unpublished typescript, LCP 1923/31, BL, 30.

who had been kind to his partner when he was dying. To show his gratitude, he pays the woman's bill, which depletes all his finances. Now destitute and desperate, he tries to hold up a pedestrian with a fake gun. He is arrested and, on his way to jail, he tells his tale of woe. Hap is released and returns to a successful career as a song and dance man. This was one of several plays that were running in 1924 in which music or musicians played significant roles.

Second, Eddie Cantor (1892–1964), one of the leading stars of Ziegfeld's *Follies*, made his first appearance as the lead in a book musical. With the opening of *Kid Boots* at the Earl Carroll Theatre, Cantor quickly and assertively proved himself to be far more than a blackface comic. His career started moving in a new direction – one that would bring him further acclaim on stage and, soon, on screen.

Cantor became famous in the *Follies* for playing the sassy son of Bert Williams, a Black actor who, like Cantor, performed in blackface. The white comedian was likewise well known for his impropriety and raunchy humour. *Kid Boots*, for Cantor, marked a decisive shift away from this unseemliness and, to a large extent, away from blackface. Percy Hammond noted this change in his review of *Kid Boots*: 'the mischievous Cantor has turned from such evil ways as he may have pursued in other capitals and is now comparatively harmless, though amusing'.[6] Throwing off blackface, though, took longer to accomplish. In *Kid Boots*, Cantor dons blackface make-up in one scene toward the end, where he plays a cameo version of himself rather than a character.

At first, Cantor was to play *Kid Boots* entirely in blackface; thus, the unsavoury practice's curtailment to one scene is significant. The idea for the show came from the songwriting team of Joseph McCarthy (1885–1943) and Harry Tierney (1890–1965), whose hit musical *Irene*, from 1919, which Florenz Ziegfeld produced, had been briefly revived in April 1923.[7] They had also contributed songs to the 1923 edition of the *Follies*, so were on good working terms with the esteemed producer. Since the songwriters knew that Ziegfeld was planning a book musical for Cantor, and since they themselves were members of a golf club, they proposed that the musical's central character would be a caddy master who also ran a bootlegging business: hence, 'Kid Boots'. The caddy master at their real-life club was Black, and

---

[6] Percy Hammond, 'New York Shows', *St. Louis Star and Times*, 12 January 1924, newspapers .com.

[7] Cantor credits the idea solely to McCarthy (Eddie Cantor, *My Life is in Your Hands* (1928, with David Freedman) and *Take My Life* (1957, with Jane Kesner Ardmore): *The Autobiographies of Eddie Cantor* (New York: Cooper Square Press, 2000), 229).

McCarthy and Tierney imagined that Cantor would perform the role in blackface. Ziegfeld and Cantor both liked the premise, and the producer hired William Anthony McGuire (1881–1940), an up-and-coming playwright who had yet to write a musical comedy, to craft the book. When time pressures mounted at an increasing rate, Ziegfeld brought in Otto Harbach (1873–1963) to assist McGuire with finishing the book.

Cantor, keenly aware of the importance of this show to his future career, decided that he did not want to be known principally as a blackface comic. Therefore, he determined that Kid Boots must be white.[8] Going beyond the appearance of his character, the actor inserted himself fully into the show's creative process. He suggested adding versions of some of his famous routines, the sort of things that audiences would expect in a show starring Eddie Cantor. These included a reworking of the perennial 'Joe's Blue Front' sketch, in which Cantor plays a salesman who, when he doesn't have what his customer comes to buy, comically convinces him to purchase something else altogether. Another was the osteopath sketch, complete with its array of contortionist twists and hard-handed pummelling. For *Kid Boots*, an electric treatment chair was added so that Cantor could have even more opportunities to showcase his unique brand of physical comedy.[9] Cantor recalled that this 'was the best physical-comedy scene I have ever played'.[10]

The star kept sending McGuire and Harbach jokes (only clean ones!) to add to the script. At first, the writers weren't interested. Eventually, though, they gave in, and, according to Cantor, his lines drew some of the show's biggest laughs.[11] The reason why the book authors weren't keen to add Cantor's jokes to the show was that they had absolutely nothing to do with the plot.[12] The quips, clever as they were, were extraneous to the storytelling and all about Cantor. Cantor, though, gave the writers ideas on how and where they could be fitted in to the storyline.[13] This reveals that in 1923, creators of Broadway musicals, including those produced by Ziegfeld, were concerned about what has become known as 'integration' – that is, the desire to make the music, the dancing, and the dialogue (i.e., everything presented on stage) serve the plot. This idea is often ascribed to musicals beginning with Rodgers and Hammerstein in the 1940s, or sometimes to

---

[8] For more on the genesis of *Kid Boots*, see Gregory Koseluk, *Eddie Cantor: A Life in Show Business* (Jefferson, NC: McFarland, 1995), 94–98.

[9] Koseluk, *Eddie Cantor*, 100–101; David Weinstein, *The Eddie Cantor Story: A Jewish Life in Performance and Politics* (Waltham: Brandeis University Press, 2018), 66–68.

[10] Cantor, *My Life*, 251.   [11] Weinstein, *The Eddie Cantor Story*, 66.

[12] Weinstein, *The Eddie Cantor Story*, 66.   [13] Cantor, *My Life*, 235.

Show Boat from 1927. What is evident here, though, is that the so-called new idea was already being practiced in 1923. Furthermore, the improvisatory nature of early musical comedy and revue, obviously not anathema to a book musical, was also present in *Kid Boots*. Cantor even added new lines at the Detroit premiere on 3 December 1923 that he kept in the show throughout its long run.[14]

Besides featuring Eddie Cantor front and centre, the show also introduced Mary Eaton (1901–1948). Ziegfeld was promoting Eaton as Marilyn Miller's successor as his premier leading lady. The critics agreed that while Eaton's singing was just fine, her acting and especially her dancing were truly exceptional. Eaton was known for doing circles of *en pointe* pirouettes in the *Follies* as well as other exquisite moves, and just as the absence of familiar Cantor sketches would have been unthinkable in *Kid Boots*, so too would have been the chance to see Eaton dance.

Also featured in a prominent role was Ethelind Terry (1899–1984), who played Carmen Mendoza, one of the romantic lead's former lovers. With her piercing dark eyes and dark hair, the Philadelphia-born actress became famous for two stage roles in which she played characters of Latinx heritage: Carmen Mendoza in *Kid Boots*, and the title role in *Rio Rita* (1927), her biggest success. Carmen is inferred to be Spanish, though she is made Anglo-white for all practical purposes in the story. Her 'Otherness' comes only through her name.

Another notable star was Jobyna Howland (1880–1936), who played Dr Josephine Fitch, a prominent golf club member. Howland, like Cantor, was known for her physical comedy and played alongside Cantor in two especially memorable scenes. First was the golf lesson. The doctor's towering stance over her teacher – Howland was six foot three inches tall – made the physical humour especially ripe for laughs (see Figure 4.1). Second was the aforementioned osteopath sketch, after which Cantor remarked that the ferociousness with which she over-convincingly played her part often left him bruised and sore.[15] Significantly, Dr Fitch is a female medical doctor, a rarity at the time, and, with her golf club membership, one who has a successful practice.

McGuire and Harbach chose as their setting the Everglades Golf Club in Palm Beach, Florida. This was not a random choice. In the mid-1920s, South Florida was in midst of a real estate boom, which reached its peak in 1925. In late 1923 and throughout 1924, the lure of Florida, with its

---

[14] Cantor, *My Life*, 245.   [15] Koseluk, *Eddie Cantor*, 104.

Figure 4.1 Eddie Cantor and Jobyna Howland in *Kid Boots*. Photo by White Studio.
©Billy Rose Theatre Division, The New York Public Library for the Performing Arts.

affordable properties and balmy climes, was very much in the air. *Kid Boots*
played into this appeal.

In the story, Kid Boots is the club's chief caddy who also gives golf
lessons, proffers advice on various topics, including romance, and is
a bootlegger. To help bolster his golf-lesson income, he owns a set of
special golf balls with extra lead added to one side so that they never go
in a straight line. By cleverly substituting his weighted golf balls for real
ones, the golfers can never get the balls to go where they want them to. Kid
tells his unsuspecting clients that all will be well if they just keep taking
more lessons, which they do. Kid's fiancée, Jane (played by the comic
actress Marie Callahan) manages the ladies' locker room at the club and
desperately wants Kid to become honest. Their relationship has direct
benefits for Kid, one of which is that he can hide his bootleg stash in her
locker room. When Dr Fitch finds him there, it sets up the osteopath scene.

Kid and Jane's romance, however, does not drive the plot. That honour is given to the millionaire semi-pro golfer Tom Sterling (played by Harry Fender, a well-known musical theatre tenor) and the very wealthy Polly Pendleton (Eaton's role), whose father runs a sporting goods manufacturing company. She, however, is engaged to Harold Regan (played by John Rutherford), the club's golf champion. Tom wants Polly to love him for who he is and not because of his money. A golf competition will take place, and if Harold wins, he can marry Polly. (This commodification of a woman as a prize is troubling, though it has plenty of precedents.) Thanks to Kid's intervention, Tom replaces Randolph Valentine (played by Robert Barrat), the champion from another club, in the tournament. One of Kid's trick balls is supposed to find its way into Harold's golf bag, but mistakenly ends up in Tom's. As things go awry, Kid confesses to the trick balls, which voids the game. All ends well, however, as Tom, the unintended victim of the prank, is declared the winner. Harold gives up his 'claim' to Polly, which allows her and Tom to be together. Tom modestly tells Boots that he cannot accept the golf trophy, to which Boots blithely replies, with a dose of metatheatricality, 'Why not? You've taken it every performance so far.'[16]

Showing the influence of the revue and furthering the golf theme, the playbill for *Kid Boots* does not list scenes but rather 'holes'. Since a game of golf has eighteen holes, the golf-infused musical is arranged in eighteen 'holes' – twelve in Act 1 and six in Act 2. Having such a large number of 'holes', some of which feature multiple 'strokes', more than hints at the format of the quintessential Ziegfeld genre: the revue. Audiences attending a Ziegfeld production would expect to see aspects of a splashly revue, no matter what. This was especially true for a show starring Eddie Cantor, for it was through the revue that he became famous enough to take the title role in a musical comedy. During the penultimate hole, just before the denouement, as the golf tournament is approaching its foregone conclusion, the audience is transported to a lavish revue that provides star turns for some of *Kid Boot*'s principal players.

Central to this homage to the *Follies* is the appearance of 'Mr. Eddie Cantor of the Ziegfeld Follies'. Here, Cantor appears not as the clever golf caddy but as himself in blackface to perform a selection of songs from his repertory, which at the time included 'Charley, My Boy', 'If You Knew

---

16   William Anthony McGuire and Otto Harbach, *Kid Boots* script, *T-Mss 1987–010, Series I: Scripts; Sub-series 1 – Play Scripts, box 2, folder 9, Flo Ziegfeld-Billie Burke Papers, Billy Rose Theatre Collection, NYPL.

Susie' and 'Dinah'.[17] Cantor told Ziegfeld that he thought having a featured band to accompany his blackface specialty would enhance its effectiveness. Ziegfeld agreed and recalled a band that Fanny Brice had recommended to him: George Olsen and His Music. Olsen, a percussionist, had been performing with his eponymous band in the Portland, Oregon area, which is where Brice heard him. According to Olsen's obituary in *The New York Times*, 'Mr. Ziegfeld wired Mr. Olsen asking how much he wanted to join Eddie Cantor in "Kid Boots." Mr. Olsen asked for $1,800 a week. Mr. Ziegfeld offered $800. Mr. Olsen, who was making $400 at the time, wired back, "We're on our way".'[18] The band's appearance in *Kid Boots* provided a substantive boost not just to the show but also to Olsen's own career and reputation. Cantor wrote that 'The unique feature of this band was its capacity for playing jazz time in a subdued and dulcet style, getting its effects through subtleties rather than noise.'[19]

The music featured in this *Follies*-esque sequence relates to the overall plot of the show in that it is performed in a 'show-within-the-show' and therefore is featured diegetically (i.e., the characters in the show see and hear the numbers). This notion of integrating or relating the musical numbers to the plot was important to the creators, just like their reticence at adding Cantor's jokes to their script.

This dictum of songs relating to the plot is especially evident in those that feature Tom, the romantic lead. In the gently syncopated duet 'When Your Heart's in the Game', Tom teaches Polly how to play golf. With lines such as 'Some golden day / Love will show you the way / If your heart's in the game', golf becomes a metaphor for the game of courtship that is at the heart of the musical. Later, when Tom's former girlfriend Carmen appears, the two reminisce about their past in a nostalgia-tinged waltz duet, 'The Same Old Way'. The waltz was becoming closely associated with the idea of memory, including of young love, at the time, and this song certainly fits that paradigm. In 'Polly Put the Kettle On', which shares its title with a popular English nursery rhyme, Tom and his friends, to Tierney's gently swaying music, envision an extremely male-oriented idea of domestic

---

[17] Weinstein, *The Eddie Cantor Story*, 69, 255. Richard C. Norton lists additional songs that may have also been performed: 'If You Do What You Do', 'Ma, He's Makin' Eyes at Me', 'A Birdie', 'The Dumber They Come They Better I Like 'Em', 'It's Just that Feeling for Home' and 'Let Me Introduce You to My Rosie' (Richard C. Norton, *A Chronology of American Musical Theater, Volume 2: 1912–1952* (New York: Oxford University Press, 2002), 349).

[18] 'George Olsen, 78, Bandleader of the 20's and 30's, Is Dead', *New York Times*, 19 March 1971.

[19] Cantor, *My Life*, 238.

bliss.[20] They imagine Polly, Tom's wealthy love interest, being married to him and cooking his meals, something new for her. Tom even states in the second verse, 'I can see her in the lovelight glow / With her pretty fingers dipped in dough'.[21] With a foreshadowing of 'When the Children Are Asleep' from Rodgers and Hammerstein's *Carousel* (1945), this male imaginary of marital bliss ends with the evocative words 'and dream with me'.[22]

Audiences would expect the show's two stars, Cantor and Eaton, to perform a duet, and Tierney gave them a lovely song of mutual support: 'Some One Loves You After All (The Rain Song)'. This was not a love song, but rather a pledge of platonic friendship. Its gentle wistfulness and weather-related lyric recall 'Till the Clouds Roll By' from *Oh, Boy!* (1917). A set of alternative lyrics in the script ties the song directly to plot points (integration), with Polly and Kid telling each other that they ultimately will be with the person they love:

After the rain – you will have Jane
After the storm – you will have Tom
Some one loves you after all.[23]

On 4 January 1924, Paul Whiteman recorded the song with his orchestra.[24] The lilting grace of Tierney's flowing melodic lines and gentle rhythmic underpinning are clearly evident in Ferde Grofé's arrangement, which features bandmembers Henry Busse (trumpet), Mike Pingatore (banjo), and Grofé and Adam Carroll (pianos).

One of the most musically complex songs in the score is the narrative counterpoint number 'Win for Me', which details the progress of the tournament. Polly, Carmen and Boots each sing about why they want Tom to win: Polly so she doesn't have to marry Harold, Carmen because she still has feelings for Tom and Boots because he made a big bet on the outcome. This particular song imaginatively integrates three distinctive plot points or character attributes. After singing their lines individually, they do so simultaneously.

The score also includes some overtly racist numbers. The 'colored caddies' sing 'Got to Have More' as a blackface minstrel number. Its inclusion evokes Cantor's reputation (and eventual appearance in the show) as a blackface performer, though its dialect lyrics concern racial

[20] 'Polly Put the Kettle On' was recorded by the American Quartet, an all-male singing foursome, in 1924 and released as HMV B1841.
[21] McGuire and Harbach, *Kid Boots* script.   [22] McGuire and Harbach, *Kid Boots* script.
[23] McGuire and Harbach, *Kid Boots* script.   [24] Victor 19244A (B-29182-2).

inequalities in 1924, namely the low-paying working conditions of the Black employees at the golf club. The white caddies are not involved; the assumption is that, because they are white, they are better paid. This glimmer of acknowledgement of racial inequalities, though presented in racist terms, is notable, not least because it foreshadows the opening atmosphere of *Show Boat* just a few years later. No such glimmer is evident in the Act 2 opening: the racially demeaning 'Mah Jong', with its ridiculing of the appropriated pastime and the Chinese culture from which it comes. Lines in pidgin English do nothing to advance the plot and only serve to accentuate the racist attitudes of the members of the exclusive white golf club.

Kid Boots was first and foremost about Eddie Cantor. After it closed on Broadway in February 1925, Cantor continued touring in the title role. This was in many ways the show that separated Eddie Cantor the physical comedian from Eddie Cantor the blackface comedian. As David Weinstein asserts, Cantor used *Kid Boots* 'to solidify his popular persona as the funny, likeable, street-smart wise guy who is not above a little criminal activity'.[25] Cantor himself said about the show: '"Kid Boots" contained' every type of comedy for which I was best suited. The pattern of its comic scenes and their sequence were skillfully designed and have rarely been excelled. The shades of fun varied from light gags and wise-cracks to human situations, and from great physical hokum to delightful nonsense.[26]

Kid Boots in many ways emblemizes what would happen throughout 1924. Old material in the form of Cantor's earlier comic routines would merge with a new image of the actor as a physical comedian. An established producer, Ziegfeld, would bring a new band with a distinctive sound to Broadway. Finally, the essentiality of the revue as a musical theatre genre would be seen through its integration into the plot of a book musical.

---

[25] Weinstein, *The Eddie Cantor Story*, 69.   [26] Cantor, *My Life*, 246.

PART II

From Winter to Spring

5 | A New Year Begins

The musicals that opened in January and early February 1924 found themselves competing with successful shows from the previous year. As always, a new musical had to make its mark. During these weeks, a fresh type of revue, one that focused on its smartness rather than visual opulence, arrived in New York from London. Adaptations of German-language works opened in Italy and the United Kingdom, reflecting the continued appeal of these transnational properties. Sprightly musical comedies also debuted, often retreading familiar paradigms, but few events could compare in significance to Paul Whiteman's 'An Experiment in Modern Music' on 12 February, when George Gershwin performed his *Rhapsody in Blue* for the first time.

André Charlot and the Making of New Broadway Stars

The French-born London producer André Charlot (1882–1956) promoted a very specific type of revue, one focused on performers, intimacy and clever wit. His revue *Puppets*, which opened at the Vaudeville Theatre on 2 January, was a vehicle for the impressive comic talents of Binnie Hale (1899–1984) and Stanley Lupino (1893–1942). Dion Titheradge's skits and Ivor Novello's songs (with Titheradge's lyrics) revolved around the pair. Among the highlights was Hale's impressions of three of the West End's leading ladies: Evelyn Laye (star of *Madame Pompadour*), José Collins (*Catherine*) and Beatrice Lillie (various Charlot-produced revues).

Charlot was listed as 'presenter' for *Puppets*, though he did not supervise its development.[1] This was for a very good reason: Charlot was in New York preparing to make musical theatre history. He hoped that his quintessentially English-style revue would succeed on Broadway, but even he almost certainly could not have envisaged what a triumph it would be. When *André Charlot's Revue of 1924* opened at the Times Square Theatre

---

[1] James Ross Moore, *André Charlot: The Genius of Intimate Musical Revue* (Jefferson: McFarland, 2005), 96.

on 9 January, it entranced Broadway audiences for eight months – well beyond the original six-week plan.

In *André Charlot's Revue of 1924*, the glamour of the revue as practiced by Florenz Ziegfeld, George White and the Shuberts came not through lavish staircases and throngs of gorgeously costumed women but rather through intimacy. Charlot's entertainments were conceived to play in smaller spaces with a smaller number of principals and a smaller ensemble than their American counterparts. Hence, when the Selwyn brothers, Edgar and Archibald, in their role as producers, brought *Charlot's Revue* to Broadway, they placed it in their 1,032-seat Times Square Theatre. While still a large number, the theatre's capacity was notably less than the 1,550 of the original configuration of the New Amsterdam or the 1,600 of the Winter Garden. For part of its lengthy run, the revue moved to the even smaller Selwyn Theatre, which sat just 740.

The actor Tom Powers saw the revue soon after it opened. Afterwards, he wrote to Beatrice Lillie, one of the revue's stars and someone with whom he had previously shared the stage, telling her,

Of course, the whole thing – your revue – I am sure it will revolutionize the production of that type of entertainment in this country. My God, how sick it must make Ziegfeld and Murray Anderson [another producer] to see your show produced with a fifth the number of principals, and a half the number of chorus, and about a sixtieth of the expense and furnishing amusement one hundred fold.[2]

Besides smaller spaces and smaller forces, London revues of the time, as David Linton writes, had a specific quality about them, one rooted in Englishness. Their very essence was based on the performance of English identity, class, empire and nostalgia.[3] Irony was mixed with comedy for what Linton calls 'a more sophisticated and select audience'.[4] Transferring this aesthetic to the bright lights of Broadway could prove challenging. Gertrude Lawrence (1898–1952), who made her US debut in *André Charlot's Revue of 1924*, explained, 'Charlot's revues were characterized by an exquisite economy, a camaraderie between all the players and the audience such as had not been known in America up to this time. It was not a rough-and-ready intimacy, and never a jocular ad-libbing, but a mental closeness hard to define, and immediate in its appeal.'[5]

Lawrence had been appearing in Charlot-produced revues since 1916, including *London Calling!* (see Chapter 1). She was one of three major

---

[2] Letter, Tom Powers to Beatrice Lillie, 1 February 1924, Beatrice Lillie Papers, NYPL.
[3] Linton, *Nation and Race*, 156.   [4] Linton, *Nation and Race*, 155.
[5] Gertrude Lawrence, *A Star Danced* (New York: Doubleday, 1945), 129.

London actors to appear in *André Charlot's Revue of 1924*, the other two being Beatrice Lillie and Jack Buchanan. Lillie (1894–1989), born in Toronto, Canada, made her West End debut in 1914 and became famous for her hilarious parodies of older singing styles and inanely engaging performance style. Her fame was such that Binnie Hale included her in her trio of impersonations in *Puppets*. As musical theatre historian Ethan Mordden quipped: 'Beatrice Lillie posed an arresting question – what do you do with a musical comedy heroine who is simply too silly to support (or abide) a love plot?'[6] The answer: put her in a revue. That is exactly what Charlot did, and it was to everyone's benefit: hers, his and especially the audience's. Tall, graceful and debonaire, Buchanan (1891–1957) was described by Charlot's biographer James Ross Moore as the man 'who ultimately became the epitome of British sophistication on the musical stage and in film'.[7] Others in the cast who would go on to have major careers included Jessie Matthews (1907–1981) and Constance Carpenter (1904–1992).

As was typical for so many revues, material that had pleased audiences previously was recycled, sometimes with the very performers who introduced it. This was the case for *André Charlot's Revue of 1924*, for the producer drew heavily upon material from three of his London revues: *A to Z* (1921), *Rats!* (1923) and *London Calling!*

The revue's opening number, significantly, was new and specific to New York. 'How D'You Do'[8] was Charlot's way of introducing the cast and his approach to the revue. The actors sang directly to the audience, breaking down the 'fourth wall' in one of the standard practices of London revue. Each then took their own turn to introduce themselves. Significantly, the self-descriptive number was played in front of the curtain: it became immediately clear that this revue would rely on the strengths of its stars and not on visual grandiosity. Charlot explained his reasoning in having the performers introduce themselves:

My principals are all on the stage five minutes after the curtain rises. This will show you how different I run my revues from the American ones. You have seen everyone in the show almost immediately after the first number has been sung. And, all during the play, these principals are on the stage almost all the time. There is no long wait between their appearances.[9]

[6] Ethan Mordden, *Make Believe: The Broadway Musical in the 1920s* (New York: Oxford University Press, 1997), 67.

[7] Moore, *André Charlot*, 53.   [8] Music by Philip Braham, lyrics by Ronald Jeans and Eric Blore.

[9] Souvenir program for *Andre Charlot's Revue of 1924 First American Tour*, MWEZ n.c. 9393 #7, Program Collection, Billy Rose Theatre Collection, NYPL.

The revue's sketches reflect a distinctively English sense of satire and wit. In 'The Green-Eyed Monster' (from *A to Z*),[10] for example, Jack Buchanan played a jealous husband who murders his wife's dancing teacher because he thinks she's having an affair with him. When the husband realizes his mistake, the players make things right by playing the entire scene in reverse.

Lillie's unique stage presence charmed the audience. She entered singing the hope-filled 'There Are Times' (from *A to Z*)[11] in front of a silhouetted chorus, which provided a stunning visual effect without the massive expense of elaborate scenery.[12] She then opened Act 2 with the delightful 'There's Life in the Old Girl Yet' (from *London Calling!*),[13] in which she played an ageing musical comedy star. As the revue moved into its final scenes, Lillie brought the house down with her rendition of 'March with Me' (from *London Calling!*).[14] In this show-stopping escapade she played Britannia, who is determined not to be overrun by her followers as she continually trips over her own feet and almost plunges herself into the orchestra pit. Tom Powers wrote to her about the audience reaction: 'Everybody around me said that they had never laughed so much in the theatre in their lives as they did in your Britannia number. ... This poor, misguided woman determined to do the number in spite of fate and the chorus and God and everybody.'[15]

While Lillie's numbers accentuated humour, Lawrence's songs conveyed anguish. Lawrence made her indelible first impression in 'Parisian Pierrot', a song she had introduced in *London Calling!*[16] Its lilting syncopated refrain, coupled with her vocal prowess, made for a deeply emotional expression of Pierrot's unrequited love for Columbine. Lawrence's crumpled pose captured what one critic called 'the pathos and wayward charm of Pierrot' (see Figure 5.1).[17]

'Parisian Pierrot' became one of Lawrence's signature songs, as did her other big number from the revue, 'Limehouse Blues'. Douglas Furber's overtly racist lyrics reek of horrific ethnic stereotypes. When Harms published the song in association with *Charlot's Revue of 1924*, Lawrence was featured on the cover in faux-Asian attire (see Plate 8). Lawrence had been

---

[10] Written by Dion Titheradge.   [11] Music by Ivor Novello, lyrics by Ronald Jeans.
[12] Moore, *André Charlot*, 89.   [13] Music and lyrics by Noël Coward.
[14] Music by Ivor Novello, lyrics by Douglas Furber.
[15] Tom Powers to Beatrice Lillie, 1 February 1924.
[16] Music and lyrics by Noël Coward.
[17] Uncited review, 'Charlot's Revue', NYPL Sub-series 5: Scrapbooks, box 62, Scrapbook – Charlot's Revue 1924, Beatrice Lillie Papers.

Figure 5.1 Gertrude Lawrence performing 'Parisian Pierrot' in *André Charlot's Revue of 1924.*

performing the number in Charlot productions since October 1921, when she and Jack Buchanan introduced it in *A to Z*. Originally, Beatrice Lillie was supposed to do the number with Buchanan, but when she became ill Lawrence replaced her. Thereafter, it became Lawrence's song. Its pulsating drone fifths, chromatic melodic descents, syncopated rhythms and harmonic quirkiness at the beginning of the refrain combine to create an aural sense of elusive Otherness. With lyrics in which the white singer claims to understand the difficulties of the Chinese immigrants living in London's Limehouse district – 'I've the real Limehouse blues',[18] she sings at one point – the song is infused with a false kinship with real victims of racial prejudice, both East Asians through 'Limehouse' and Black people through

---

[18] Douglas Furber and Philip Braham, Limehouse Blues [sheet music] (London: Ascherberg, Hopwood & Crew, 1922), 5.

'Blues'. Using overtly offensive language to describe the very people with whom she claims emotional bonds, the singer exerts her internalized racially superior attitude as she sings of her forlorn state. Despite – or perhaps partly because of – its overt racist tone, the song became a massive hit, and not only because of Lawrence's rendering.

In addition to these two signature songs, Lawrence also performed 'I Don't Know', a sultry number that she referred to as 'a quiet little song',[19] and the sentimental duet 'You Were Meant for Me' with Jack Buchanan.[20] This was the same non-syncopated Sissle and Blake song that she and Noël Coward introduced in *London Calling!*

The revue ended optimistically, reprising the mood of Lillie's first song, 'There Are Times'. In 'Night May Have its Sadness' (from *A to Z*), Ivor Novello's melodic lyricism blends with Collie Knox's evocative lyric to proffer hope in the midst of gloom. The undulating verse, indicated to be performed 'very smoothly', captures the languid atmosphere suggested in the grief-filled narrative. The refrain, carrying the notation 'slowly, but very marked rhythm', offers a sense of anticipation. It begins not with the stability of a tonic harmony but rather on a more active dominant chord. According to the principals of tonal harmony, a dominant chord should resolve to the tonic. Since the words 'Night may give its sadness' overlie a dominant harmony, they too must resolve to 'gladness in the morning', just as the tonal motion must resolve to the tonic. Such understatement reveals an affecting blend of words and musical process.

André Charlot's Revue of 1924 closed on 20 September after 298 performances. It then embarked on a successful, extensive and eventful tour, but that story comes later.

Elsewhere, Namely Milan and Madrid

Madame Pompadour's unqualified success in Berlin, Vienna and especially in London proved that audiences adored the glamourous costume operetta. The work's formidable early legacy continued when an Italian version opened on 15 January 1924 at the 3,000-seat Teatro Dal Verme in Milan. Performed by the Compagnia Regini Lombardo (Regini Lombardo Company) and translated by Angelo Nessi, this *Madame Pompadour* came from the same esteemed ensemble that brought *Il paese del*

---

[19] Lawrence, *A Star Danced*, 128.
[20] In some playbills, the song's title appears as 'I Was Meant for You'.

campanelli to the stage the previous November. In the title role was Nella Regini, the company's soprano who had delighted audiences as Nela in *Il paese del campanelli*. Regini received enormous praise for her performance: one critic wrote that her success in the difficult role affirmed her as the greatest Italian operetta prima donna.[21]

Three days later, on 18 January, *La leyenda del beso* (The Legend of the Kiss) opened at the Teatro Apolo in Madrid. This work, which would become part of the standard zarzuela repertory, featured a nearly operatic story of cultural encounter by Enrique Royo, Antonio Paso Díaz and Silva Aramburu and an evocative score by Reveriano Soutullo and Juan Vert. The plot concerns Count Mario, who falls in love with Amapola, a Romani traveller who, with her community, is staying on his land. As Amapola's mother was dying, she uttered a troubling prophecy: whoever kisses Amapola's lips will die. Iván, another Romani, is besotted with Amapola, though she does not reciprocate his feelings. During a spectacular Romani celebration, Mario invites Amapola to meet him secretly on the castle steps. At the climax of their impassioned duet, they kiss, invoking the prophecy. Iván enters, ready to kill Mario, when Ulita, a wise older woman, arrives and implores all the Romani to leave immediately, which they do. Mario is left to contemplate the truth of the prophecy, and when his friends enter, they find him in a state of complete despair. The fatal kiss has indeed caused death, not a physical death, but the death of all of Mario's hopes and desires.

The Romani feature prominently in several numbers, including the quirky 'Qué vaivén tiene el fox' (How the Foxtrot Sways) and the lavish spectacle 'Tiene el son de mi cantar' (It Has the Sound of My Singing). In the former, Gorón, Mario's friend from Madrid, tries to teach the Romani how to dance the latest Parisian sensation, the foxtrot. The group is grounded in flamenco, and so the attempted merger of the new foxtrot and the familiar flamenco offers the zarzuela's dance director an opportunity to create some humorous choreographic moments. A seriousness underpins this juxtaposition, though, for it is as if Gorón is trying to teach the Romani how to be modern and sophisticated by dancing the foxtrot, and their challenges in this regard suggest that this may not be possible. This racist portrayal shows the Romani to be intellectually and physically 'inferior' to the upper-class characters in the zarzuela. Their treatment is akin to the racist depictions of African American and Indigenous

---

[21] *Cronaca dei theatri Milanese* (Chronicle of Milan Theatre), 26 January 1924; quoted in Anna Dell'Orto, 'Scienze spettacolo Lombardo', thesis, n.d., academia.edu.

characters in shows that were playing on Broadway at the same time. The second number is a massive *zambra*, a particular type of flamenco associated with the Romani in Spain and often performed nowadays for tourists. This is its context in *La leyenda del beso*, for the Romani are performing their culture (or more precisely, Suotullo and Vert's version of it) for Mario and his friends.

In order to move the action from the public spectacle of the zambra to the ultimately tragic final meeting of Mario and Amapolo, and to do so without words, Soutullo and Vert created a transitory orchestral inter-mezzo. This rapturous interlude, which sometimes features on orchestral concerts, begins with splendid largesse and progresses to a smaller, more intimate sound world that sets up the atmosphere for the duet '¿Vendrás, mujer? Mi corazón te aguarda' (Will You Come, Woman? My Heart Awaits You). Here, Mario, on the verge of complete psychological collapse, expresses his intense ardour to Amapolo as their inevitable kiss draws increasingly nearer.

La leyenda del beso was not the first work by any means to deal with cultural encounters in Spain. One can certainly think of Georges Bizet's opéra comique *Carmen* (1875) in this regard, though it is of course French and not Spanish. In *La leyenda del beso*, however, it is the male protagonist who suffers an emotional death, rather than the female protagonist a physical one, as in Bizet's tragedy.

Musical Comedies Come and Go

Two Broadway musical comedies opened seven blocks away from each other on the evening of 21 January: *Lollipop* at the Knickerbocker Theatre on 38th Street and *Sweet Little Devil* at the Astor Theatre on 45th Street. Neither show would last beyond May, even though they boasted scores by two of the decade's most celebrated composers: Vincent Youmans (*Lollipop*) and George Gershwin (*Sweet Little Devil*). Their brief runs prove the fragility of the musical theatre business.

Lollipop's story was by Zelda Sears (1873–1935), one of a comparatively small but significant number of women writing for Broadway in the 1920s. Sears was an accomplished actor, librettist, lyricist, screenwriter, novelist and businesswoman. In *Lollipop*, the orphan Laura Lamb, known as Lollipop, finally gets adopted by the wealthy Mrs. Garrity. Things do not turn out well for the youngster, for she is accused, falsely, of stealing from her adoptive mother. Nonetheless, Lollipop's eternal sense of optimism and hope, befitting a musical comedy heroine, ensures a happy ending, complete with a romantic union with her only friend from the orphanage, the plumber Bill Geohagen. Sears's plot thwarted the popular American Cinderella paradigm, for Lollipop was neither employed nor did she end up with a wealthy suitor. Playing the title role was Ada-May (1896–1978), born Ada May Weeks, a fine dancer who was the show's biggest draw. Creating the role of Mrs. Garrity was none other than the show's librettist, Zelda Sears, who already in 1919 was being described as 'The Greatest of Stage Old Maids',[22] a perfect description of her character in *Lollipop*.

For composer Vincent Youmans, *Lollipop* held personal and professional significance, for this was his first solo score for Broadway. He'd written songs for *Wildflower*, the long-running hit from 1923 that was still playing when *Lollipop* opened, but that score was co-written with Herbert Stothart, as was *Mary Jane McKane*, which had opened in December. Thus, for several months in 1924, Vincent Youmans's music was being featured – and praised – in three different Broadway shows. Among *Lollipop*'s admittedly few treats was the delightful foxtrot 'Take a Little One Step'. Its charming metrical trippings led Youmans to add it to *No, No, Nanette* after that show opened on Broadway in 1925.

Another notable feature of *Lollipop* was the inclusion of twelve Tiller Girls in the production. Their presence did nothing for the plot, but that really didn't matter, for they were there for no other reason than to show off their precision dancing and synchronized back flips.

Opening seven blocks north of *Lollipop* was *Sweet Little Devil*, a musical comedy that wholly embraced the mistaken identity archetype for its plot. *Sweet Little Devil* was created as a vehicle for the silent-screen starlet Constance Binney (1896–1989), who had performed the dance-based role of Parker in *Oh, Lady! Lady!!* back in 1918. Laurence Schwab and Frank Mandel crafted the storyline about a young woman who answers her older cousin's fan mail, and George Gershwin, working with the veteran lyricist Buddy De Sylva, wrote the musical comedy's genre-defining songs. This was Gershwin's fifth musical comedy (after *La-La-Lucille!*, *A Dangerous Maid*, *Flying Island* and *Our Nell*) and the first of four shows with music by Gershwin that would open in 1924.

Binney played Virginia Arminta Culpepper, the 'sweet little devil' whose older cousin is Joyce West, a beautiful New York showgirl. Tom Nesbit,

---

[22] Ada Patterson, 'The Greatest of Stage Old Maids', *Theatre Magazine* 13 (April 1911): 127. https://babel.hathitrust.org/cgi/pt?id=ucl.32106011629943&view=1up&seq=231&q1=%27greatest%20of%20stage%20old%20maids%22.

a young American engineer working in Peru, reads about Joyce and writes her a fan letter. She responds (or so he thinks), and an increasingly amorous exchange of letters begins. In reality, Joyce is only interested in wealthy men and discards Tom's letter. Virginia rescues it, answers it and keeps the correspondence going. Tom learns he needs to come to New York to sell his latest invention for a sizeable sum and proposes that he and Joyce meet in person. Virginia becomes concerned, for she doesn't want Joyce meeting Tom and flinging herself at him because of his money. So, Virginia convinces Tom of her cousin's greed. In retaliation for stringing him along through their letters (or so he thinks), Tom takes Joyce with him back to Peru and makes her work in the mines. Virginia, realizing that she wants Tom for herself, goes to Peru to sort things out. She and Tom unite as Joyce sets her sights on another man.

Among the score's many highlights are the metrically kinetic 'Jijibo' and the satirical march 'Hooray for the USA'. 'Jijibo', which forms the basis for the Act 1 finale, describes a new dance that can help you either lose or gain weight, whichever you want. The song plays into the decade's obsession with physical fitness. The uneven rhythms of the jazzy refrain give it an innate perkiness, which is further enhanced by a clever mixture of metric groupings. While the orchestra moves swiftly along with its four-pulse groupings, the melody trips along in three-beat ones. The metric effect is accentuated through an emphasis on the third syllable of the dance's name (Jiji**bo**), which forms a clever incessant rhyme with 'know' and 'go'. The song also creates interest from a harmonic perspective, for it features a lowered seventh scale degree in its opening ascending figure, negating the effect of a 'leading tone' (ti in solfege; 'tea' if one thinks of 'Do, Re, Mi' from *The Sound of Music*) that pushes a melody toward a satisfying conclusion. Also known as mixolydian mode, this harmonic opening creates a sense of Otherness that, in terms of musical dramaturgy, points to the absence of Black characters and the white commodification of Black culture on Broadway.

While the jijibo is a fictional dance for the purposes of the musical, such dances formed a major part of the Broadway canon at the time. Jazz dances, according to dancer and dance historian Liza Gennaro, showed white audiences how jazz rhythms were 'translated on to bodies' and how the dancefloor became 'a place from which to draw energy and express rhythm'.[23] Steps with animal names like the bunny hug, turkey trot and pigeon walk represented, writes Robert Hylton, another dancer and dance

---

[23] Gennaro, *Making Broadway Dance*, 12.

historian, 'a balance of cultural transmission and appropriation'.[24] Hylton continues, when discussing the white dancers and dancing teachers Irene and Vernon Castle: 'Black social dances were taken and adapted to suit white consumers, enabling dancers such as the Castles to have a career unavailable to Black dancers. This lack of opportunity stemmed from the racist simultaneous perception of Black culture as capital but Black people as inferior – a reality of appropriation still present today.'[25] 'Jijibo' is a prime example of this sort of cultural capital.

'Hooray for the USA', by contrast, is a parody of a patriotic march with its celebratory pomp. The lyrics satirize life at home when a trio of secondary characters (Sam, May and Rena) arrive in Peru after a long and arduous journey. They miss their native land, even with its faults. Just as 'Jijibo' played on the popularity of syncopated dances with roots in Black culture, 'Hooray for the USA' offered a satirical parody of election-year patriotism, for in November 1924 Calvin Coolidge would be re-elected as US president.

The week after the premieres of *Lollipop* and *Sweet Little Devil*, another musical comedy opened on Broadway. *Moonlight*, which debuted on 30 January at the Longacre Theatre, had as its premise a Long Island gentle-man who bets his party guests that with the right combination of mood, music and words, it is possible for any man and any woman to fall in love. Con Conrad provided the love-inducing music, William B. Friedlander the lyrics and William Le Baron the book. What critics praised, though, were the dancing and the sets.[26] Like its January siblings, it had a modest run and closed in June.

Viennese Operetta in London, via Italy: *The Three Graces*

When it comes to the stage works associated with Franz Lehár (1870–1948), it is the music that makes us most remember them. So much so, in fact, that sometimes the story seems extraneous. Such is the case with *The Three Graces*, whose roots lie in Lehár's unsuccessful Viennese operetta *Der Sterngucker* (The Stargazer, 1916), with book and lyrics by Fritz Löhner. The score, though certainly not the story about a young astronomer who seems to have become engaged to three of his sister's friends, captivated the

---

[24] Hylton, *Dancing in Time*, 59.   [25] Hylton, *Dancing in Time*, 59.
[26] Dan Dietz, *The Complete Book of 1920s Broadway Musicals* (Lanham: Rowman and Littlefield, 2019), 192.

attention of the Italian impresario Carlo Lombardo (1869–1959). (This is the same Lombardo who was behind *Il paese dei campanelli* and the Italian version of *Madame Pompadour.*) Lombardo persuaded Lehár to use the music for an entirely new libretto, one which he himself conveniently provided. The result was *La danza delle libellule* (The Dance of the Dragonflies), which opened in Milan in 1922 to great acclaim. Its popularity prompted a translation into German by A. M. Willner as *Der Libellentanz*, also a success. It is noteworthy that there were now two completely different German-language libretti for the same musical score. Since the Lehár–Lombardo operetta had earned profits on both Italian and German musical stages, it comes as no real surprise that an English-language version would eventually join its continental siblings.

The well-known English playwright Ben Travers set about doing just that, and the result, *The Three Graces*, opened on 23 January at the Empire Theatre in London, where it played for nearly three months. This was the first production of a new and relatively unknown Lehár operetta (not a familiar favourite like *The Merry Widow*) to be staged in London after the Great War.[27] Continued resentment toward Austria resulted in some booing at some performances.[28] The piece itself, however, was lauded. Even so, the comparatively short run had a great deal to do with its venue. The Empire was a variety theatre, not an operetta house. *The Three Graces*, lovely as it was, was not the type of fare that would draw audiences to the Empire. The Empire's offerings, even as its name implies, would be very pro-British, and a continental import, especially five years after hostilities ended, was going to struggle.

As did several musical theatre offerings of the time, *The Three Graces* includes a show-within-a-show in which the characters who play the romantic leads in the show-within-a-show end up falling in love. There's also a ubiquitous rescue narrative: a wealthy man marries a newly destitute woman, one result of which is that she can resume her privileged lifestyle. Here, it is Countess Helene (played by Winifred Barnes) of the Castle Nancy, who is to be evicted from her home after a legal case brought forth by Charles, Duke of Nancy (played by Thorpe Bates). Both claim ownership of the castle and find themselves at odds over the entanglement. Helene arranges for a festive gathering to take place at what she considers to be her castle, part of which will be a new Mount Olympus-themed

---

[27] Scott, *German Operetta*, 95.

[28] Richard Traubner, *Operetta: A Theatrical History* (Garden City: Doubleday, 1983; paperback ed., Oxford: Oxford University Press, 1989), 255.

musical revue written by her uncle and guardian, Count Pommery. To add to the prestige of the event, they've hired Max Rory, a famed Parisian actor, to play Adonis. When Charles arrives to discuss the ownership situation with Helene, he is mistaken for Rory and gladly takes on the role. The real Max Rory, though, is insulted at being asked to perform with a group of amateurs and sends Bouquet, a buffoon actor, in his place. Helene herself plays Venus in the entertainment, which includes the splendid 'Mythological Quartet' (see Figure 5.2), and of course she falls in love with the actor playing Adonis, Charles, during 'The Love Scene'. Charles is recognized, and after he is forced to reveal his true identity, his irate co-star tells him to leave immediately. He returns the next morning with news that the court has ruled in his favour and that Castle Nancy is now his. Helene, distraught, succumbs to Charles's amorous appeals and decides to marry him, thus becoming a duchess while also remaining mistress of Castle Nancy.

The show's hit was 'Gigolette', performed not by Helene or Charles but by Helene's friend Tutu. Ben Travers's troubling lyric follows its Italian and German predecessors in its tale of a dancing girl who will 'dance' all night to help men forget their troubles. The lyric is a thinly veiled description of

Figure 5.2 The 'Mythological Quartet' from *The Three Graces*, from *Play Pictorial* 44 (no. 265), p. 107.

the song's title character, a little female gigolo, or a sex worker. The seductiveness of the song is set up musically in the sultry-sounding verse, cast in the minor mode with ample chromatic slippages. The lilting refrain, in the major mode, is the man's call to his 'sweet charmer of the night'. The song's popularity through the Italian version, including recordings and dance-band arrangements, meant that it could have already been familiar to London audiences when *The Three Graces* opened.

The connection between 'Gigolette' and a sex worker is solidified in the dance that concludes the number, an apache (pronounced ah-PASCH). This was an extremely sexualized dance of the time derived from the tango that was part choreographic display and part melodrama. Its prescribed narrative recounts a vicious bar-room encounter between a pimp and a sex worker, and its highly problematic sexual and gendered power relations kept it in the realm of theatrical performance and away from the world of social dance.[29] The dance's popularity in 1924 was such that it appeared in many musicals, not just *The Three Graces*.

Over time, the show really didn't find success in either German or English, but the Italian version, *La danza delle libellule*, remains known in Italy and has been produced there several times in the twenty-first century.

February in New York

A few weeks into the run of *Sweet Little Devil*, on 12 February, Gershwin was catapulted to further fame when his *Rhapsody in Blue* was featured on Paul Whiteman's 'Experiment in Modern Music' concert at Aeolian Hall. Gershwin biographer Richard Crawford notes that Gershwin at first declined Whiteman's request for a work to be featured on the concert because he was working on *Sweet Little Devil*,[30] while Ryan Bañagale writes that Gershwin 'supposedly forgot' that he had agreed to write something for Whiteman at the time.[31] Regardless, Gershwin began working on *Rhapsody in Blue* in earnest in early 1924. A frequently told story, Gershwin himself among its proponents, recounts how Gershwin was on the train to Boston for the tryout of *Sweet Little Devil* when he envisioned

---

[29] Hylton, *Dancing in Time*, 66–68.
[30] Richard Crawford, *Summertime: George Gershwin's Life in Music* (New York: W. W. Norton, 2019), 122.
[31] Ryan Raul Bañagale, *Arranging Gershwin: 'Rhapsody in Blue' and the Creation of an American Icon* (New York: Oxford University Press, 2014), 15.

Rhapsody in Blue: 'I suddenly heard – and even saw on paper – the complete construction of the rhapsody, from beginning to end.'[32] As enticing as this genesis story may be, as Bañagale has shown, manuscript evidence proves otherwise.[33]

A week after *Rhapsody in Blue*'s premiere, another rags-to-riches musical comedy, this one with music at its core, opened on 19 February at the Lyric Theatre. Starring Eleanor Painter (1885–1947), an accomplished opera singer, *The Chiffon Girl* told the story of a young Italian woman from New York's 'Little Italy' neighbourhood whose wealthy patron sends her to Italy to study voice. Four years later she returns a great prima donna. Her romantic interest, Mario, meanwhile, has become a bootlegger. Critics praised the score by 'Carlo and Sanders' – the husband-and-wife team of Monte Carlo (born Hans von Holstein, 1883–1967) and Alma Sanders (1882–1956) – and Painter's 'quite gorgeous' voice, but that was about it.[34]

The musical's reputation certainly wasn't helped by concerns about the leading man. During *The Chiffon Girl*'s out-of-town tryout, the show's producer, Charles Capehart, felt that George Reimherr, who was playing Mario, was not right for the part, so he engaged Joseph Lestora to take over for the Broadway opening. But during the final rehearsals it became obvious that Lestora wasn't ready, so Reimherr was called back to sing the premiere. Lestora took over the role later in the week. His performances were still wavering, so the management again asked Reimherr to return. The situation came to a head on 25 February, when both Lestora and Reimherr showed up at the Lyric Theatre to sing Mario. The off-stage drama, alas, was probably more exciting than that of the actual libretto. Lestora was forced to vacate his dressing room, and, while he was screaming breach of contract, Reimherr played Mario for the rest of the musical's short run.[35]

---

[32] Quoted in Crawford, *Summertime*, 123.   [33] Bañagale, *Arranging Gershwin*, 66–67.
[34] '"The Chiffon Girl" Opens', *New York Times*, 20 February 1924.
[35] '2 Appear for Same Role', *New York Times*, 26 February 1924.

6 | A Tale of Two Operettas

Until 1924, Franz Lehár (1870–1948) had been closely associated with the famed Theater an der Wien, where many of his best-known operettas, including *Die lustige Witwe* (The Merry Widow), debuted. Lehár's works had dominated the theatre's stage for some time, but this reign ended on 28 February when *Gräfin Mariza* (Countess Maritza) opened there with a score not by Lehár but rather by Emmerich Kálmán (1882–1953). Hubert Marischka (1882–1959), the theatre's new director and also its leading actor, wanted to bring a new style of operetta to his theatre, one rooted in the glamour of the revue and which would highlight modern syncopated dances. Marischka aimed to project an aura of contemporary confidence for the Theater an der Wien in what was a new, post-war theatrical marketplace.[1] The change in direction displaced Lehár and his increasingly operatic approach to the genre, along with several of the theatre's leading stars. Lehár responded to this series of events with *Cloclo*, which opened eight days later at the Bürgertheater. *Cloclo* proved that Lehár, like Kálmán, was wholly capable of creating a score that reflected established operetta traditions alongside newer styles of popular music.

The opening night of *Gräfin Mariza* was an eagerly anticipated event. Because the audience demanded that nearly every musical number be repeated several times, the performance lasted nearly six hours.[2] The entire production exuded opulence, colour and panache. Importantly, its musical and visual splendour provided much-needed relief from the harsh realities of the economic and social hardships in post–Great War Vienna.

Though set before the war, Julius Brammer and Alfred Grünwald's often poignant libretto directly addressed many of the issues facing the Viennese public in 1924. It included plenty of barbed lines that contemporary audiences would have enjoyed, including one about the hefty entertainment tax

---

[1] Marischka took over the theatre after the death of his father-in-law, Wilhelm Karczag, in 1923. He bought out the venue's other shareholders and thus became the sole owner of a Viennese theatre, a rarity at the time (Micaela Baranello, *The Operetta Empire: Music Theatre in Early Twentieth-Century Vienna* (Oakland: University of California Press, 2021), 124–125).

[2] Stefan Frey, *'Laughter under Tears': Emmerich Kálmán – An Operetta Biography*, translated by Alexander Butziger (Culver City: Operetta Foundation, 2014), 153.

that all theatres, including the Theater an der Wien, were having to pay on box office receipts.[3] The librettists crafted a careful balance of specificity and universality that make *Gräfin Mariza* quintessentially Viennese and also wholly appealing elsewhere (see Plate 9).

As the curtain rises, a sense of mystery, loss and displacement immediately starts to emanate from the stage. Hungary, where the operetta is set, was no longer directly connected to Austria in a political sense, and the loss of the Dual Monarchy is keenly felt. Such emotional and psychological voids come to the fore as Manja, a Romani fortune teller, proffers her adage that 'Glück ist ein schöner Traum' (Happiness Is a Beautiful Dream) before delivering an array of coloratura flourishes, an aural manifestation of her magical abilities. The minor mode and expanded harmonic palette, along with a repeated distinctive *short-LONG-short-short-short-LONG* rhythmic pattern, add to the melancholic élan that permeates the entire operetta.

Béla Törek is the new property manager at the estate of the young widow, Countess Maritza. In reality, though, he is the impoverished Count Tassilo of Endrődy-Wittemburg, who had to sell his lands to pay off his father's debts. The count took this job, incognito, to rebuild a dowry for his beloved sister. Tassilo is no longer the 'csardas cavalier' he once was. He misses his past life, as he sings in the expansive 'Wenn es Abend wird' (When Evening Comes), a slow, languid waltz filled with references to Vienna, the waltz and the Danube. Kálmán here employs the trope of a slow waltz in a classic dramaturgical fashion as a conduit to memory and, as is so often the case, loss. Tassilo is like many former aristocrats who lost their estates in the war and then became the victims of war profiteers.[4] His privileged lifestyle, like those of so many sitting in the theatre, is a thing of the past.

Maritza soon makes her grand entrance accompanied by the full chorus, as befits a title character in an operetta. She is bewitched by the csardas, as she proves in 'Lustige Zigeunerweisen' (Happy Romani Life), with its alternation of slow (*lassan*) and fast (*frissen*) sections. Here, the confluence of Romani and Hungarian cultures is celebrated through a stunning vocal display. Maritza is delighted to be back at her estate and also to confirm her engagement to Baron Kolomán Zsupán, which has recently been reported in the press. She tells a confidante that she really isn't engaged, and cannot be, for Zsupán isn't real – she took his name from the title character in Johann Strauss, Jr's operetta *Die Ziguenerbaron* (The Gypsy Baron). Maritza concocted the entire plan just to get rid of all the wannabe suitors

---

[3] Frey, *'Laughter under Tears'*, 153.   [4] Frey, *'Laughter under Tears'*, 154.

who keep approaching her, including the lecherous Romanian prince Moritz Dragomir Populescu.

Among Maritza's entourage is none other than Lisa, Tassilo's sister. When Lisa and Tassilo see each other, the disguised count immediately begs her not to reveal his identity, and they sing of their pleasant childhood memories in 'Schwesterlein/Brüderlein' (Little Sister/Little Brother). This is another memory-evoking waltz, but lighter in character than 'Wenn es Abend wird'. These are happy memories of childhood and not of recent loss. The siblings also pledge hope and assurance to each other as their gentle duet draws to a close.

Amidst this happy reunion, a surprise visitor arrives: Baron Kolomán Zsupán! He read about his engagement in the paper and decided that he must come meet his fiancée. Maritza is more surprised than anyone else at Zsupán's appearance: she never thought that someone who shared his name with an operetta character could actually exist. Like Maritza, he is a pig farmer and invites her to join him on his estate in the foxtrot 'Komm mit nach Varasdin' (Let's Go to Varasdin). Varasdin (German: Warasdin; Croatian: Varaždin) was a town that experienced several shifts in political rule in the early twentieth century. At the time of the operetta's setting, Varasdin was the county seat for Varasdin County within the Kingdom of Croatia-Slavonia, an autonomous domain within the Kingdom of Hungary and part of the Dual Monarchy. In 1920, as a result of the Treaty of Trianon, which saw the disintegration of many Hungarian lands, it became part of the Kingdom of Serbs, Croats and Slovenes. In 2024, Varaždin is in the northern part of Croatia.

As the first act speeds towards its dramatic conclusion, Tassilo offers his own show-stopping czardas, 'Auch ich war einst ein feiner Csárdáskavalier/Komm Zigáni' (I Too Was Once a Csardas Cavalier/Come Romani). Tassilo's csardas is more complex in design than Maritza's. It includes a sombre *lassan*, in D minor, filled with words that evoke the painful memories of its singer, followed by a more metrically stable invitation, in D major, for the Romani to join him in his sorrow. During this passage, which is repeated, Marischka, who created the role, would drink a bottle of wine, holding it upside down to show the audience that it was indeed empty. Then, he would pick up a violin – Marischka was also a fine violinist – and join the band as the second part of the csardas, the *frissen*, began. There are no words in the *frissen*, it is pure instrumental music and dance. The life-affirming sequence gets faster and faster, and Marischka would join the dancers in their revelry. It was a truly dazzling number.

Maritza enters while Tassilo is impressing everyone with his singing, fiddling and dancing. Since she missed the beginning of the showpiece, she commands Tassilo to do it all again for her, from the beginning, since she, as we know, loves csardas. He refuses. The theatre audience would have been on Maritza's side at this moment – they would have liked nothing more than to hear the number again. Kálmán biographer Stefan Frey notes the metatheatrical paradox that emerges here, for while the actor playing Tassilo (especially someone like Marischka) would happily give an encore, the character of Tassilo resolutely would not.[5] Since Tassilo refuses Maritza's command, the tempestuous countess fires him on the spot.

Maritza's guests, meanwhile, are preparing to go to the cabaret in the boisterous syncopated choral number 'Tabarin' (the name of the popular cabaret where the guests are heading). The association with the popular Charleston dance comes not just in the dance itself but also in the shared syllabic structure of the words Tabarin and Charleston. This duality is triangulated when one considers Zsupán's hometown, Varasdin. Charleston–Tabarin–Varasdin: musical (and dramatic) connections are thus established between a popular dance, a cabaret and a foxtrot.

In midst of the celebrations, Manja returns with a prophecy: Maritza will fall in love with a wealthy man within a month's time. Maritza responds to this news with a glowing waltz, 'Eh ein kurzer Mond' (A Short Month), in which she expresses her sincere hope that the prophecy will come true. Her guests wholeheartedly support her. As they leave, Lisa remains behind. When Tassilo comes to tell Maritza that he is going, she 'un-fires' him. Alone on stage, he offers a delicate reminiscent reprise of his csardas. She hears him from her balcony and responds, gently singing his music. This is the first time the two will have sung the same music in the operetta. Either he has captured her heart or she has conquered his. Or perhaps both.

In Act 2, Zsupán realizes that he is far more interested in his fiancée's friend, Lisa, than in his fiancée. Lisa has also taken a liking to the pig farmer from Varasdin, as they sing in their lyrical foxtrot 'Wenn ich abends schlafen geh' (When I Go to Sleep at Night). They are becoming the modern couple who dance foxtrots and enjoy syncopated sounds. By contrast, Maritza and Tassilo revel in the worlds of the waltz and the csardas, the musical identifiers of the two parts of the former Dual Monarchy: the waltz for Austria and the csardas for Hungary. They imagine what being in love would be like in the bright waltz duet 'Herrgott, was ist den heut' los' (Lord, What's Going on

---

[5] Frey, *'Laughter under Tears'*, 144.

Today). The soon-to-be lovers plan to just 'waltz our worries away', as did so many in Vienna prior to the Great War.

A month has passed since the end of Act 1, and the chorus gleefully returns. Since Maritza didn't go to the Tabarin, her friends bring the Tabarin to her with a reprise of its celebratory song. Manja's prophecy seems to be coming true, for Tassilo and Maritza soon sing a glorious, expansive waltz duet, 'Mein lieber Schatz' (My Dear Sweetheart), complete with impassioned sustained high notes.

But just as Tassilo and Maritza are realizing their love, Lisa and Zsupán are dissolving theirs. They do so in the jaunty duple-metre duet 'Junger Mann ein Mädchen liebt' (Young Man Loves a Girl), which is distinguished by its dotted rhythms and three punctuated notes at the ends of phrases. These punctuations provide a kinship to Zsupán's 'Komm mit nach Varasdin', which includes similar phrase endings.

The conniving Prince Populescu convinces Maritza that Tassilo is just a fortune hunter who really is in love with Lisa, not her. In another fit of anger, Maritza literally throws money at Tassilo, which he, in turn, passes along to the Romani. Considering the massive inflation going on in Austria at the time, this 'banknote delirium'[6] would surely have resonated with audiences. A series of musical reprises begins that deftly propels the plot to the act's finale. First, Maritza mockingly sings 'Mein lieber Schatz' at – not to – Tassilo, and he responds, expressing similar scorn. Tassilo then calls for a reprise of 'Komm Zigáni', during which he defiantly dances with Manja just to infuriate Maritza. Tassilo then finds Lisa and sings 'Schwesterlein' to her as a pledge of his love for her, no matter what happens. Maritza yet again overhears him (as she did at the end of Act 1 when he performed his csardas) and realizes that Lisa is his sister and not his lover. The countess revels in this new knowledge, for now she is sure that Tassilo truly loves her.

In Act 3, Tassilo's eccentric Aunt Bozena arrives. The family hasn't spoken to her in years. She has come into some money and wants to tell Tassilo that she has bought back his estates for him. She is accompanied by her comic and not always competent Bohemian servant, Penizek. Tassilo, unaware of what his aunt has done, tells Lisa and Zsupán the reality of the family's financial situation. Zsupán is elated, for in order to get his inheritance, he must marry someone who is poor, so everything is perfect. He can be with Lisa! Zsupán and Lisa rejoice in a reprise of 'Komm mit nach Varsadin'. Kálmán then gives Tassilo (or, more precisely, Marischka) one

---

[6] Frey, *'Laughter under Tears'*, 146.

more chance to show off his glorious tenor voice in the emotive romance 'Fein könnt' auf der Welt es sein' (It Could Be Fine in The World). As Tassilo yet again prepares to leave (recalling the end of Act 1), he asks Maritza for a reference, which she writes in front of him. When she hands him the note, he reads not a reference letter but a marriage proposal, which he gladly accepts. They sing a reprise, this time lovingly, of 'Mein lieber Schatz', joined by the chorus. To celebrate the double engagements, everyone heads to the cabaret in a joyful reprise of 'Tabarin'. The extensive use of reprise in Act 3 provides musical and dramatic continuity and closure to the various plot lines. Interspersed with new songs, the act's musical blend of the new and the familiar offers yet another example of this year-defining confluence.

The score is a cornucopia of musical riches. The two large-scale csardas numbers, one for Maritza and one for Tassilo, are vocally demanding showpieces not easily forgotten. The waltzes – those evoking memories, such as the pensive 'Wenn es Abend wird', and those expressing the passion of love, such as 'Mein lieber Schatz' – remain hallmarks of the Viennese operetta tradition. The fast-paced Charleston-style songs such as 'Komm mit nach Varasdin' and 'Tabarin' reflect a strong sense of urban modernity with their rhythmic energies.

Politics also come into play, particularly the results of the Treaty of Trianon. Here is a Viennese take on relationships between Hungary and its new post-war neighbouring nations. Baron Zsupán is a pig farmer, thus envisioning his homeland of Croatia (part of the Kingdom of Serbs, Croats and Slovenes) as a purely agricultural area, but one where they dance foxtrots. Romania gained a lot of Hungarian territory from the treaty, and it comes as no surprise that the Romanian character, Populescu, is portrayed as a self-serving dishonest tyrant. Finally, Czechoslovakia, which also received former Hungarian lands, is represented by the Bohemian servant Penizek, a comic figure who likes to misquote lines from plays he managed during his days in the theatre. We are bemused by Zsupán, have disdain for Populescu and laugh at Penizek. Furthermore, the Croatian, Romanian and Bohemian characters are all presented fairly one-dimensionally; none of them possess the complicated, often conflicting emotional states of Tassilo, Maritza or even Lisa.

Hubert Marischka, who for the first time was the sole manager of the Theater an der Wien, had his own ideas about what and who should appear on its historic stage. He wanted his operettas to be more than entertainment – the genre's inherent social and political commentaries were essential to him. He was similarly insistent on correct casting. This included himself as Tassilo and the marvellous Betty Fischer (1887–1969) as Maritza. Marischka had the role of Tassilo created expressly to show off his own distinctive talents as actor, singer, dancer and violinist.[7] His 'Auch ich war einst ein feiner Csárdáskavalier/Komm Zigány' csardas became his personal showpiece. Fischer trained as a seamstress before beginning her musical career. She was continuously praised not only for her three-and-a-half octave range, but also for her glamourous costumes, which made her a sort of fashion guru.[8] Fischer became an icon of Viennese operetta, and Kevin Clarke, director of the Operetta Research Center, describes what her performance of Maritza most likely would have sounded like, based on recordings of some of her other roles: 'bathed in melancholia, a certain nostalgic flair, and an effortless delivery from top to bottom, and the other way round'.[9] Ah, what we have missed.

To play Lisa and Zsupán, Kálmán wanted to secure the same actors who had been critical to the success of his previous operetta, *Die Bajadere* (1921): Louise Kartousch and Ernst Tautenhayn.[10] Kálmán became concerned when he learned that Tautenhayn had been approached to appear in Lehár's *Cloclo* and knew that if Tautenhayn joined that show, then so would Kartousch.[11] Kálmán implored Marischka to prevent their departure from the Theater an der Wien, where they were the long-standing comic leads, but the pair was already on their way to the Bürgertheater.

Wanting fresh faces to succeed Kartousch and Tautenhayn, Marischka engaged Elsie Altmann (1899–1984) as Lisa and Max Hansen (1897–1961) as Zsupán. Altmann was known for her dancing and soubrette roles, and an image of her taken by the Viennese fashion photographer Madame d'Ora showing the star's half-naked breasts was used to market the operetta and its up-to-datedness. Hansen subsequently became a well-known cabaret and operetta singer in Berlin. In addition to Altmann and Hansen, another newcomer to the Theater an der Wien was the one who played the non-singing role of Penizek. The librettists created the part especially for a then little-known character actor by the name of Hans Moser. Moser (1880–1964) became one of the biggest stars of Austrian cinema, and one critic described his

---

[7] Frey, *'Laughter under Tears'*, 143.

[8] Kevin Clarke, 'The Royal Voice of Betty Fischer on Truesound Transfers', 11 June 2020, Operetta Research Center, http://operetta-research-center.org/royal-voice-betty-fischer-truesound-transfers/, accessed 13 May 2021.

[9] Clarke, 'The Royal Voice of Betty Fischer on Truesound Transfers'.

[10] Frey, *'Laughter under Tears'*, 149–150.   [11] Frey, *'Laughter under Tears'*, 149–150.

portrayal of Penizek as that of someone 'who single-handedly makes the operetta worth watching'.[12]

Marischka was also concerned about the look of the show. This visual dimension was critical to his goals for the production and, by extension, for the theatre. His wife, Lilian Karczag-Marischka (1901–1981), designed costumes that were intended to transport audiences back to what Frey describes as 'the lost paradise of the Dual Monarchy, with its pomp, gypsies, and uniforms'.[13] It was not just the aural world of waltzes and the czardas that evoked nostalgia for the pre-war Empire but also the eye-catching glamour of the sets and costumes.

One week and one day after *Gräfin Mariza* opened at the Theater an der Wien, Lehár's *Cloclo* debuted at the Bürgertheater. Although the Bürgertheater had been staging operettas since 1910, it lacked a resident ensemble. Hence, *Cloclo* does not feature any full-stage choral spectacles or dance sequences. It is, as Frey calls it, a chamber operetta.[14] With only four principal roles and several minor ones, it provided a sense of intimacy in performance that was notably different from what was happening at the Theater an der Wien. It could be seen as a Viennese corollary to the small-scale revues of André Charlot and the modestly scaled musical comedies that were appearing on New York and London musical stages.

In Béla Jenbach's playful libretto, Severin Cornichon (whose surname means 'little pickle'), the fictional mayor of the actual French city of Perpignan, financially supports Cloclo, a coquettish revue performer whom he fancies, having seen her on stage – and off – years earlier. Cloclo is in love with the young and dashing Maxime, who, although wealthy, cannot access his fortune. When the mayor's wife, Melousine, intercepts a letter from Cloclo to her husband in which the Parisian performer begs him to send her money and addresses him as 'Papa', Melousine assumes that Cloclo must be her husband's love child. After hitting a policeman, Cloclo escapes to Perpignan, where Melousine takes her under her protective wing. After a series of slapstick antics, all ends well, including Cloclo being reunited with Maxime.

This was not a new libretto, for Jenbach had written it in 1922 for Leo Fall. Fall wrote eight numbers for his version of *Cloclo* before shifting his attention to *Der süße Kavalier* (The Sweet Cavalier), which would be his last operetta. At that point, Jenbach took back his libretto and offered it to

---

[12] Frey, *'Laughter under Tears'*, 150.   [13] Frey, *'Laughter under Tears'*, 154.
[14] Stefan Frey, *Franz Lehár: Der letzte Operettenkönig* (Vienna: Böhlau, 2020), 237 ('Kammeroperette').

Lehár, who gladly accepted it, especially after he learned that the famed star of the Theater an der Wien, Louise Kartousch, would play the title role.[15]

Just as Cloclo thwarts the expected behaviours of the title character in a Viennese operetta – she is no Merry Widow or Maritza – the entire work in some ways inverts the prevalent rags-to-riches Anglo–American musical comedy paradigm. Rather than someone from a modest background achieving fame and/or fortune, but almost always love, here the reverse happens: the revue star escapes from the city to the countryside, where her very presence wreaks havoc, though she still ends up with her man.

Cloclo displays other influences of musical comedy, ones it does not subvert. These include its various syncopated dances as well the addition of saxophones to the orchestration, the first time the jazz-associated instruments appear in any of Lehár's works. Furthermore, the idea of a comic lead needing sanctuary after hitting a police officer recalls *Oh, Boy!* the Guy Bolton–P. G. Wodehouse–Jerome Kern hit from 1918, for that is exactly what happens in that show.

Lehár's most popular song in *Cloclo* was not an elegant waltz but rather a salacious foxtrot, Melousine's 'Ich habe "La Garconne" gelesen' (I Have Read 'La Garconne'). As the mayor's wife, Melousine is expected to model respectability, something she decides to abandon after reading Victor Margueritte's scandalous 1922 novel *La Garconne* (translated variously as The Flapper, The Tomboy, or The Bachelor Girl). It follows that she will sing of her newfound freedom in a musical idiom audiences would have associated with modern views: a foxtrot. Melousine informs us that she was never like Messalina, the promiscuous wife of the Roman emperor Claudius, nor did she behave as Madame Pompadour. She always remained faithful to her husband, at least until she read *La Garconne*. Now, she has become sophisticated, wants to float from man to man and would like to try her hand at the power that being a man in a male-dominated society can offer. The foxtrot's kinetic rhythmic figures, chromatic inflections and pizzicato (plucked) strings in the orchestra mark this song as something very distinctive from not just typical waltz fare but also the other dances featured in the score. In the mid-1920s, the term 'la garconne' also referred to the silhouette of a flapper dress; its youthful look actually inspired a change in fashion, whereby looser waistlines dropped below the hips.[16] Melousine craves this flapper culture and all it represents.

The effect of the song would have been heightened in performance, since the actor who sang it, Gisela Werbezirk (1875–1956), was known for her

---

[15] Frey, *Franz Lehár*, 237.   [16] Hylton, *Dancing in Time*, 119.

austere, even prudish appearance. Werbezirk had an uncannily keen sense of timing that she used for dramatic and sometimes humorous effect. To have her throw off the patina of responsibility expected of a mayor's wife and perform a foxtrot brought an unexpected turn to her character, one that she negotiated with comic aplomb. Werbezirk recorded the song in 1925; her vivid declamation of the lyrics in a somewhat speech-sung style infuses them with unmistakable character-driven sass.[17]

The foxtrot was not the only popular dance to appear in *Cloclo*. A tango and a java, which has been called 'a faster, more lascivious version of the waltz',[18] feature in Act 2, which is set in Perpignan. The tango was extremely popular on both sides of the Atlantic in 1924, and had strong associations with Paris. Its sense of hypermasculinity and reputation as a dance in which men would try to attract the attention of women (or other men) made it a visual spectacle. That year, the Argentine dancer Casimiro 'El Vasco' Aín (1874–1940) danced a tango for Pope Pius XI. Aín was dressed in tails and his partner in a long, dark blue skirt. In their performance, they gave only a hint of the dance's sensuality, though they ended their performance with a small run and a freeze, a move Aín learned on the streets of Buenos Aires. The Pope was said to have been pleased.[19] A similar sense of glamourous allure was seen in *Cloclo*'s tango, set as solo number for Severin. Concerning the java, Cloclo and Severin proved the popularity of the dance, via Lehár, in 'Feurige Tänzer' (Fiery Dancers) with its accentuated percussive underpinning and angular feel. Also in Act 2, Cloclo shows her awareness of other contemporary dance trends by performing the shimmy 'Olé-Olá-Olé'.

As was typical in 1924, this operetta's forward-looking aspects were balanced by its nods to the past, particularly the quirkiness of memory. Astute fans of Lehár's *The Merry Widow* may have recognized the title character's name, for she shares it with one of Chez Maxim's dancing girls in that operetta. Also, Cloclo's love interest shares his name with the famed establishment, though now with a final 'e'. Musical reverberations of *The Merry Widow* are also present. 'Wenn man über fünfzig ist' (When You're Over Fifty), a choral number led by Severin, echoes the boisterousness of 'I'm Off to Chez Maxim' (as does 'Tabarin' in *Gräfin Mariza*), while Cloclo's luscious waltz refrain for 'Gehen die Mädchen zu Bette' (The

---

[17] Odéon A 312737, recorded 1924.

[18] 'Clo Clo', Folks Operetta, https://folksoperetta.org/event/clo-clo/, accessed 4 November 2021.

[19] Hylton, *Dancing in Time*, 66.

Girls Go to Bed) recalls the introspective glow of 'Lippen schweigen' (Lips Stay Silent/Love Unspoken).

The balance of old and new is further emphasized in two duets for Cloclo and Maxime. The lusciousness of their waltz 'Nur ein einziges Stündchen' (Just a Single Hour) is complemented by the lively syncopated song 'Kinder, es ist keine Sünde' (Children, It's Not a Sin). The stylistic difference in these duets reveals the demands placed on operetta singers at the time, for they had to be able to perform not only flowing *bel canto* numbers but also faster-paced, jazzy ones.

Such stylistic demands are especially notable in Cloclo's music beyond these duets. Lehár created the role with Louise Kartousch in mind. Kartousch, described as a 'soubrette dancer',[20] had recently been criticized in the press for not being able to sing convincingly in a coloratura-infused style. So, for *Cloclo*, Lehár created music that would not rely so much on this sort of virtuoso display (leave that to Betty Fischer in *Gräfin Mariza*) and would instead highlight the multiple strengths of her voice and stage persona. This plan worked extremely well from a dramatic perspective, for Cloclo is a revue performer and, as such, she'd be expected to have a voice

Figure 6.1 Louise Kartousch and Ernst Tautenhayn, the stars of *Cloclo*, in the 1918 film *Wo die Lerche singt* (Where the Lark Sings).

---

[20] Norbert Linke, *Franz Lehár* (Reinbek bei Hamburg: Rowohlt Taschenbuch Verlag, 2001), 79 ('Soubrettentänzerin').

ideally suited to slightly syncopated songs, rather than revel in extensive coloratura flourishes.

Kartousch had appeared for years alongside the comic actor Ernst Tautenhayn at the Theatre an der Wien, as well as in several silent films, including *Wo die Lerche singt* (Where the Lark Sings, 1918; see Figure 6.1). Tautenhayn played Severin in *Cloclo*, continuing the legacy of him and Kartousch sharing the stage. Severin's music, and therefore Tautenhayn's, was more in the comic baritone vein and certainly not that of a soaring operetta tenor. Those dulcet tones belonged to the character of Maxime, played by the noted Austrian tenor Robert Nästlberger (1887–1942).

Gräfin Mariza and *Cloclo* are both emblematic of Viennese musical theatre in 1924. Traditional elements capitalizing on the past (e.g., overt references to *Die Ziguenerbaron* in *Gräfin Mariza* and *Die lustige Witwe* in *Cloclo*) play alongside new directions in the form of current popular dances such as the Charleston, the foxtrot and the shimmy. Established stars were continuing to build their legacies, namely Hubert Marischka and Betty Fischer at the Theatre an der Wien and Louise Kartousch and Ernst Tautenhayn, now at the Bürgertheater. Kartousch and Tautenhayn's departures from the Theater an der Wien allowed new stars to take their places. Musically, the familiar worlds of the waltz and csardas were meeting new syncopated dances. The social realities of post-war Europe and new identities for women, such as Melousine in *Cloclo*, were likewise being performed on stage. Not to be forgotten are the roles of producers and theatre owners such as Marischka, who, like his contemporaries elsewhere, brought his own vision to his productions. Unlike his contemporaries Florenz Ziegfeld or André Charlot, however, and echoing the practices of nineteenth-century actors–owners–producers, Marischka not only produced his shows in his own theatre but also starred in them. Yet again, an old practice is reinvented and reinfused with the exuberant glamour of the 1920s.

7 | The Coming of Spring

With the coming of spring came a sense of joy and occasional abandon. Wrongs could be made right if you only sang about them, at least on stage. This unabated sense of hope permeated many of the revues and musical comedies that appeared from March through May, though an underlying seriousness was emerging in how popular musical theatre was being viewed on the whole and how such works were being constructed. The seasoned dynamism of the old and the innovative vigour of the new continued to meet, evocative new soundworlds were emerging and, nearly everywhere one turned, a glamourous glow was lighting the way.

Taking the Revue Seriously

When Albert de Courville's (1887–1960) *The Whirl of the World* debuted at London's Palladium on 4 March, it was obvious that the producer was more a disciple of Florenz Ziegfeld than of André Charlot. It played on its largesse, most notably in the 'Mantle' scene. A goddess and her attendants descend a large staircase. The goddess then returns up the steps and, as she does so, her cloak opens to envelop the entire ensemble, the staircase and most of the stage.[1] This sort of visual effect would have made Ziegfeld proud. The revue was also noted for its confluence of US American and London cultural references. This was especially evident in songs by Frederick Chappelle (music) and Donovan Parsons (lyrics) with titles such as 'Ragging the Westminster Chimes' and the uncomfortable 'In My Little Wigwam Wembley Way'.

Leap Year, which opened later in the month at London's Hippodrome on 20 March, also featured transnational aspects. The British comedian George Robey (1869–1954) led the cast with his glorious misadventures in otherwise everyday situations. Robey was a legendary music hall performer whose signature character was the Prime Minister of Mirth (see Figure 7.1).

---

[1] Bruxellons, www.overthefootlights.co.uk/London%20Revues%201920-1924.pdf, accessed 2 December 2023.

Figure 7.1 George Robey as the Prime Minister of Mirth.

Critics who saw *Leap Year* remarked on his especially riotous rendition of Guy Fawkes and his portrayal of a father who becomes overly anxious about his son daring to marry an actress. Robey's famous 'look of shocked surprise, and then the sly, slow smile' were on full display.[2]

While Robey epitomized the established, the Gertrude Hoffman Girls from the USA embodied the new. The troupe dazzled audiences and critics with its famed web routine (see Figure 7.2), which they had introduced in Ziegfeld's *Follies* the previous year. They began by ascending twelve ropes suspended from rigging hanging just behind the proscenium arch. Sunny Stalter-Pace describes what happened next: 'Suspended by one foot, upside down, and sideways, they moved through a bevy of patterns, sometimes

---

[2] 'London Hippodrome. "Leap Year"', Daily Telegraph (London), 21 March 1924.

Figure 7.2 The Gertrude Hoffmann Girls. Wake Forest University Special Collections and Archives.

holding on to one rope and sometimes to two.'[3] For a spectacular finish, the girls would swing out over the audience. Beyond their skilful athleticism, what made this troupe distinctive was their individuality. Each performer displayed her own unique physicality and personality in the heterogenous ensemble. They were not like the Ziegfeld girls or the Tiller Girls, with their physical sameness and uniform precision movements. This celebration of individuality was also reflected in the playbill, where solo dancers were listed by their first names. *Leap Year* featured, among others, Margaret in the Buck Dance, Catherine in the Ballet Dance and Emma in Peacock's Mirror Dance.

Not all was pure delight, for *Leap Year* included some significant condescension of people who did not look like its relatively affluent white able-bodied audience. In one sketch, Ratoucheff's Russian Lilliputians, a troupe of little people who had been on the vaudeville circuit, took on the roles of mechanical figures who are seen as the operators of 'automated'

---

[3] Sunny Stalter-Pace, *Imitation Artist: Gertrude Hoffman's Life in Vaudeville and Dance* (Evanston: Northwestern University Press, 2020), 150.

machines. Their routine would have provided a stark contrast to the anti-mechanical moves of the Hoffman Girls. The implication was that those displaying physical difference from the people in power could be and were being exploited for the benefit of those in power. This was also the case with the song 'Fried Chicken', in which Laddie Cluff, in blackface, furthered racist stereotypes about African Americans and the southern USA. Then, in the finale, a special lighting effect designed by Adrian V. Samoiloff, whose lighting experiments at the Hippodrome had been going on since 1921, made the entire white company appear Black. By being white, the scene implied, one had the agency to assume other ethnicities and then return to a white privileged status. This effect would also feature in Irving Berlin's *Music Box Revue* that December (see Chapter 13).

On 24 March, in New York, the Shubert-produced *Artists and Models*, which had been playing successfully at the Shubert Theatre since August of the previous year, moved to the Winter Garden Theatre. With this shift of venue came a new segment – one that reflected an increasingly sophisticated approach to the popular genre. The Russian coloratura soprano Vera Lavrova, the Baroness Michael Royce Garrett, made her US debut in the production. Lavrova sang two arias in the revue: the 'Hindu Song (Song of the Indian Guest)' from Nikolai Rimsky-Korsakoff's *Sadko*, and 'Juliette's Waltz Song' from Charles Gounod's *Roméo et Juliette*. Her presence added to the artistic elegance of the production. When the revue went on tour in May, Lavrova remained in New York and joined the ensemble of another Shubert-produced revue, *Innocent Eyes*.

The Winter Garden held cultural significance in 1924 beyond being the home of glamourous Shubert revues, for it was there that the noted author and cultural critic Gilbert Seldes (1893–1970) announced the appearance of his latest book, the hugely influential *The Seven Lively Arts*.[4] In this and other writings, Seldes claimed the legitimacy of popular culture, arguing that pieces in the popular vein did not pose any threat to 'high-brow' arts but that the common enemy to all types of art were second-rate bogus works.[5] He stated: 'The battle is only against solemnity which is not high, against ill-rendered profundity, against the shoddy and the dull.'[6] Seldes's reason for choosing the Winter Garden, according to modern culture scholar Michael North, was that it was 'the center of an aesthetic, one

---

[4] Michael North, *Reading 1922: A Return to the Scene of the Modern* (New York: Oxford University Press, 1999), 151.

[5] Gilbert Seldes, *The Seven Lively Arts* (New York: Harper & Brothers, 1924; reprint ed., New York: Dover, 2001), 311.

[6] Seldes, *The Seven Lively Arts*, 348.

that linked modernism and popular culture in an alliance against the censor'.[7] For *Artists and Models* was showing a new approach to the revue, arguably modernist because of its fragmentation and ties to classical ideals (e.g., the human body) and one which, with its on-stage nudity, certainly caught the eye of censors.

On 27 March, *Vogues of 1924* took over the recently vacated Shubert Theatre. The comedians Fred Allen (1894–1956) and Jimmy Savo (1895–1960) were the main features. The musical star was the French-born violinist–singer–actor Odette Myrtil (1898–1978), who had appeared in Ziegfeld's *Follies* back in 1915 as the 'Apache Violinist'. After appearing on stages in London and touring Europe, she returned to the USA in 1923, first in vaudeville and then in *Vogues* (see Figure 7.3). With sketches and lyrics by Fred Thompson and Clifford Grey and music by Herbert Stothart, Myrtil's numbers evoked a myriad of exotic settings: 'Katinka' (Russia), 'Pierrot' (France) and 'Eldorado' [sic] (South America).[8] The revue also featured the warm baritone of J. Harold Murray (1891–1940) and the acrobatic dancing of Alice Manning. A second edition of the revue began on 25 June as *Vogues and Frolics*.

Such was the state of the revue in March. Classical opera, a violin-playing singing actor, well-established comedians and discriminatory images were all part and parcel of the wide-encompassing genre.

Rodgers, Hart and Fields: Before They Became Famous

It is rare for a musical theatre composer to have two different works open just days apart, but such was the case for Richard Rodgers (1902–1979) in March 1924. First was *Temple Belles*, billed as 'a comedy in one act', which had a single performance on 20 March. Presented by the children of the Religious School of the Park Avenue Synagogue, the work was part of the synagogue's Purim Entertainment and Dance. Rodgers contributed five songs to the show, with lyrics by Lorenz Hart (1895–1943) and additional lyrics by Dorothy Crowthers, in addition to writing the libretto and conducting the

---

[7] North, *Reading 1922*, 151.

[8] Myrtil would continue to appear on Broadway in the years to come; her most notable accolades include creating the role of Odette in Harbach, Hammerstein and Kern's *The Cat and the Fiddle* (1931) and succeeding Juanita Hall as Bloody Mary in the original production of Rodgers and Hammerstein's *South Pacific* in the early 1950s.

Figure 7.3 Odette Myrtil, featured performer in *Vogues of 1924*, arrives in New York in 1923.

orchestra.[9] Herbert Fields (1897–1958) provided stage direction. Then, on 23 March, the Benjamin School for Girls presented *The Prisoner of Zenda* at the Selwyn Theatre. The genuine Ruritanian romance – for the name Ruritania comes from Anthony Hope's novel on which the musical was based – featured lyrics by Fields, who again directed. Dorothy Fields (1905–1974), who was then a student at the school, played the title role, wearing a beard. As Rodgers had done just a few days earlier, he conducted the show's orchestra.

These school musicals were extremely significant in furthering the working relationship of Rodgers, Hart and Herbert Fields – three future icons of the American musical theatre. The next year, on 18 September, the trio would see the opening of *Dearest Enemy* at the Knickerbocker Theatre,

---

[9] Geoffrey Block, *Richard Rodgers* (New Haven, CT: Yale University Press, 2003), 15.

the first of their eight Broadway musicals with Rodgers as composer, Hart as lyricist and Fields as librettist. Dorothy Fields, star of *The Prisoner of Zenda*, would likewise go on to become one of the most important lyricists of the twentieth century. And here we are in 1924, where these future legends of Broadway are beginning to be noticed.

Doña Francisquita Goes to South America and the Astaires Return to London

Amadeo Vives (1871–1932) was not only a composer of zarzuela, including *Doña Francisquita* (see Chapter 3), but also an impresario. His *Compañia Española de Zarzuelas* (Spanish Zarzuela Company) arrived in Buenos Aires, Argentina, on 20 March, where it began final preparations to present *Doña Francisquita* at the Teatro Victoria. The premiere on 25 March was to a sold-out audience and rave reviews. Vives thoroughly enjoyed his celebrity status and the numerous accolades he received. In August, he took his company across the Río de la Plata to Montevideo, Uruguay, for seventeen performances at the Teatro Solís.[10] To conclude the South American sojourn, they returned to Argentina for performances in Rosario, Mendoza and at the famous Teatro Colón in Buenos Aires.[11] A lavish farewell to the company took place on 30 October, by which time the *Compañia* had given 200 performances of *Doña Francisquita*, along with other works.[12]

On 28 March, just days after *Doña Francisquita* opened in Buenos Aires, Adele and Fred Astaire returned to London's West End in what was called a revival of *Stop Flirting*, their hit from the previous year. In reality, this was the musical's eagerly anticipated post-tour return to the British capital. Even though the Astaires continued to fill the Strand Theatre night after night, they were eager to return to the USA, especially after the death of their father earlier in the year. Despite their stardom in London (or perhaps because of it), they were becoming increasingly concerned about their continued absence from New York. So, they arranged with their producers

---

[10] Susana Salgado, *The Teatro Solís: 150 Years of Opera, Concerto, and Ballet in Montevideo* (Middletown: Wesleyan University Press, 2003), 346.

[11] 'El Teatro Colon 1921-1929', blog post, 8 September 2014, 'Rosario y su Zona: Historias y Curiosidades', http://rosarioysuzona.blogspot.com/2014/09/el-teatro-colon-1921-1929.html, accessed 4 February 2023.

[12] 'Amadeo Vives. *Doña Francisquita* en Buenos Aires', 18 February 2007, Casal Argentina Barcelona, www.casalargentino.org/inicio.php?sec=30&not=505, accessed 4 February 2023.

Alex A. Aarons and Sir Alfred Butt to end *Stop Flirting*'s popular and profitable run. Fred recalled Butt quipping, 'I'm sure this show could run several more years if you wanted to stay.'[13] Sadly for Butt, they did not.

During the revival's run, Lennox Robinson wrote in *The Observer*, somewhat wistfully, 'One of these days someone will take Adele and Fred by the scruffs of their necks, bid them stop flirting, dress them beautifully, invent a story and a setting for them – and I shall rent a stall by the year.'[14] How elated the critic would have been to know that his wish was in the process of being granted. *Black-Eyed Susan*, as the new musical was being called at the time, would mark the Astaires' eagerly anticipated return to the New York stage and would feature songs by another pair of siblings, George and Ira Gershwin.

The Return of Bolton, Wodehouse and Kern: *Sitting Pretty*

The Astaires were not alone in returning to familiar ground in March 1924. During the teens, a series of 'Princess Theatre' musicals played on Broadway. Named after the theatre where most of them played, they promoted an intimacy of approach not only in the size of the venue (just 299 seats) but also in their claim that everything that happened on stage would be about telling the story. This meant not just the dialogue but also the songs and the dances. These shows, produced under the intrepid Sam H. Harris (1872–1941), featured books and lyrics by Guy Bolton (1884–1979) and P. G. Wodehouse (1881–1975) and music by Jerome Kern (1885–1945). Princess Theatre shows such as *Very Good Eddie* (1915), *Oh, Boy!* (1917) and *Oh, Lady! Lady!!* (1918) were heralded as something very special. Their vibrant farce-filled stories were complemented by enchanting songs from Jerome Kern, some of which, like 'Look for the Silver Lining' from *Sally*, became evergreens.

In 1924, several creators who had enjoyed earlier successes were trying to recapture the undefinable magic that had brought them their previous acclaim. Though it resulted from a somewhat accidental reunion, a new musical by Bolton, Wodehouse and Kern, the Princess Theatre triumvirate, became part of this phenomenon. When *Sitting Pretty* opened on 8 April, *The New York Times* proclaimed, 'the followers of the trio may now rejoice anew, for the new musical piece at the Fulton is well up to the standard'.[15]

[13] Astaire, *Steps in Time*, 121.
[14] Lennox Robinson, 'At the Play', *Observer* (London), 22 June 1924, newspapers.com.
[15] '"Sitting Pretty" Gay and Lavishly Staged', *New York Times*, 9 April 1924.

The legacy of the Princess Theatre shows on the new venture became even more apparent when it was advertised as 'The Seventh of Their Series of the Princess Musical Comedies', 'their' being listed on playbills and sheet music as simply 'Bolton, Wodehouse and Kern'.[16] First names were not necessary, for this was an established trio of Broadway creators whose names were immediately recognizable.

Sitting Pretty was intended to be a star vehicle for the Duncan Sisters (Rosetta (1894–1959) and Vivian (1897–1986)), a well-known vaudeville team, with music and lyrics by Irving Berlin and book by Bolton and Wodehouse. Berlin was delayed in writing the songs since he was busy with his own *Music Box Revue*, as was the show's producer, Sam H. Harris. The Duncan Sisters, in the meantime, had created their own show, *Topsy and Eva* (see Chapter 14), which was quickly becoming an unexpected hit. As a result, the sisters were no longer available for *Sitting Pretty*, and Berlin, not seeing how the show could possibly work without their unique talents, also pulled out.[17]

While in London rehearsing *The Beauty Prize*, Wodehouse, who still believed in the show's potential, showed a draft libretto to Kern, who offered to write the music for the new show. Bolton sailed to England so they could finish the script, and thus the creative team behind the Princess Theatre musicals was reunited.[18] To replace the Duncan Sisters, Harris hired Gertrude Bryan (1888–1976) and Queenie Smith (1898–1978). Although the character list specifies that the female leads are twin sisters, having them played by actual twins was neither in the original concept (the Duncan sisters were born about two and a half years apart) nor in the original cast (see Figures 7.4 and 7.5).

Wodehouse and Bolton's plot centres on the identical twin orphans May and Dixie Tolliver, who live adjacent to the sprawling estate of the irascible William Pennington. Pennington is a great believer in eugenics, as were many others at the time. Frustrated with his family's attitude towards their wealth and privilege, he summons his relatives to tell them that they are all being disinherited. To create an improved breed of Pennington, he will adopt a young man and a young woman to begin the line anew. To everyone's dismay, Pennington introduces the young man he will adopt. Horace

---

[16]   Gerald Bordman, *Jerome Kern: His Life and Music* (New York: Oxford University Press, 1980), 246.

[17]   P. G. Wodehouse and Guy Bolton, *Bring On the Girls! The Improbably Story of Our Life in Musical Comedy with Pictures to Prove It* (Pleasantville: Akadine Press, 1997 [originally published New York: Simon and Schuster, 1953]), 180–181.

[18]   Banfield, *Jerome Kern*, 136.

Figure 7.4 Gertrude Bryan, who played May in *Sitting Pretty*. LC.

Figure 7.5 Queenie Smith, who played May's 'identical' twin, Dixie, in *Sitting Pretty*.

is a waif who lacks both education and social graces. He is not as innocent as he seems, for his adoption is part of a dastardly plan hatched by his Uncle Jo, a jewel thief, to rob the Pennington estate. When Jo comes to tell his nephew their next steps, Horace starts having second thoughts and escapes into the garden, where he meets Dixie. It is love at first sight. They dream of an uncomplicated life together in the lilting duet 'Mr and Mrs Rorer'. Horace doesn't want to be a criminal; he yearns for a peaceful life with Dixie. Shortly thereafter, Dixie inadvertently insults Mr Pennington, who vows never to adopt her, thus ending her dream of being with Horace. Meanwhile, Mr Pennington's nephew Bill has problems of his own. His money-grabbing fiancée, Babe, called off their engagement when she learned of his disinheritance. May approaches Bill, and, as happened with her sister and Horace, they immediately fall in love. Bill promises his newfound sweetheart that he will go out into the world, earn his own fortune and return to marry her. They sing of their love in the yearning duet 'A Year from Today'. In the Act 1 finale, the senior Pennington announces that he has decided to adopt May. Hence, she must marry Horace, who therefore cannot be with Dixie, and May can no longer wed Bill.

Six months later, at Mr Pennington's Florida estate, a costume ball is in full swing. Bill, in the meantime, has become a famous private investigator and comes to offer his services to his uncle. He and May are elated to see each other and, in the wistful waltz 'All You Need is a Girl', Bill sings to her that she was his inspiration to succeed. Jo, meanwhile, has got himself hired as Horace's tutor and is putting the finishing touches on plans for the robbery. Horace is becoming increasingly concerned that criminals always go to jail, and his uncle nostalgically recalls the joys of prison life in the satirical Victorian parlour ballad 'Dear Old-Fashioned Prison of Mine'. Dixie shows up unexpectedly in her new role as a seamstress for the famous dressmaker who designs May's ball gowns; Dixie's job is to make sure they fit properly. The sisters are elated to see each other and pledge to never again be separated in the score's outstanding hit, 'On a Desert Island with You'. Horace is likewise overjoyed to see Dixie and proposes. Bill follows suit with May, and they dream of their own domestic bliss in the aurally evocative duet 'The Enchanted Train'. As the plot quickly wraps up, Horace thwarts his uncle's plans and gives full credit for its unravelling to Dixie. Just as May inspired Bill to become financially self-sufficient, Dixie convinced Horace to forsake his criminal ways. Dixie accepts Horace's marriage proposal, after which Mr. Pennington gives his blessing to both couples: his adopted 'children' and Bill and May.

For John McGlinn, who conducted performances of *Sitting Pretty* and recorded the score in 1989,[19] this work showed Kern embracing a new approach to musical comedy: one where each and every score would have 'a particular tone, a style unique to itself'.[20] For McGlinn, *Sitting Pretty* reflected 'a sense of yearning for an unobtainable ideal, the melancholy of unfulfilled longing'. Kern's richly nuanced score provides 'ballast' (McGlinn's word) for the frivolity of the story with its loveable crooks and perky twin orphans. As McGlinn points out, all the major characters have songs in which they desire 'a state of bliss that doesn't exist in the real world – or even in their fairy-tale stage world'.[21]

Kern's approach to a score was certainly shifting in *Sitting Pretty*.[22] In order to create the pervading aesthetic quality that McGlinn hears, rather than a song-by-song approach, Kern was starting to envision the score as a larger, organic unity. *Sitting Pretty* does not contain the musical tightness of what will happen in *Show Boat* just a few years later, where small melodic fragments recur in multiple songs to link them and their dramatic situations together,[23] though hints of such a treatment are present.

Horace's songs reflect this sort of thinking: the comic trio 'Bongo on the Congo', the dreaming-of-a-domestic-future-together duet 'Mr and Mrs Rorer' and the charming title song. The first two songs, which appear next to each other in Act 1, feature rhythmically even notes in their verses, while the refrains are characterized by alternations between longer and shorter values (dotted rhythms) that give them a more kinetic, dance-like feel. While this treatment suggests a commonplace use of rhythm in popular song and an everyday approach to show-tune writing, Kern subtly uses it to depict the duplicity in Horace's character and his eventual turnaround. The even-noted verses could be heard as depictions of his underlying honesty, while the uneven rhythms in the refrains are aural manifestations of his less savoury surface-level behaviour.

In Act 1, while Horace and Jo are discussing their plans for the robbery, young Bill's friend, Judson, interrupts them. Horace and Jo quickly shift their conversation to the improbable topic of life in Africa. Wodehouse's lyrics for 'Bongo on the Congo' are filled with highly problematic sexualized racism. Kern, though, wrote an absolutely captivating soft-shoe refrain

[19] New World Records 80387–2 (1990), 2 discs.
[20] John McGlinn, 'How Kern Took a New Turn', *New York Times*, 9 April 1989.
[21] McGlinn, 'How Kern Took a New Turn'.
[22] For a detailed musical analysis of the score, see Banfield, *Jerome Kern*, 138–153.
[23] See, for example, Geoffrey Block's analysis in *Enchanted Evenings: The Broadway Musical from 'Show Boat' to Sondheim and Lloyd Webber* (Oxford: Oxford University Press, 2009), 27–43.

for the cringe-worthy song. He didn't write an actual bongo (Bongo is a place name in the lyric), but rather created a lilting schottische whose directness and alternation between even notes and dotted rhythms give it a simple – and easily memorable – allure. Horace is charming, but, like the song itself, something sinister is also present.

In Horace's duet with Dixie that follows, another problematic lyric, this one misogynistic, comes to the fore. 'Mr and Mrs Roper' suggest that women only need to cook good meals for husbands to keep them faithful. The verses emphasize even note values, while the refrain is a rollicking jig with uneven rhythms. In these two numbers, it is not just the problematic criminal behaviour of Horace that is evident but also the problematic white male vantagepoint of the lyrics.

The title song offers something different. The penultimate number in the show, 'Sitting Pretty' provides a lovely means for Horace and Dixie to declare their mutual love. Horace has been redeemed, and now the pretty pair just want to 'sit and sit and sit'. The uneven rhythms have been vanquished, and the implied honesty of the even ones have taken over. While even note values were heard in the verses of Horace's earlier songs – showing his fundamental morality – they come to the fore here. Horace has overcome the dramaturgical implications of uneven, or perhaps 'crooked', rhythms and has entered Dixie's metrically ordered world.

There is a significant potential problem with this reading, which gets to the heart of how much can be read into any work in terms of musical dramaturgy. The title song was actually cut from the original production, so Horace's musical even-note denouement never happens. A fundamental sense of close musical integration and a musical plot existing amidst a dramatic one were not overriding considerations when it came to the practicality of performance. The song was cut not because of plot or time but because the actor who played Horace, Dwight Frye, had a slight speech impediment that caused his 's's to sound like 'sh's. With the song's repetitive words, and the fact that it also included the show's title in the lyrics, the difficult decision was made to cut the joyful duet. John McGlinn restored the number in 1989, which provides a sense of musical resolution in this regard.

Late in the show come two duets featuring May, the first with Dixie and the second with Bill. In the wistful 'On a Desert Island with You', the twins dream of always remaining together and leaving all their troubles behind. Languid triplets and sparkling descending figures suggest an ethereal location in the middle of the Pacific Ocean. In 'The Enchanted Train', the idyllic Pacific gives way to idyllic Long Island. May and Bill sing of the 'magic' train that will carry commuters, including Bill, to domestic bliss every evening after a full day's work in Manhattan. Wodehouse's cartographical lyric includes a list of stations on the Long Island Rail Road while Kern's music, with its steady chugging accompaniment and various train effects, depicts the railroad itself.

Among the many charms of *Sitting Pretty* is its vibrant orchestration.[24] When it comes to the Broadway musical, the innovations made in the sounds emanating from the pit can easily be overlooked. Two especially notable figures – Robert Russell Bennett (1894–1981) and Max Steiner (1888–1971) – created the orchestrations for *Sitting Pretty*. Each worked on specific numbers, and sometimes they contributed to the same song. Bennett began orchestrating for Broadway in 1922, and by 1924 he was the most sought-after orchestrator in the business. He provided orchestrations for many of Kern's biggest hits, including *Show Boat* (1927) and nearly all of Rodgers and Hammerstein's shows. Bennett was largely responsible for what has been called the 'Broadway sound', with its rich, mid-range sonorities and full string sections. Born in Vienna, Steiner fled his homeland during World War I, spent time in London and then worked on Broadway before going to Hollywood in 1929, where he became one of the leading film composers and music directors. Among the most famous of his more than 300 film scores are *Gone with the Wind* (1939) and *Casablanca* (1942). Steiner also served as music director for *Sitting Pretty*. The truly captivating sounds of *Sitting Pretty* result from the artistry not only of Kern but also of Bennett and Steiner.

Both orchestrators contributed to *Sitting Pretty*'s evocative sound palette. Bennett's orchestration for 'On a Desert Island with You' includes large bells, muted strings and an English horn doubling the vocal line. Combined, they give the song an exotic, almost Orientalist quality. In the encore, Bennett calls for the melody to be doubled in the flute and the trumpet.[25] The shimmering timbre is like a beautiful aural reflection on placid Pacific water.

Similarly affecting are the locomotive effects in 'The Enchanted Train'. The snare and bass drums create a sonic rendering, through rhythm, of the engine starting up and chugging along. Bennett gives instructions in the orchestral score for how this is to happen: 'Dr[um] to imitate train (in rhythm). Rolls on downbeats for 4 measures, then on beats 1 and 2

---

[24] Orchestral materials for *Sitting Pretty* are preserved in the Jerome Kern Collection at the Library of Congress.

[25] 'On a Desert Island with You', full orchestral score, box 68, folder 6, Jerome Kern Collection, LC.

afterwards. Move to solid eights, then sixteenths.'[26] What happens is this: the engine gets going (drum rolls every fourth beat, then every other beat, then every beat), the train starts moving (eighth notes) and gains speed (sixteenth notes). Bennett calls for this same 'train effect' later in the number.[27] In the final refrain, Steiner adds a highly cinematic effect by scoring an actual steam whistle.[28]

Like its theatrical siblings, once *Sitting Pretty* closed on Broadway, it toured. In many respects, the tour was more successful than the Broadway production. First, the famous Dolly Sisters, the identical twins Rosie (1892–1970) and Jenny (1892–1941), played the identical twins May and Dixie. Described as 'the world's most beautiful and famous twins',[29] the Hungarian-born Dolly Sisters had been vaudeville favourites before achieving further fame and fortune in Europe. They returned to the USA, their adopted country, for the *Sitting Pretty* tour. Their performances did not disappoint, with one reviewer noting 'the charm of their intricate steps which are brimming over with cadence at one moment and jazz at the next'.[30] Second was having the Vincent Lopez Syncopated Band in the pit. Lopez (1895–1975) was one of the most popular American bandleaders of the decade and a formidable rival to Paul Whiteman. The 'sparkle and brilliancy'[31] the band brought to the score was mentioned by critics throughout the tour as one of the production's highlights.

Musical Comedies of Various Sorts

Several common plots, or variants thereof, filled musical comedies in 1924. These included rags-to-riches tales, commentaries on social class and wealth and stories involving mistaken identity. Such tropes were set to music that ran the gamut from nearly spoken music hall–style numbers to exuberantly expansive lyrical outpourings. Most common, though, were songs with varying degrees of syncopation that might appeal to dance bands and record companies and hence become popular outside the theatre. Like the plots, it was all too easy for the music to become commonplace. When stories and songs seemed recycled and predictable, audiences stopped coming.

---

[26] 'The Magic Train', full orchestral score, box 69, folder 1, Jerome Kern Collection, LC.
[27] 'The Magic Train', full orchestral score.   [28] 'The Magic Train', full orchestral score.
[29] 'Entrancing Dolly Sisters at Teck in Musical Revue', *Buffalo Courier*, 22 February 1925, newspapers.com.
[30] 'Dolly Sisters' Dances Delight', *Evening News* (Harrisburg, PA), 29 April 1925, newspapers.com.
[31] 'Dolly Sisters' Dances Delight'.

Such was the case with *Paradise Alley*, which opened on 31 March at the Casino Theatre in New York and lasted less than two months. The ambitious Bonnie Brown, played by the 'lark-like'[32] Helen Shipman, goes from the New York slum Paradise Alley to London, where she becomes a musical comedy star. She receives various marriage proposals, but returns to wed Jack Harriman, the American lightweight boxing champ with whom she is in love. Charles W. Bell and Edward Clark provided the book and Howard Johnson the lyrics, while the show's director and producer, Carle Carlton, wrote most of the songs. The biggest hit was the title song, a perky foxtrot that was taken up by dance bands and recorded by both Paul Whiteman and His Orchestra[33] and Harry Raderman's Dance Orchestra.[34]

While *Paradise Alley*'s recyclings brought about its early demise, *Our Nell* fared somewhat better in London. It opened on 16 April at the Gaiety Theatre, where it played for just over four months. Following the successful musical retellings from the previous year of courtly ladies of history, *Catherine* and *Madame Pompadour*, here was one about a British figure, Nell Gwynne (1650–1687), mistress of Charles II (see Plate 10). *Our Nell* was the third musical to be produced by Robert Evett (1874–1949) and starring the venerable José Collins (1887–1958) to play at the Gaiety Theatre, the other two being *The Last Waltz* (1922) and the aforementioned *Catherine*. Evett and Collins were hoping to establish the Gaiety Theatre as a venue for long-running, successful musicals akin to what was happening at Daly's Theatre, home to *Madame Pompadour*. Personal animosity was also involved, for Evett and Collins had both been working at Daly's until their quarrels with its manager, Jimmy White, became so insurmountable that they both left.[35] This fuelled their motivation to succeed at the Gaiety.

Sadly, though, *Our Nell* seems to have fallen flat. This certainly wasn't the fault of its star, who received strong reviews. As was typical, critics blamed the book, this one by Louis N. Parker and Reginald Arkell. *Variety*'s reviewer described it as having 'the ambling gait of one of the pensioners mentioned in the text'.[36] He was also distraught at anachronistic references in the dialogue (e.g., terms such as 'leading lady' and 'stalls') and levelled a similar criticism at the songs by Harold Fraser-Simson and Ivor Novello,

---

[32] Percy Hammond, 'New York Shows', syndicated article, 12 April 1924, *St. Louis Star and Times*, newspapers.com.
[33] Victor 19353-A.   [34] Edison Diamond Disc 51351-R.
[35] Collins, *The Maid of the Mountains*, 189.
[36] 'New Plays Produced in London and Paris', *Variety*, 7 May 1924, 18.

stating that the score 'hardly ever catches the spirit of the period'.[37] What the creators were doing, though, was to use contemporary language and music as a conduit to tell the story in a mode familiar to the audience. Collins did this as well when she used recognizable accents to reflect the change in her character, morphing from an East London sound to 'top story tones'.[38] *Our Nell* ended with the king promising to build a home in Chelsea for old soldiers, what became the Royal Hospital Chelsea, home to the Chelsea Pensioners, and culminated musically in the stirring march (for 1924) 'Our England' by Novello and Arkell, about which Collins remarked, 'It is not exaggerating to say that this patriotic song was the best ever written.'[39]

Also looking to the past, *To-night's the Night* had been a massive success when it played at the Gaiety Theatre in 1915, the very venue where *Our Nell* was playing in spring 1924. A summer revival of the previous decade's hit opened at the Winter Garden Theatre on 21 April. With a book by Fred Thompson, music by Paul A. Rubens and lyrics by Rubens and Percy Greenbank, the musical comedy, based on the French farce *Les Dominos roses* (The Pink Dominos), concerned two women who test the fidelity of their husbands. The score included an interpolation by Jerome Kern, 'They Didn't Believe Me', which became one of Kern's early hits. *To-night's the Night* featured the male stars of the Winter Garden's previous production, *The Beauty Prize*, George Grossmith, Jr and Leslie Henson, both of whom had been in the original *To-night's the Night*. Grossmith reprised his role as the Honourable Dudley Mitten, and Henson's role of Henry, 'that irrepressible nephew', was expanded to showcase more of the actor's talents.[40]

Sex featured prominently in the libretto for *Gosse de riche* (Rich Kid), a *comédie musicale* with music by Maurice Yvain (1891–1965) that opened at the Théâtre Daunou in Paris on 2 May. The work was by the same composer whose *Ta bouche* (literally, Your Mouth) Clare Kummer had adapted as *One Kiss* for Charles B. Dillingham in late 1923. In the book by Jacques Bousquet (1883–1939) and Henri Falk (1881–1937), Achille Patarin is horrified to discover that he shares the same mistress as his future son-in-law, the painter André Sartène. All of course works out by the end, and Patarin's daughter, Colette, is with her painter. This was an extremely cosy production, with only 8 characters, no chorus, and at a theatre with just 450 seats. Yvain's vivacious score showed the strong

---

[37] 'New Plays Produced in London and Paris'.   [38] 'New Plays Produced in London and Paris'.
[39] Collins, *The Maid of the Mountains*, 238.
[40] 'The Winter Garden: 'To-night's the Night', *The Stage*, 24 April 1924, britishnewspaperarchive .com.

influence of American dances such as the foxtrot appearing alongside the Parisian favourite, the java. The cast included the talented soprano Alice Cocéa (1889–1970) as Colette and Henri Defreyn, the tenor who created the role of Danilo in the French premiere of *The Merry Widow* in 1909, as André. *Gosse de riche* became one of Yvain's most popular works and is still performed in France in the twenty-first century.

J. Hartley Manners's play *Peg O' My Heart* had been delighting audiences since it first appeared in 1912, so there was great anticipation in New York for its musical version. Unlike the original, *Peg O' My Dreams* didn't succeed. It opened at Jolson's 59th Street Theatre on 5 May for a mere thirty-two performances. There simply wasn't enough about the production to keep it going. Manners prepared the musical adaptation himself and kept the plot intact. Peg, a poor Irish girl living in New York, is set to become an heiress after her uncle in England dies. There's a twist, of course: Peg must go to England and live with relatives who will teach her 'proper' manners, and she must not know of the plan. Peg acquires a suitor, Jerry, who turns out to be none other than Sir Gerald Adair, executor of her uncle's will. After various mishaps, all ends happily. Hugo Felix and Anne Caldwell's songs melded musical comedy perkiness with operetta expanse, and the vocal demands of the title role required someone with operatic training. Suzanne Keener, a young singer on the roster at the Metropolitan Opera, made her first and only Broadway appearance as Peg. Curiously, no solo songs for her are listed in the playbill. The show's early demise indicated that even when based on a popular play from twelve years earlier, the rags-to-riches tale of a young Irish immigrant had just been seen too often.

Yet another rags-to-riches tale, this one about a young woman who has an idea for a new type of doll, *Plain Jane* opened at the New Amsterdam Theatre on 12 May. In McElbert Moore and Phil Cook's story, Jane Lee cannot pay her rent and so gives her landlady's daughter a rag doll she has made. The landlady's son, Kid McGuire, is a boxing manager and decides to help Jane by entering her creation in a contest for new dolls sponsored by the multi-millionaire owner of a doll company, Julian Kingsley. The fancy 'doll king' discards the rag doll, but all is not lost, for his son, Dick, rescues it from the dustbin. But Jane needs money to make an industry out of her doll, so Dick, having fallen in love with Jane, enters a boxing match, promoted by Kid, that includes a $25,000 prize. He of course wins, Jane is elated and the two become engaged. Tom Johnstone wrote the music, which featured lyrics by Phil Cook. Among the score's highlights was the romantic duet 'Along the Road to Love'. The musical comedy centred more on the talents of its principal comedian, Joe Laurie, Jr as Kid McGuire, as it did on the romantic leads Lorraine Manville and Jay Gould. In this way, it bore a resemblance to *Kid Boots* with its emphasis on Eddie Cantor as Kid and a sport-themed plot.

Opening in London on the same date as *Plain Jane* was *Toni*, starring the debonair Scottish actor Jack Buchanan (1891–1957). Buchanan made his successful Broadway debut in *André Charlot's Revue of 1924* in January (see Chapter 5) and left Charlot's production to return to the United Kingdom for *Toni*.[41] The story by Douglas Furber and Harry Graham concerns Princess Stephanie (played by a charming dancer listed with the single name June) of the imaginary Ruritanian kingdom of Mettopolachia who is forced out of her country and makes her way to England. There, she befriends the women's clothier Anthony Prince, aka Toni (Buchanan's role). The princess persuades Prince to return with her to Mettopolachia and decide which of the three groups vying for political power should be allowed to rule. After hearing from the leaders of the groups (the Ruling Classes, the Middle Classes and the People), Toni famously responds that their words mean nothing to him, for he doesn't speak Mettopolachian. Of course, Toni and the princess fall in love and all ends happily.

Though the plot practically screams operetta, the songs by the teams of Hugo Hirsch and Douglas Furber and Stephen Jones and Harry Graham are filled with lilting syncopated melodies rather than luxuriant waltz refrains. The score is, on the whole, breezy and light, ideal for the dance floor. The importance of dance in the musical becomes especially evident when Toni enters to the foxtrot 'Take a Step', the lyrics of which are all about dancing. Indeed, *Toni* was very much a dancing show, and Jack Buchanan himself is credited on the playbill with designing the dances and ensembles.

Typical of operetta, socio-political commentary infuses the work. Here, it critiques the role and significance of British foreign policy in the 1920s, especially concerning the newly formed Kingdom of Serbs, Croats and Slovenes. The musical implies that British policy is internationally respected and that other nations will therefore ask Britain for advice, even if the envoys are not qualified (Toni is a women's clothier) and do not understand the situation or the language. The dancing Jack Buchanan thus becomes a personification of British foreign intervention. His star quality and effervescence kept the show running until mid-December.

---

[41] Moore, *André Charlot*, 93.

On the Topic of Musical Style

The evening after *Plain Jane* and *Toni* opened on opposite sides of the Atlantic, a play that dealt directly with the relationship between Central European concert music and Tin Pan Alley song opened on Broadway at the Central Theatre. *The Melody Man* starred Lew Fields (1867–1941) as Franz Henkel, an Austrian composer who is miserable working as a jazz arranger for a New York popular music publisher. When the owner of the firm, Al Tyler, wins the affections of Henkel's daughter, Elsa, as well as steals a melody from Henkel's 'Dresden Sonata' for his jazz hit 'Moonlight Mamma', Henkel is incensed. In this insightful commentary on the politics of musical style, the authors – called 'Herbert Richard Lorenz' on the playbill, and in reality the trio of **Herbert** Fields, **Richard** Rodgers and **Lorenz** Hart – address some of the very issues they themselves would be facing in subsequent decades. (Lew Fields was Herbert and Dorothy's father.) Adapting classical melodies for the musical stage was of course nothing new, and it was certainly something audiences would have heard in 1924 in shows such as *Catherine* (Tchaikovsky) and a revival of *Blossom Time* (Schubert). Fields began his career in vaudeville, so here was someone whose career was formed in the realm of popular entertainment playing a European composer who despises jazz and popular music styles.

These eternal relationships between the old and the new, the venerated and the innovative, the original and the transformed are at the heart of not just *The Melody Man* but also the world of musical theatre in 1924, including the spring months. Old-style plots were being presented with new-style music, as in *Toni*, and creators from the previous decade reunited for a new work, as in *Sitting Pretty*. Established stars returned in new productions, such as José Collins in *Our Nell* and George Grossmith and Leslie Henson in a revival of *To-Night's the Night*. Newer stars were continuing to make their marks, such as Adele and Fred Astaire and Jack Buchanan. It was an exciting few months for the musical, and more glories were on the way.

8 | The Resplendence of the Revue

Some revues offer awe-inspiring visual feasts while others are much more modest in scope. Some revel in their wholesomeness while others do just the opposite. Whatever the approach to the songs, sketches and overall aesthetic, producers hoped to achieve what an unnamed reviewer admired in the revue *Innocent Eyes*: 'The amazing scenes ... are disclosed in kaleidoscopic fashion. Never a hitch, never a delay.'[1]

The revues that opened in the spring (and indeed throughout the year) represent only some of what was happening, for revues were ubiquitous in the 1924 musical theatre landscape. Especially in the United Kingdom, many toured on various circuits. These included such audience draws as *Mr Tower of London*, the show that propelled comic actor Gracie Fields (1898–1979) to fame, and *Risk It*, which featured the Scottish comic Sandy Connor.[2]

Not All Revues Succeed

Revues, with their non-narrative structure, offer plenty of opportunities for innovation. Sometimes things work, other times they do not. A case of the latter is *Cartoons*, which opened at the Criterion Theatre in London on 19 April. What was unique here was that animated cartoons drawn by Tom Webster appeared alongside the live sketches. This innovative use of mixed media – live and pre-recorded, humans and drawings – seems so forward looking. But technology cannot replace content. As one reviewer noted, the animations showed Webster at his best, while the remainder was 'quite banal and conventional'.[3] The visual dimension must have been truly striking, for the playbill included an index to the 'generally elaborate and often bizarre'[4] costumes by Webster and Dolly Tree.

---

[1] 'Week's Review of Stage Offerings', *Times Union* (Brooklyn, NY), 11 November 1924, newspapers.com.
[2] 'Variety Stage', *The Stage*, 6 November 1924, BNA.
[3] 'The Criterion: 'Cartoons', *The Stage*, 24 April 1924, BNA.   [4] 'The Criterion: 'Cartoons'.

There are many ways to successfully begin a revue; insulting the audience is not among them. When *Come In*'s composer, Clay Smith, greeted the audience with 'ladies and gentlemen – and you', the malicious addition to the familiar salutation did not go over well. Produced by Lee White at the Queen's Theatre in London, *Come In* opened on 1 May. Critics uniformly blasted the show. White took their criticisms to heart and made revisions during the first week of the run. Some sketches were dropped, though the songs associated with them remained. The revised version still did not work, and *Come In* lasted just three weeks.

Five New Revues over Four Days

It was a different situation for revues in New York. Five new revues opened over four days in the latter part of May. First was *I'll Say She Is*, on 19 May, which featured the Broadway debut of the Marx Brothers, four of the most iconic comic stars of the century. The next evening featured the premieres of *Innocent Eyes*, a vehicle for Mistinguett,[5] the Parisian singer and dancer famous enough to be known by one name, and *The Grand Street Follies*, performed at the Neighborhood Theatre in Manhattan's Lower East Side. Completing the quintet were *Round the Town* on the 21st, created by journalists, and *Keep Kool* on the 22nd, with strong links to vaudeville.

Revue No. 1: I'll Say She Is

I'll Say She Is best remembered – and rightly so – as the show that featured the Broadway debuts of the Marx Brothers (see Plate 11).[6] The opening night playbill lists the siblings with their real names: Leonard (1887–1961), Adolph (1888–1964), Julius (1890–1977) and Herbert (1901–1979), ones they later replaced with the more familiar Chico (pronounced 'Chick-o'), Harpo, Groucho and Zeppo.

---

[5] On occasion, the name is spelled as 'Mistinguette', with an 'e' added to the end.

[6] Noah Diamond resurrected *I'll Say She Is* with a staged reading and Fringe Festival performance in 2014 and an off-Broadway production in 2016 in which he played Groucho. Since no complete script or score is known to have survived, Diamond reconstructed the show based on extant fragments and comments and quotations from reviewers who saw the show at various times, either on Broadway or during its pre- and post-Broadway tours. He recounts his journey in *Gimme a Thrill: The Story of 'I'll Say She Is', The Lost Marx Brothers Musical and How It Was Found* (Duncan: BearManor Media, 2016).

The plot of *I'll Say She Is* concerns a character simply called Beauty, a young society lady whose sole desire is to be thrilled. The brothers do their best to accommodate. Beauty finds herself in a Chinatown opium den, where she is accused of murder, and later, when they take her a hypnotist, she becomes the Empress Josephine. In these and other scenarios, the Marx Brothers performed some of their classic routines, many of which had already become audience favourites when the siblings had been playing vaudeville.

Playing Beauty to the brothers' antics was an actor billed as 'Lotta Miles'. That wasn't her real name; she was the generic young woman who would appear in ads for the Kelly-Springfield Tire Company. 'Lotta Miles' indicated the long life of the tyres she marketed. While there were many Lotta Miles over the years, Florence Reutti (1893–1937) was the only one who continued using the name after she left the company. In a very clever bit of marketing, she appeared as 'Lotta Miles' in an advertisement for Kelly-Springfield Tires that was printed in the playbill for *I'll Say She Is* and as Beauty in the show itself.

The thin storyline was the brainchild of Will B. Johnstone, who also wrote the show's lyrics to music by his brother Tom, composer for the musical comedy *Plain Jane* (see Chapter 7). But, as actor and playwright Noah Diamond puts it, much of the show 'was written out loud, with the best improvisations made permanent'.[7]

One of the Marx Brothers's most popular vaudeville sequences, the theatrical agency sketch, featured in *I'll Say She Is*. The brothers filmed the scene in 1931 for *The House that Shadows Built*, a promotional film for Paramount Studios. This is the only preserved audio-visual documentation of all four Marx Brothers performing material from their first Broadway show. One by one, they enter the agent's office, telling him of their talents. The fast-paced metric patter is filled with clever rhymes (e.g., 'don't slam the door' and 'Ethel Barrymore'), dovetailed entrances and the same sort of rhythmic precision that one might find in a Rossini *buffa* ensemble, rap or the musical *Hamilton*. The matching of fast-paced verbal counterpoint, punctuated pronunciation and precise physical gestures remains as captivating today as it was in 1924.

The aforementioned opium den scene culminated in an aggressive Apache dance performed by Harry Walters and Cecile D'Andrea. Their characters, called 'Hop Merchant' and 'White Girl' in the playbill, furthered negative stereotypes of Asian men and their abuse – and

---

[7] Diamond, *Gimme a Thrill*, 54.

murder – of white women. Beauty is arrested for 'White Girl''s death, which provides Julius one of the show's classic lines: 'You are charged with murder and if you are convicted you will be charged with electricity.'[8]

At one point in Act 2, Beauty, unmoved by finery, longs for poverty, a state in which she thinks she might finally find her sought-after thrill. 'What I wouldn't give for a single cinnamon bun and a piece of scrapple', she wishes.[9] Just then, Julius, dressed in drag as a fairy godmother, enters and 'Cinderella Backward' begins. Rather than just a ball, Beauty goes to a full-fledged dance marathon. She watches the graceful 'Pygmalion Ballet', 'The Awakening of Love', set to Felix Mendelssohn's 'Spring Song' in an elegant classical turn for Walters and D'Andrea. This is a Marx Brothers show, though, and not a dance revue, so immediately after the dancers leave the stage, Julius, Adolph and Herbert enter for their own 'Tramp Ballet', 'The Death of Love', a parody of 'The Awakening of Love' danced to the same music.

As 'The Death of Love' ends, Leonard enters and announces that he is a hypnotist. Thus begins the famous Napoleon Scene. Beauty is the Empress Josephine and Julius is Napoleon. The three other brothers, ostensibly Napoleon's advisors, charge their way towards the empress as soon as they enter, wooing her in their own ridiculous manners. The scene features harp and piano specialties as well as a waltz for the 'Court Singer' (performed by Ruth Urban), 'Glimpses of the Moon'. When Napoleon arrives, the advisors hide. When he leaves, they emerge. He returns, they hide. He leaves, they emerge. He returns, they hide. He leaves, they emerge, and so on. The speed of the entrances, exits and dialogue increases to a truly frenetic speed. All is precisely timed, and Julius ultimately finds Josephine atop Adolph's lap. The audience went wild.

I'll Say She Is played at the legendary Casino Theatre, a venue famed for its earlier operetta productions and Moorish-inspired interior. By 1924, it had become more than a bit dilapidated, which gave it a quaintness that was, as Diamond asserts, a 'mixture of splendor and ruin'.[10] The antic-filled revue, with its patina of faded vaudeville – the antithesis, in so many ways, of Ziegfeld glamour – had found a perfect home.

---

[8] Quoted in Lee Davis, *Scandals and Follies: The Rise and Fall of the Great Broadway Revue* (New York: Limelight, 2000), 210.
[9] Diamond, *Gimme a Thrill*, 126.   [10] Diamond, *Gimme a Thrill*, 103.

Revue No. 2: Innocent Eyes

Physicality of a different sort was key to the first of the two revues that opened the next evening. Described by one reviewer as a 'garmentless concoction',[11] the satirically titled *Innocent Eyes* opened at the Winter Garden. Nudity was a shared feature between *Artists and Models* and *Innocent Eyes*, both of which were Shubert productions. According to an unnamed critic, 'The difference between the two revues is that "Artists and Models" emphasizes its boldness by the spoken world. "Innocent Eyes" simply presents its scenes and its chorus and permits its audience to "take or leave" it.'[12] Presentation dominated in *Innocent Eyes*. The revue was designed to showcase the Parisian *chanteuse* and *danseuse* Mistinguett (Jeanne Florentine Bourgeois, 1873–1956) in her US debut (see Figure 8.1). It certainly played into the popularity of French culture in the USA during the 1920s, especially its more salacious aspects. Whereas such elements had been tamed in Clare Kummer's operetta adaptation *One Kiss*, here they came to the fore. As critic Burns Mantle noted, 'it is as naked as the law permits, even nakeder in spots'.[13] The revue's journey to Broadway began several months earlier, at Nixon's Apollo Theatre in Atlantic City on 8 January, after which it visited other cities, including Chicago, en route to New York.

Mistinguett had been starring in Parisian revues since the late 1890s, appearing at the Casino de Paris, the Folies Bergère and the Moulin Rouge. By 1924, the peak of her fame had passed. Her US sojourn could be seen as a way for her to recapture her former glory with new audiences. She was known for her flamboyant theatricality and was said to have helped create the ferociously dramatic 'Apache Dance', which she performed in *Innocent Eyes*. This is the same dance that featured in the opium den scene in *I'll Say She Is*. But it was Mistinguett's physical appearance for which she was most renowned, especially her legs and ankles. Articles about Mistinguett and reviews of her performances inevitably mentioned her physicality, and more often than not made it the focus of the story.

The Shuberts' resident scriptwriter, Harold Atteridge, created the revue's sketches, which took place in the environs of the famous Moulin Rouge and included a tyrannical father selling off his daughter (Mistinguett) to a brutish man.[14] This scenario provided the dramatic context for the 'Apache Dance'. *Innocent Eyes* was very much a Shubert

[11] 'Week's Review of Stage Offerings'.   [12] 'Week's Review of Stage Offerings'.

[13] '"Innocent Eyes" and Mistinguett Are Here', *Daily News* (New York), 22 May 1924, newspapers.com.

[14] John Corbin, 'The Play', *New York Times*, 21 May 1924.

Figure 8.1 Mistinguett, star of *Innocent Eyes*, at the Moulin Rouge.

house production, for in addition to Atteridge, who also wrote some of
the show's lyrics, the score featured songs by Jean Schwartz and Sigmund
Romberg, among others. The title song, a foxtrot, became popular
through sheet music sales and thus provided additional publicity for the
revue.[15]

The most attention-grabbing feature of *Innocent Eyes*, though, was not
Mistinguett, at least not directly, but rather the production's varying degrees
of on-stage female nudity. While playing in Chicago, a delegation from the
mayor's and the district attorney's offices visited the theatre to see for
themselves if the women appearing on stage were sufficiently draped, per
their previous instructions. Gillman Haskell, the company's manager, took

---

[15] Music by Fred Coots, with Jean Schwartz; lyrics by McElbert Moore.

them backstage to ensure their satisfaction. He kept the women covered for the performance that followed, just in case the officials stayed to watch.[16]

Such covering, however, was not typical. J. J. Shubert, in his concept of the show, wanted the women barely dressed. Haskell wrote to the producer about the situation in Chicago:

> Except on nights when the police women come in to look us over (last time was night before last) I put the Inspiration and Venus tableaux on just as you had them, but drape the three models in the first act a little; when the police are here, I drape everything so to save trouble ... We keep the drapes ready at hand for using at a moment's notice.[17]

It was not at all unusual for members of the chorus to remain in New York when a show began its post-Broadway tour. Such was the case with Lucille LeSueur (1904?–1977), who was in the chorus of *Innocent Eyes*. After the show closed at the end of August, she joined the chorus of its Winter Garden successor, *The Passing Show of 1924*. When that revue closed, LeSueur moved to Hollywood, made her screen debut as the uncredited body double for Norma Shearer in *Lady of the Night* (MGM, 1925), changed her name to Joan Crawford and subsequently became one of the most acclaimed movie stars of the century.

Revue No. 3: The Grand Street Follies

A revue of a wholly different type, this one also featuring women at its centre, but now as creators and producers, shared its opening date with *Innocent Eyes*. This revue's location was as far from the bright lights of Broadway as was its sense of impropriety. Called 'the brightest of the local revues',[18] *The Grand Street Follies* was produced at and by the Neighborhood Playhouse, located at 466 Grand Street (hence its title) in Manhattan's Lower East Side. The revue offered good-humoured burlesques, with music, of its own productions and featured many of its players burlesquing their own performances. The revue, befitting its genre, also lampooned broader aspects of New York's theatrical scene.

---

[16] Letter, Gilman Haskell to J. J. Shubert, 16 March 1924, 'Innocent Eyes' correspondence file, Shubert Archive.

[17] Letter, Gilman Haskell to J. J. Shubert, 24 March 1924, 'Innocent Eyes' correspondence file, Shubert Archive.

[18] Burns Mantle, *The Best Plays of 1923–1924 and the Year Book of the Drama in America* (Boston: Small, Maynard & Company, 1924), 10.

The 1924 production was the second to be created and staged at the venue, the first having taken place in 1922. The philanthropists Alice Lewisohn (1883–1972) and Irene Lewisohn (1886–1944) founded the playhouse in 1915 as an art theatre with a small resident company. It was located in the Henry Street Settlement House, and was therefore part of the Settlement House philanthropic movement, the goal of which was to provide educational, recreational and artistic programmes to urban residents. When the sisters couldn't find an experimental play they liked to conclude their 1921–1922 season, Alice recalls suggesting that they just open their annual in-house satire of the season to the public.[19] The somewhat tentative audience who came to the first of the three public performances, not knowing what to expect, was absolutely delighted. Word spread quickly, and ten more performances were added. People were clamouring to get in, many pretending to be season subscribers since that was the only way to get a ticket. From then on, the *Follies* became an integral part of the Playhouse's season.[20]

Except for the next year. For, shortly after *The Grand Street Follies* made its public debut, the Neighborhood Playhouse announced that it would not produce any shows the next season. During this sabbatical year, as it was called, the Lewisohn sisters travelled throughout Europe, India and the eastern Mediterranean to explore the roots of theatre. They were concerned about the commercial influences on the art form they so loved, and upon their return they decided to replace 'repetition with original theatrical value', as Neighborhood Playhouse biographer John P. Harrington puts it.[21]

This 'original theatrical value' was certainly evident when the next edition of *The Grand Street Follies* opened on 20 May 1924. Agnes Morgan (1879–1976) and Helen Arthur (1879–1939) resumed their roles as the show's principal co-creators and performers. Morgan had been directing productions at the Neighborhood Playhouse from its earliest days. She began writing material for the venue in the early 1920s. Arthur was the Playhouse's business manager and Agnes's partner. She was also an attorney and a theatrical manager.[22] Particularly significant among the women who joined them to create the 1924 show were Agnes Hyland

[19] Alice Lewisohn Crowley, *The Neighborhood Playhouse: Leaves from a Theatre Scrapbook* (New York: Theatre Arts Books, 1959), 116.

[20] Crowley, *The Neighborhood Playhouse*, 117.

[21] John P. Harrington, *The Life of the Neighborhood Playhouse on Grand Street* (Syracuse: Syracuse University Press, 2007), 164.

[22] Crowley, *The Neighborhood Playhouse*, 117.

(1885 or 1886–1962) and Aline Bernstein (1880–1955). Hyland had been associated with the Neighborhood Playhouse since its founding as the resident pianist, playing for silent films and live productions. She composed original music for all five editions of *The Grand Street Follies*. Bernstein made her name as a set and costume designer at the Neighborhood Playhouse, volunteering her time to do so. This put her in good stead for when, in 1926, she battled to become the first female member of the Designers Union. Bernstein went on to design many Broadway productions and wrote several important books, mostly about clothing. In 1950, she won the Tony Award for Best Costume Design for Marc Blitzstein's Broadway opera *Regina*.

The 1924 *Grand Street Follies* was a smart revue that lampooned not only the Neighborhood Playhouse's own productions but also theatre in general. For example, 'Who Killed the Ghost?' was a Shakespearean hodgepodge in which members of the company offered impersonations of famous actors in canonic roles. The earnestness of 'John Barrymore as Hamlet' appearing opposite the sparkle of an imaginary 'Fanny Brice as Ophelia' resulted in a delightfully incongruous scene. Hyland and Morgan's lilting ballad 'The National Sport of England', in which the singer prides himself on chasing women (the sport), was included in the scene. Albert Carroll performed it as John Barrymore as Hamlet. Many in the audience would have found the lyrics to include clever allusions to Barrymore's very public private life.

But it was the Neighborhood Playhouse's own productions that provided the majority of the source material. Oftentimes, the burlesques included mash-ups with characters from other popular or famous plays. For example, in 'The Shewing-Up of Jo Leblanco', based on George Bernard Shaw's *The Showing-Up of Blanco Posnet*, which the Playhouse had produced the previous autumn, Sadie Thompson, the prostitute in W. Somerset Maugham's play *Rain*, makes an appearance. This is the same character that George Rosener was lampooning at the time in an *Artists and Models* sketch. Just as Rosener cross-dressed for the role, so did Dan Walker (see Figure 8.2). In a way, this was Dan Walker playing George Rosener playing Sadie. Walker took on another female role part in the show when he impersonated the famed singer Elsie Janis (1899–1956), who at the time was touring on both sides of the Atlantic, in 'A Recital at Town Hall'. Janis famously considered herself *not* a singer of art song and classical repertories, so this skit must have been truly splendid in its incongruity, since Town Hall was known for exactly that sort of music.

The management at the Neighborhood Playhouse knew that the 1924 *Grand Street Follies* would be an audience draw and planned for a long run.

Figure 8.2 Dan Walker puts finishing make-up touches on Agnes Morgan, one of the driving creative forces behind *The Grand Street Follies*. NYPL. https://digitalcollections .nypl.org/items/a1612d9b-69cc-8890-e040-e00a180634be.

As Burns Mantle noted, New Yorkers 'made a fad of it'.[23] Mervin L. Lane of New Rochelle, New York, was so impressed with the revue that he wrote a letter to the Dramatic Editor of the *New York Times*:

The other night I made a trip to the other end of town for the purpose of witnessing 'The Grand Street Follies' at the Neighborhood Playhouse. Small wonder there were no vacant seats! The spontaneous cleverness exhibited by this group of players is a revelation, and when one thinks, by comparison, of the stupidity which dominates the average Broadway revue the reason for the success of the production is readily understood.[24]

The 1924 *Grand Street Follies* played an impressive 172 performances and did not close until the end of November. Its popularity inspired new versions in the coming years, though, as Alice Lewisohn remarked, the later editions lacked the charm of the earlier ones, back when 'everything was subordinated to the spirit of play'.[25] Like so many things, its distinctiveness was curtailed as it became institutionalized.

---

[23] Mantle, *The Best Plays of 1923–1924*, 10.
[24] 'News and Comment from the Mail Bag', *New York Times*, 15 June 1924.
[25] Crowley, *The Neighborhood Playhouse*, 119.

Revues Nos. 4 and 5: *Round the Town* and *Keep Kool*

The aesthetics of *Innocent Eyes* and *Grand Street Follies* could hardly have been further apart. Yet another approach to the especially malleable genre, this one coming from the world of print journalism, was seen on 21 May when *Round the Town* opened at the Century Roof Theatre. Journalists wrote – and some even appeared in – this doomed show, which closed after just thirteen performances. Theatre critic Alexander Woollcott decreed: 'Silence of the tomb, however, shall enshroud "Round the Town".'[26] The revue proved that just because a writer achieves fame in one medium, even theatrical criticism, it does not guarantee success in another.

The fifth in this quintet was *Keep Kool*, which opened at the Morosco Theatre on 22 May. Its title was a take on the current political slogan 'Keep it Cool with Coolidge'. At the time, Coolidge was in the midst of his re-election campaign. *Keep Kool* was produced by E. K. Nadel, who had been a vaudeville manager for twelve years and was thoroughly rooted in the genre and its workings.[27] Paul Gerald Smith (1894–1968), a vaudeville writer who was gaining increasing recognition for his sketches, wrote the entirety of *Keep Kool*, and another vaudeville veteran, Jack Frost (born Harold G. Frost, 1893–1959) composed the music. Considering its producer and creators, it comes as no surprise that *Keep Kool* was rooted firmly in the vaudeville aesthetics of pure entertainment and comedy.

Vaudevillians familiar and new appeared in *Keep Kool*. Among the long-standing performers were Hazel Dawn (1890–1988), Charles King (1886–1944) and Johnny Dooley (1886–1928). Dawn, born to a Mormon family in Utah, became famous playing the title character in the London production of *The Balkan Princess* in 1910 and achieved further stardom when *The Pink Lady* opened on Broadway the following year. She then appeared in eleven feature films from Famous Players-Lasky in the mid-teens. Dawn had been touring in vaudeville before joining the *Keep Kool* company. Her talent was to play violin on stage as well as sing, similar to Hubert Marischka at the Theater an der Wien in Vienna and Odette Myrtil in *Vogues of 1924*. King featured in *Little Nellie Kelly* before *Keep Kool*, and in 1928 he went to Hollywood, where he appeared in several early film musicals, including the Academy Award-winning *The Broadway Melody* (1929). The third member of the veteran trio,

[26] Alexander Woollcott, 'The Reviewing Stand', syndicated article, *Buffalo News*, 31 May 1924, newspapers.com.

[27] 'Who's Who in 'Keep Kool', *Brooklyn Daily Eagle*, 11 May 1924, newspapers.com.

Dooley, was a popular 'knockabout comedian'[28] who brought his sense of physical humour to the show. Another famous vaudevillian left *Keep Kool* before it reached Broadway: William Frawley (1887–1966), who later became beloved to millions as Fred Mertz in the television series *I Love Lucy*.[29] Leading the newcomers were the Australian-born dancer Ina Williams (born Queenie Williams, 1896–1962) and the future film and television actor Dick Keene (1899–1971). The variety of performances and the combination of experience and youth kept *Keep Kool* running until September.

Meanwhile in London

Four new revues featured in London's summer season. First was *The Punch Bowl*, which opened at the Duke of York's Theatre on 21 May. In three parts, the entire second part was devoted to 'Punch-and-Judy Up-to-Date', a modernist reworking of the British puppet staple. The sequence is envisioned as a dream – or more of a nightmare – that the tired Showman, played by Alfred Lester with tremendous dryness, experiences after an indifferent day. In the end, the Showman and his wife realize that some things should not be updated, including Punch and Judy. In a year during which so many 'old' things were being renewed or returned to theatrical stages, the sketch offered a reminder that this is not always a good idea. It included ballet music by the modernist composer Norman O'Neill (1875–1934). O'Neill taught composition at the Royal Academy of Music and, along with C. Armstrong Gibbs and Cyril Scott, was among the 'serious' composers whose music appeared in London musicals in 1924. Another feature of the show, and in musical contrast to Punch and Judy, was Nora Blaney's emotive interpretation of Irving Berlin's new song, 'What'll I Do?', written the previous year.

An eponymous revue featuring its American star, *Elsie Janis at Home* delighted audiences at the Queen's Theatre from 3 June to 9 August (see Plate 12). Janis (1889–1956) had given concerts in Europe during the Great War and became known as the 'Sweetheart of the AEF' (American Expeditionary Force). As such, she remained a beloved presence on the London stage. She delighted audiences with her quick wit and various caricatures, especially those of a French mademoiselle who doesn't speak much English trying to sing 'I'm Just Wild about Harry', an Italian

[28] 'Johnny Dooley, Actor, Dies at 41', *New York Times*, 8 June 1928.
[29] Frawley's name appears in the cast list that appears in Gordon Whyte, 'Musical Comedy: Revue, Operetta, Spectacle', *The Billboard*, 17 May 1924.

signorina who flings roses at the audience and a volatile diamond-glazed dancing master in 'On with the Dance'.[30]

Janis shared the stage with several notable performers. She sang duets with a Canadian baritone with 'a pleasingly modulated voice'[31] credited as Walter Verne Pidgeon. This singer was none other than the future film star Walter Pidgeon (1897–1984), who had begun singing with Janis the previous year. Also appearing in the revue was the team of Layton & Johnstone, an African American singing duo formed of Turner Layton (1894–1978), who also played piano, and Clarence 'Tandy' Johnstone (1885–1953). They went to London for *Elsie Janis at Home* and ended up staying in the United Kingdom, where they performed in swanky clubs and made many recordings until their partnership dissolved in 1935 (see Figure 8.3). Layton & Johnstone were praised for their wide and eclectic repertory, which audiences would have seen and heard in *Elsie Janis at Home*.

Elsie Janis at Home had a limited run due to other engagements for its principals. It was significant in several important respects. First, its American performers reflected the transnational dimension of the revue. Second, its multi-ethnic cast placed more Black performers in the UK music industry. Third, even with its progressive aspects, racism remained, for Janis performed one of her characters in blackface.

The third of these London revues, *Yoicks!*, opened at the Kingsway Theatre on 11 June. Produced by and featuring Donald Calthrop (1888–1940), the revue is perhaps best remembered for its burlesquing of performance styles rather than specific performers. For example, one segment offered reinterpretations of the children's tale 'Babes in the Wood' first as performed by the Russian Ballet and then in an experimental staging with overly exaggerated lighting effects in a parody of Basil Dean. As was typical of revues, material was changed during its eight-month run as performers left or joined the cast.

The Odd Spot, which opened at the Vaudeville Theatre on 30 July, rounded out this quartet of revues. It featured the humorous Binnie Hale (1899–1984), whose impressions of Elsie Janis, Phyllis Dare and even the singer, actor and composer Ivor Novello did what they could to save the otherwise second-rate show. Hale's impressions had been a highlight of the revue *Puppets*, which had played at the same theatre earlier in the year. André Charlot's protégé Dion Titheradge (1889–1934) wrote many of the sketches and also produced the show. A team of composers and lyricists contributed the songs. One critic noted that the revue 'has some odd spots

---

[30] '"Elsie Janis at Home." At the Queen's', *The Era*, 4 June 1924, BNA.
[31] 'Elsie Janis at Home'.

Figure 8.3 Layton & Johnstone (Turner Layton [left] and Clarence 'Tandy' Johnstone [right]), who made their London stage debuts in *Elsie Janis at Home*.

that are good',[32] while another said it would 'teach the audience to appreciate other theatres'.[33] It offered further proof that the style of Charlot was something distinctive and not always repeatable by others.

The Big Series in New York: Ziegfeld's *Follies* and *George White's Scandals*

The five revues that opened on Broadway over four days in May and the London summertime quartet demonstrated fresh approaches to the

[32] S.H.B-S. 'New Vaudeville Revue. "The Odd Spot"', *The Sportsman* (London), 1 August 1924, BNA.

[33] 'Our Captious Critic: "The Odd Spot", at the Vaudeville', *Illustrated Sporting and Dramatic News*, 16 August 1924, BNA.

established genre. However, at least in New York, revue remained closely associated with large-scale, corporate productions, as was evident in new editions of Ziegfeld's *Follies* and *George White's Scandals*.

After Ziegfeld's *Follies of 1923* closed at the New Amsterdam Theatre on 10 May 1924, it began its post-Broadway tour. Its successor, *Follies of 1924*, opened at the New Amsterdam on 24 June. Thus, two different editions of the same revue were playing simultaneously, though in different cities. This was typical, as was having especially popular sketches and songs move between editions: for example, by mid-July, the shadowgraph scene from the 1923 edition had returned to the New Amsterdam Theatre.[34]

Critics found the 1924 edition to be of better quality than its immediate predecessor, though none thought it to come close to the genre-defining spectacles of the late teens. The *Follies* had become a brand in and of itself, and the 1924 edition gave audiences exactly what they expected. As *The New York Times* critic noted, 'Mr. Ziegfeld this year has made no departure from type'.[35] This particular *Follies*, however, was significant in that it included the final appearances of long-standing *Follies* favourites and introduced future famous faces to the series. Saying their farewells were the sprightly dancer Ann Pennington (1893–1971) and the wise humourist and rope-twirler Will Rogers (1879–1935). Making their debuts were the versatile singer Vivienne Segal (1897–1992) and the British musical comedy star Lupino Lane (1882–1959). Segal would become famous for creating leading roles in *The Desert Song* (1926, Margot), *Pal Joey* (1940, Vera Simpson) and the revival of *A Connecticut Yankee* (1942, Morgan le Fay), while Lane would introduce 'The Lambeth Walk' in the 1937 musical *Me and My Girl* and its 1939 film adaptation. As happens so frequently in this eventful year, past and future stars met in the present.

In addition to individual performers, two ensembles made their *Follies* debuts in the 1924 edition: George Olsen and His Music and the Tiller Girls (actually two sets of Tiller Girls). Olsen and his orchestra had been significant contributors to the success of *Kid Boots* (see Chapter 4), and now they were being spotlighted in Ziegfeld's high-profile revue. The famed Tiller Girls made their dramatic entrance jumping phosphorescent ropes across a dark stage. Two different troupes of Tiller Girls were featured in the *Follies* as the result of family rivalry. Ziegfeld arranged for John, the father and originator of the precision-dancing enterprise, to send one of his long-established troupes. However, John's son Lawrence, who had broken away

---

[34] van der Merwe, *The Ziegfeld Follies*, 184.
[35] 'New "Follies" Opens with Will Rogers', *New York Times*, 25 June 1924.

from his dad to form his own company, had already sent his 'Empire Girls'. Hence, Ziegfeld had two troupes of precision dancers on the bill. Tiller historian Dormey Vernon notes that there was very little difference in dancing technique between them; the variance came from their attitude: 'Johns' were more staid while 'Lawrences' were more lively.[36] The musical number in which they made their debut, 'The Beauty Contest', holds significance as the last number written expressly for the *Follies* by the highly esteemed composer, conductor and cellist Victor Herbert (1859– 1924).

Herbert, an American music icon in the decades surrounding the turn of the twentieth century, passed away on 26 May 1924. Although he enjoyed a wide-ranging musical career, he remains best known for the operettas he wrote around the turn of the twentieth century. It was this repertory that featured in a tribute sequence in the *Follies of 1924*:

'Gypsy Love Song' from *The Fortune Teller* (1898), sung by Irving Fisher
'I Can't Do the Sum' from *Babes in Toyland* (1903), sung by Ann Pennington
'Kiss Me Again' from *Mlle. Modiste* (1905), sung by Vivienne Segal
'Toyland' from *Babes in Toyland*, sung by Gloria Dawn and then Bernice
  Ackerman
'March of the Toys' from *Babes in Toyland*, sung by Lupino Lane and Mae Daw and
  featuring the Tiller Girls and the Empire Girls

The set glowed with nostalgic splendour. Some critics saw the set as further proof of how old-fashioned and lacklustre the *Follies* had become.[37] However, it also showed the timelessness of Herbert's music and its continued appeal to later generations of performers and audiences.

Herbert's music played in stark contrast to syncopated dances such as 'Biminy', a foxtrot by the perennial Ziegfeld songwriting team of composer Dave Stamper and lyricist Gene Buck. At first, Ann Pennington sang the jaunty number, but when it was decided that she should she become its featured dancer, the lyrical tenor Irving Fisher took over the vocal duties.[38] George Olsen and His Music recorded an instrumental version of the song with a prominent banjo part that gives it a highly distinctive sound.[39]

On 30 June, the sixth edition of *George White's Scandals* opened at the Apollo Theatre. Critics again called out the predictability of the production with all its grandeur. The critic for *The New York Times* remarked that

---

[36] Vernon, *Tiller's Girls*, 100.   [37] Ommen van der Merwe, *The Ziegfeld Follies*, 185.
[38] Ommen van der Merwe, *The Ziegfeld Follies*, 182.
[39] Recorded 19 August 1924. Victor 19429-B.

White 'has evolved a standardized product',[40] echoing similar remarks about Ziegfeld.

This was the fifth and final *Scandals* for which George Gershwin composed all or most of the music.[41] The lyrics were by Buddy De Sylva, sometimes on his own and at other times with Ballard MacDonald. The outstanding song from the show was 'Somebody Loves Me', sung by the 'breezy and bewitching singer'[42] Winnie Lightner. Ira was proud of his brother's contributions, writing to him in London: 'I enclose some reviews, one of which goes to far as to dare to say it is better than the Follies which had opened the week before.'[43] Of course, it comes as no surprise that comparisons between these two brands of revue would be made.

---

[40] 'New "Scandals" Open; An Elaborate Show', *New York Times*, 1 July 1924.
[41] Neimoyer, 'After the Rhapsody', 106.   [42] 'New "Scandals" Open'.
[43] Ira Gershwin to George Gershwin, 25 June 1924, Gershwin Correspondence, box 140, folder 13, George and Ira Gershwin Collection, LC.

Plate 1 Sheet music cover for *Shuffle Along*. NYPL. https://digitalcollections.nypl.org/ items/510d47e3-c352-a3d9-e040-e00a18064a99.

Plate 2 Publicity advertisement for *Artists and Models*. The Shubert Archive.

"STOP FLIRTING," AT THE QUEEN'S

Miss Adèle Astaire, Miss Marjorie Gordon, and Mr. Fred Astaire
in one of the scenes in this bright little show which is carrying on
with undiminished success in its new home at the Queen's Theatre

Plate 3 Adele Astaire, Marjorie Gordon and Fred Astaire in *Stop Flirting*. Alamy.

Plate 4 Fred Stone and Dorothy Stone, the father and daughter stars of *Stepping Stones*.

Plate 5 Poster for *Il paese dei campanelli* (The Land of the Bells) featuring its star, Nella Regini.

Plate 6 Evelyn Laye in *Madame Pompadour*, from *Play Pictorial* 44 (no. 264), pp. 60–61.

Plate 7 Poster for *Doña Francisquita*.

Plate 8 Sheet music cover for 'Limehouse Blues' featuring Gertrude Lawrence.

Plate 9 Original sheet music cover for *Gräfin Mariza* (Countess Maritza).

Plate 10 José Collins in *Our Nell*, as seen on a *Play Pictorial* cover.

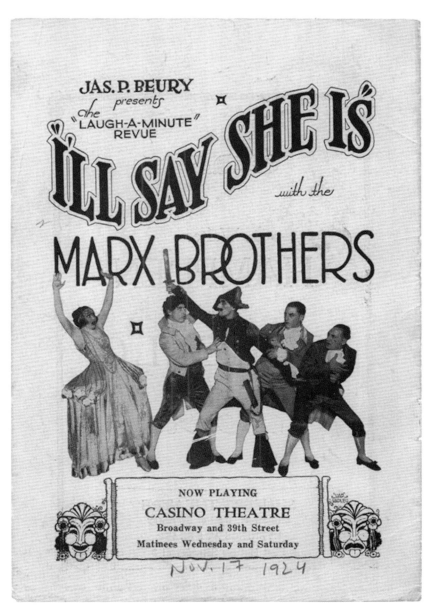

Plate 11 Advertisement for *I'll Say She Is*. NYPL. https://digitalcollections.nypl.org/items/d80e87f0-9eed-0130-2770-58d385a7bbd0.

Plate 12 Elsie Janis, star of *Elsie Janis at Home*.

Plate 13 Marie Tempest, star of *Midsummer Madness*.

Plate 14 Dorothy Dickson in *Patricia*, as seen on a *Play Pictorial* cover.

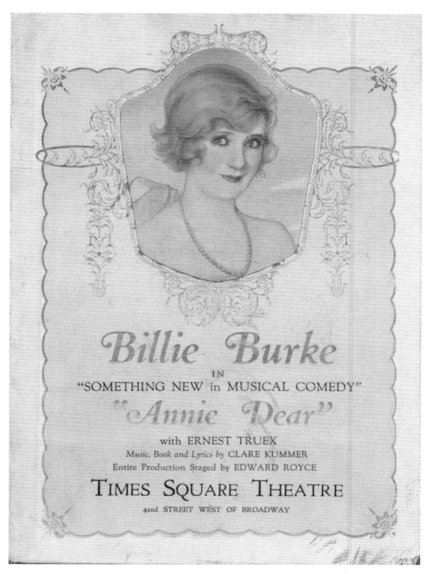

Plate 15 Billie Burke, star of *Annie Dear*, featured on an advertisement for the musical.

Plate 16 Sheet music cover for 'Peter Pan (I Love You)', featuring Marilyn Miller.

Plate 17 Publicity poster for *The First Kiss*. © Victoria and Albert Museum, London.

Plate 18 Poster for the 1954 film version of *Il paese dei campanelli* (The Land of the Bells) featuring Sophia Loren. Puglia Digital Library, Creative Commons License.

Plate 19 Poster for the 1936 film version of *Rose-Marie*, starring Jeanette MacDonald and Nelson Eddy.

PART III

From Summer to Autumn

9 | Summertime Frolics

As the summer continued, a variety of musical theatre possibilities were on offer. These included a revival of a classic operetta, musical comedies of various sorts, a modernist piece of musical theatre and a time-travel fantasy. The old and the new were yet again colliding as the 1924–1925 theatrical season got underway.

In 1923, Evelyn Laye had proven her ability to head an operetta cast in a London revival of *The Merry Widow*. Her success was such that she was subsequently cast in the title role of *Madame Pompadour* at Daly's Theatre. That same revival of *The Merry Widow*, now starring Nancie Lovat (1900–1946), opened at the Lyceum Theatre on 28 May, where it played until November. Carl Brisson (1893–1958) reprised his role as Prince Danilo, as did George Graves (1876–1949) as the Masovian Ambassador Baron Popoff. In another evocation of the past in the present, Graves was playing the role he originated in the original English-language version of *The Merry Widow* back in 1907. On opening night, according to one reviewer, 'when the well-known waltz was played the roof was nearly lifted off the theatre by the cheering'.[1] Lehár's most famous operetta continued to delight.

The same could not be said for *Flossie*, which opened in New York on 3 June at the Lyric Theatre. An unnamed reviewer predicted that the show would not 'leave an indelible impression'[2] – that person, unfortunately, was correct. Armand Robi's bedroom farce concerned a young woman (Flossie, played by Doris Duncan) and a young man (Archie, played by Sydney Grant) who are forced to spend a night together in a studio apartment and the ensuing misunderstandings. The overused scenario had music by Robi that was deigned largely forgettable (except for the production number 'Walla-Walla') and a cast deemed 'undistinguished'.[3] With so many splendid offerings available, if a musical had nothing special to offer, it was doomed. *Flossie* closed before the end of the month.

---

[1] '"The Merry Widow." At the Lyceum,' *The Era* (London), 4 June 1924.
[2] 'Coney Island Lights Outshine Broadway as Theater Season Dies and Summer Begins', syndicated column, *Lansing State Journal*, 28 June 1924, newspapers.com.
[3] 'The First Summer Show', *New York Times*, 4 June 1924.

Unlike *Flossie*, *The Street Singer*, which opened later in the month in London, had a great deal to offer. The 'pretend' riches-to-rags tale, with a book by Frederick Lonsdale (1881–1954), lyrics by Percy Greenbank (1878–1968) and music by Harold Fraser-Simson (1872–1944), opened at the Lyric Theatre on 27 June (see Figure 9.1). The Duchess of Versailles

Figure 9.1 Phyllis Dare and Harry Welchman in *The Street Singer*, from *Play Pictorial* 50 (no. 271), p. 79.

(played by Phyllis Dare) has fallen in love with an impoverished and not very good painter, Bonni (played by Harry Welchman). She disguises herself as Yvette, the street singer of the title, in order to gain his attention. She buys one of his paintings with money she says she earned from her singing, and he is elated. A massive soirée is then held in Yvette's honour at the atelier. Through a dealer, the duchess buys all of Bonni's paintings, and Bonni thinks his talent has finally been recognized. Invited to meet his patron, he leaves the fête – and Yvette – behind in his search for fame. When the duchess's carriage arrives soon thereafter, the cast realizes what the audience has known all along: Yvette is the duchess. After a massive row, which includes Bonni destroying his last painting, a portrait of Yvette, the two reconcile for the requisite happy ending. There's also a sub-plot about a vivacious young widow, Violette (played by Julie Hartley-Milburn), who pursues and wins over the misogynistic valet Francois (played by A. W. Baskcomb). In both instances, a woman conquers the obstacles that keep her from being with the man she decides to love.

Audiences revelled in seeing Phyllis Dare (1890–1975) alongside Harry Welchman (1886–1966). The two had appeared together previously in *The Lady of the Rose* (1922), and their stage chemistry was reignited in *The Street Singer*.

Fraser-Simson's music hearkened back to the composer's greatest success, *The Maid of the Mountains* (1917). Musical highlights included Bonni's lilting 'Take Life as It Comes', Yvette's 'Heart's Desire' and the couple's waltz duet, 'Just to Hold You in My Arms'. Another notable song was Francois's ''Ow I 'ate Women'. Here, Greenbank's misogynistic lyrics that bemoan women ('They screech and they chatter and yell') are at odds with Fraser-Simson's graceful waltz melody. This stylistic mismatch between music and lyrics makes one pay closer attention to the harrowing, though beautifully set, words. The effect is similar to that of 'A Little Priest' from Stephen Sondheim's *Sweeney Todd: The Demon Barber of Fleet Street* (1979), where Mrs. Lovett and Sweeney Todd ponder how people from different professions would taste and do so to the strains of a jubilant waltz.

As was typical of musical comedy, *The Street Singer* included interpolations. In this instance, they were by Ivy St Helier (born Ivy Janet Aitchison, 1886–1971), a British actor, lyricist and composer who later appeared in the original 1929 production of Noël Coward's *Bitter Sweet*. Her songs included two for Estelle, one of Bonni's admirers, played by the comic actress Phoebe Hodgson (1885–1972). The buoyant 'A Perfect Little Lady' and the sprightly 'That's the Sort of Man' became highlights of the production. St Helier also wrote the march-like 'Follow Yvette' for Phyllis

Dare and the chorus. The vivacious number, which includes a whistled refrain and plenty of dancing, became one of the show's most popular songs and 'caused a furore'[4] at the premiere.

A sentimental and somewhat nostalgic atmosphere infused *The Street Singer*, as it did *The Merry Widow* and *Madame Pompadour*. The popularity of those works and their continental origins was alluded to during the curtain call on opening night. As one critic noted:

> When [Frederick Lonsdale] was suddenly dragged on he told us that Fraser-Simson's music had proved that we need not go to Germany for good musical comedy. And Frederick Lonsdale was right. The music by Fraser-Simson and the additional number [sic] by Ivy St. Helier are quite as good as anything we have had from Vienna or Berlin.[5]

British national pride was on full display.

The Modernist Musical Return of Marie Tempest

When a beloved star from years past returns to the musical stage, there can be tremendous excitement. This was certainly the case when it was announced that Marie Tempest (1864–1942) would be appearing in a new musical (see Plate 13). Decades earlier, Tempest had played the title role in Alfred Cellier and B. C. Stephenson's 'comedy opera' *Dorothy* (1886), and then earned legions of loyal fans at Daly's Theatre in the 1890s, originating the romantic female leads in long-running musical comedies such as *The Geisha* (1896), *A Greek Slave* (1898) and *San Toy* (1899). Even though Tempest continued to appear in dramatic roles after leaving Daly's at the turn of the twentieth century, her return to the *musical* stage was an event of note. The vehicle for her return was a somewhat unorthodox choice. Tempest was not going to be appearing in a revival of a Daly's show or some other sort of large-scale production, but in an experimental work with a cast of four and an orchestra of ten. *Midsummer Madness*, which opened on 3 July at the Lyric Theatre in Hammersmith, away from the glitz of the West End, was not a romantic-tinged rhapsody, but rather a modernist creation for the musical stage.

In 1918, the producer Nigel Playfair (1874–1934) became manager at Hammersmith's Lyric Theatre. With a seating capacity of 550, he made it

---

[4] 'Brilliant New Actress: Woman Who Will Be Famous – "The Street Singer" at the Lyric', *Daily News* (London), 28 June 1924, BNA.

[5] 'Brilliant New Actress'.

a prestigious venue for new plays, stunning revivals and legendary performers. After reading Clifford Bax's 'play for music' *Midsummer Madness*,
Playfair decided not only to produce it at his theatre but also to have Cecil
Armstrong Gibbs (1889–1960) create the music and, in a casting coup,
secure Marie Tempest for the principal role.

Bax's play concerns a quartet of actors that arrives at a pub garden to
perform *The Mollusc*, Hubert Henry Davies's 1907 play about a woman
who spends an enormous amount of time trying to do absolutely nothing.
When no one turns up to see the play – everyone has gone to the movies –
the troupe decides to put on their own new work, 'Midsummer Madness',
for themselves. Even if no one else is there, we are told, 'the thrushes will
like the music and the hollyhocks appreciate the color'.[6] Leading the
players are Pat Nolan (played by Frederick Ranalow) and his wife, who
lacks a first name and is simply called Mrs Nolan (played by Tempest).
They travel with a younger couple who, very much in love, squabble
incessantly: Chloe Mobin (played by Marjorie Dixon) and Harley Quinn
(played by Hubert Eisdell).

In the show-within-a-show, a 32-year-old widow, Mrs Pascal (played by
Mrs Nolan), finds herself among three characters drawn from the *commedia dell'arte* tradition, though with some distinctive traits: Pantaloon, the
skinflint, who is now a purveyor of ladies' pantaloons (played by Mr
Nolan); Harlequin, the youthful trickster, who can be more than a bit
temperamental (played by Harley Quinn); and Columbine, Harlequin's
traditional love interest, now a serving maid, who often outwits her partner
(played by Chloe Mobin). It is no coincidence that the characters who
become Harlequin and Columbine have names close to those of their
commedia dell'arte counterparts. As expected, the lines between the characters in the play-within-the-play and those playing the roles can and do
get blurred. At the end of their 'private' performance, the Nolans realize
that an audience has indeed been there all along and speak directly to those
seated at the Lyric Hammersmith. The plot of the play-within-the-play is
not complicated: each character shows a romantic interest in both characters of the opposite gender. Since there is a clear division according to age,
the final pairing resolves itself neatly along those lines.

The show and its concept were different to a typical West End musical
comedy. This reflected not only the wide range of aesthetic approaches that
could appear on commercial musical stages but also the backgrounds of its
creators. Clifford Bax (1886–1962), whose family enjoyed independent

---

[6] Clifford Bax, *Midsummer Madness: A Play for Music* (London: Ernest Benn, 1923), 8.

wealth, was already known as a playwright, poet and translator when he wrote *Midsummer Madness*. Among his contributions in the latter category were works by the influential Venetian playwright and opera librettist Carlo Goldoni (1707–1793). Among Bax's favourite pursuits was to create literary works with direct connections to other artistic media. He called *Midsummer Madness*, when it was published in 1923, 'A Play for Music'. Not 'with music' but 'for music'. The play's reason for being was to be set to music. Furthermore, when his trilogy *Studio Plays: Three Experiments in Dramatic Form* was published in 1924, it included illustrations in an art deco style designed by Dorothy Mullock (1888–1973), who was (and still is) perhaps best known for her iconic posters for the London Underground. Clifford Bax was no stranger to music, for his brother was the distinguished composer Sir Arnold Bax (1883–1953), who was regarded largely for his orchestral works and, in 1942, was appointed Master of the King's Music.

Creating the music for *Midsummer Madness* was not the playwright's brother but Cecil Armstrong Gibbs. Gibbs was especially renowned for his choral music, songs and support of amateur choruses. He taught at the Royal College of Music and was thus part of the British musical establishment and not someone for whom the popular musical stage was a familiar artistic home. His music for *Midsummer Madness* combines modernist innovation, such as piquant harmonies and added beats to disrupt the musical flow, with knowing retrospection. There are clever versions of patter songs in the Gilbert and Sullivan style (e.g., Pantaloon's 'How Little They Know of the World' and Columbine, Mrs Pascal and Pantaloon's trio 'You Must Decide Between Us') and keen evocations of English folk song (e.g., Harlequin and Pantaloon's duet 'A Glass, A Glass' and Columbine's 'The Mind of a Man is a Toy'). To accentuate his love of the old, Gibbs saves one of his best surprises for the epilogue, in which he inserts a splendid display of unaccompanied vocal writing in the style of a Renaissance madrigal.

The show's lofty atmosphere was noted by critics, one of whom called the score 'over-refined'.[7] Another reviewer noted echoes of John Gay and Carlo Goldoni[8] in the production, not surprising considering that Ranalow had been appearing in revivals of Gay's *The Beggar's Opera* and that Bax had published translations of the Venetian playwright's works. On the whole, the critics panned everything except Tempest. Bax was of course elated to have a star of Tempest's magnitude starring in one of his plays.

[7] 'A New Musical Play', *The Guardian* (London), 4 July 1924, newspapers.com.
[8] 'In the Limelight', *Sunday Pictorial* (London), 6 July 1924, newspapers.com.

He recalled how he would 'watch her from the wings, trying to discover the method of her unique magic. And what did I see? Perfect timing of every phrase and every turn of the head; yes, but I saw too that she acted even with her little fingers. They were epigrams in themselves.'[9]

On the Road: The Case of *Tilly*

As *Midsummer Madness* proves, not everything new and noteworthy in British musical theatre happened in London's West End. Another example is the musical comedy *Tilly*, which opened as a touring production at the Empire Theatre in Leeds on 21 July. Originally intended for the variety circuit, it travelled throughout the provinces, including three weeks in Manchester, before playing for just one week at the Alhambra Theatre in London in early November.

Herbert Clayton and Con West based their libretto on Ian Hay's 1919 play *Tilly of Bloomsbury*. With music by the popular light music composers Haydn Wood and Jack Waller and lyrics by Bert Lee and R. P. Weston, it was a familiar rags-to-riches scenario, with working-class Tilly Welwyn (played by Maudie Dunham) and aristocrat Richard Mainwaring (played by James Prescott) as the lovers who eventually end up together. Along the way, the libretto provides ample commentary about social class. In Act 1, Richard brings Tilly to his family home, where he regales them with tales of their adventures together, such as getting engaged on the upper deck of a bus. His family is not impressed. Tilly realizes that to succeed in the world, you must put on a pretence, what she calls 'Swank' in her song of the same name. Tilly's brother Percy (played by Harry Gould) arrives at the Mainwarings, where he entertains them with his music hall song, 'When Father Swept the Chimney'. The stalwart Mainwarings are not amused, unlike Richard, who is keen to learn songs like that.[10]

The situation is reversed in Act 2, when the Mainwarings visit Tilly's family, who run a boarding house in Bloomsbury. While the Mainwarings are there, Samuel Stillbottle (played by Arnold Richardson) arrives with two associates to repossess the Welwyn's furniture. The Welwyns leave to quickly earn money through several outrageous schemes and Richard settles their debt. Stillbottle, meanwhile, uses the Welwyn home to rehearse his choir for an upcoming wedding. The mirth-filled rehearsal was

---

[9] Hector Bolitho, *Marie Tempest* (Philadelphia: Lippincott, 1937), 211.

[10] Herbert Clayton and Con West, 'Tilly', unpublished typescript, LCP 1924/22, BL.

a highlight of the production, with musical wanderings, according to a reviewer, that included music hall, Richard Wagner, Franz Schubert and George Friderick Handel.[11] Once Tilly and Richard sing the love duet 'We Never Knew', the Welwyns return, and the Mainwarings forgive their son for paying off Stillbottle and offer their best wishes to the couple.

A New Season Begins on Broadway

The 1924–1925 theatrical season on Broadway began in August with a quartet of musicals that individually may not have been terribly significant but, when taken together, offer valuable insights into the state of Broadway musical comedy at the time. All include a meet–separate–reunite scenario for the romantic leads, though it is the reason behind the separation that differs in each show. It is the theatre industry itself in *Marjorie*, capitalism in *No Other Girl*, time travel in *The Dream Girl* and financial responsibility in *Bye, Bye, Barbara*.

First to open, on 11 August at the Shubert Theatre, was *Marjorie*, which had a huge all-male creative team: three book writers, four librettists and five composers. The libretto by Shubert staff creators Fred Thompson, Clifford Grey and Harold Atteridge concerns Marjorie (played by Elizabeth Hines), a young woman who falls in love with the theatrical producer Brian Valcourt (played by Roy Royston). Marjorie shows Brian a play written by her brother, which the producer assumes is her own work, and decides to stage it. Marjorie doesn't dissuade him with the truth. After the expected sorts of professional-cum-personal trials, the couple come together at the end. The show's hit was Sigmund Romberg's lyrical ballad 'My Twilight Rose', with lyrics by Grey. The metatheatrical musical, which critics either loved or hated, hints at the novelty of having a play written by a woman, for if Marjorie had insisted that the play was by her brother early on, it likely would not have made it to the stage.

Two days later, *No Other Girl* opened at the Morosco Theatre. Aaron Hoffman's light-hearted book and Bert Kalmar and Harry Ruby's catchy songs concerned a young Quaker man, Ananias Jones (delightfully played by Eddie Buzzell), who comes up with a plan to revitalize Quakertown, the sleepy community where he lives. He proposes building a highway to connect Philadelphia and New York City that will pass through the heart of the town. Electric advertising billboards would pay for half the

---

[11] 'Tilly', *The Era* (London), 30 July 1924, BNA.

construction costs, while the government would cover the rest. The elders are suspect, so Ananias leaves everything behind, including his love interest (played by Helen Ford), goes to New York, finds investors, makes the highway happen and returns to Quakertown a wealthy capitalist ready to marry his sweetheart. Her name, Hope, is not accidental, for it reveals Ananias's fundamentally optimistic attitude towards love and life.

The third show was *The Dream Girl*, which opened on 20 August at the Ambassador Theatre. The laudatory *New York Times* review began, 'Victor Herbert left this life on a high note'.[12] Herbert, the show's composer, had died on 26 May, one month after *The Dream Girl* began previews in New Haven. Thus, the production was in some ways, like the sequence of Herbert selections in Ziegfeld's *Follies of 1924*, an homage to the esteemed composer.

Rida Johnson Young (1875–1926) created the libretto. This was the first time Young and Herbert had worked together since the massively popular *Naughty Marietta* of 1910. Young based her libretto on the play *The Road to Yesterday* by Beulah Marie Dix and Evelyn Greenleaf Sutherland. She and Herbert began *The Dream Girl* as early as 1921, according to Young's biographer Ellen Peck.[13] To provide topical humour, the Shuberts brought in their staff writer Harold Atteridge, who, according to Peck, seems to have written material only for the vaudeville actor Billy B. Van to perform in the character of Jimmie Van Dyke. His quip-filled part is notably different in tone from the rest of the highly romantic work.[14]

In the time-travel fantasy, a group of American women are visiting a London painters' studio. One of the painters is looking for the ideal male model for his painting of a fifteenth-century knight. When Jack Warner (played by Walter Woolf), an American athlete, comes to the studio to meet his female friends, they convince the artist that Jack should be the model. He refuses until he learns that Elspeth (played by Fay Bainter) will soon be arriving. Jack has only seen Elspeth's picture, but thinks he knows her though he cannot remember how. One of the women, Malena (played by Vivara), believes she was Romani in a previous life and wants to go back in time. It's Midsummer Eve, and Malena tells her friends that this is a night filled with magic, and whatever they wish can come true. Jack dresses for the painting, and Malena is sure she has seen him dressed that way before. Elspeth arrives, and Jack wonders if she might be his 'dream

---

[12] 'Herbert Melodies in "The Dream Girl"', *New York Times*, 21 August 1924.
[13] Ellen M. Peck, *Sweet Mystery: The Musical Works of Rida Johnson Young* (New York: Oxford University Press, 2020), 133.
[14] Peck, *Sweet Mystery*, 135.

girl' from another life. She falls asleep, and in Act 2 she goes back in time 300 years. In this earlier reality, all the characters from Act 1 are there, although Elspeth is the only one who is aware that she is from another time. Elspeth is being forced to marry the evil Lord Strangevon, and Jack, dressed as a knight, rescues her. In Act 3, Elspeth wakens from her dream. Jack is still in his costume, and she thinks that she somehow conjured him from her dream. They realize they were in love in a past life and decide to marry in the present one.

One of the reviewers noted the various genres at play in *The Dream Girl*, calling Act 1 a musical comedy, Act 2 an operetta and Act 3 a burlesque.[15] This astute observation clearly shows how normal it was for different musical aesthetics to appear in the same work. Walter Woolf (1899–1984), an operetta baritone, was featured prominently in the soaring 'My Dream Girl' in Act 1 and the heroic march 'The Broad Highway' in Act 2, while the delightful musical comedy dancer Fay Bainter (1893–1968) led the ensemble in Act 1's 'Dancing Round'. When it was decided during the pre-Broadway tryout that she needed a dramatic song to conclude her dream, Sigmund Romberg and Atteridge wrote 'I Want to Go Home', which became her only solo number in the show. (Herbert had, by now, passed away.) Adding to the operetta atmosphere in Act 2 was 'Gypsy Life', led by Vivara. Here was a direct reference to Hungarian-flavoured operettas such as *Countess Maritza*, although Herbert's 'Hungarian-ness' relies on syncopation and remains grounded in tonal harmonic principles.

It wasn't a fortune teller but rather the title of *Bye, Bye, Barbara* that predicted its fate. The musical comedy that opened at the National Theatre on 25 August closed after just two weeks. With music by the husband-and-wife team of Monte Carlo and Alma M. Sanders, whose musical *The Chiffon Girl* played earlier in the year (see Chapter 5), and book by Sidney Toler (1874–1947) and Alonzo Price (1884–1962), the show earned mediocre reviews at best. Set in present-day California, the story focused on the illusionist The Great Karloff (played by Jack Hazzard) who dons various disguises and engages in all sorts of activities, including ballooning and parachute jumping, to keep from paying alimony to his ex-wife. The romantic plot featured Barbara (played by Janet Velie), whose father opposes her being with Stanley, the man she loves, until he comes up with $50,000 to prove he can support her. Audiences devoured Hazzard's recycled jokes, such as when he is asked if he is Russian: 'Sure I'm Russian.

---

[15] Max Lief, '"Dream Girl" a Dream; – Sometimes a Yawn', *New York Daily News*, 22 August 1924, newspapers.com.

I'm rushin' for a place to hide'.[16] The show's humour and music hearkened back to the past, though without the ballast to secure it in the present.

An Early September Assemblage

The first four days of September was an especially rich time on Broadway, with six shows in which music played a significant role – either musicals or a play about a composer – opening in close succession. First was *Top Hole*, which opened on 1 September at the Fulton Theatre. *Top Hole* played on the success of the golf-themed *Kid Boots* by also including a golf theme. Bob Corcoran (played by Ed Glendinning) is more concerned about winning trophies in various sports than working in his father's business. His father has had enough of paying his son's debts and tells him to go earn the $1,000 that he owes his creditors. So, Bob heads to California (rather than *Kid Boots*'s Florida), saves a young woman from an accident on the way, falls in love with her, becomes a golf instructor at a swanky club, is accused and acquitted of a robbery, wins a golf tournament that includes a $1,000 prize, gains the woman's affections and reconciles with his father. Its hit song was Jay Gorney, Harry Richman and Robert Braine's syncopated 'When You're in Love', which, according to one reviewer, audience members were whistling as they left the theatre.[17] The musical played four months – not a bad run, though nothing like *Kid Boots*.

The same day *Top Hole* opened, *Stepping Stones*, starring Fred and Dorothy Stone, returned to the Globe Theatre for forty performances after its successful multi-city tour. This sort of performance trajectory hearkens back to nineteenth-century practices, when a New York residency was part of a tour, and the idea of a long run as the main marker of a show's success was not yet established. It is difficult to really call this a 'revival', since it was essentially the same production (with some cast changes) that had played on Broadway earlier in the year.

On 3 September, *Be Yourself!* opened at the Sam H. Harris Theatre. Comedian Jack Donahue (*c.*1892–1930) played Matt McLean, who travels to backwoods Tennessee and finds himself embroiled in a generations-old family feud between the McLeans and the Brennans. He manages to dance and sing himself out of any trouble with the help of Tony Robinson, played

---

[16] Max Lief, '"Bye Bye, Barbara" Just Another Show', *New York Daily News*, 26 August 1924, newspapers.com.

[17] Arthur Yokom, 'In This Case a Song Saves a Whole Show', *Daily News* (New York), 3 September 1924, newspapers.com.

by the delightful Queenie Smith (1898–1978), who had appeared in *Sitting Pretty* in the spring. The book and lyrics by George S. Kaufman and Marc Connelly were lauded for their rustic humour, though Lewis Gensler and Milton Schwarzwald's music received mixed reviews. The show's outstanding song was 'My Road', which recurs throughout the score as a unifying device. The lilting ballad, with its languid triplets flowing over a duple-metre accompaniment, is sung not by the principals but rather by the romantic pair Marjorie Brennan (played by Dorothy Whitmore) and David Robinson (played by Barrett Greenwood). The delightful dancing of Donahue and Smith was not enough to keep *Be Yourself!* going, and it closed in November.

Though not a musical, *Great Music* by Martin Brown opened on 4 September at the Earl Carroll Theatre for forty-four performances. The play shared its underlying premise with several musical comedies that appeared throughout 1924, including *Top Hole*: a young man has to prove himself to his father. Here, though, the ending is tragic. Thanks to the support of his stockbroker father, Erik Fane (played by the film and stage actor Tom Powers (1890–1955)), goes to Rome for a year to compose. Ultimately, he contracts leprosy and travels to the Marquesas Islands, where he notates his great symphony – which has been heard throughout the play – just before he dies. The play's distinctions included its subtitle – *The Dramatic Interpretation of Erik Fane's Symphony in D Minor* – and its arrangement in four movements, each of which gives the locale of that scene's action: Theme (Rome), Scherzo (Paris), Largo (Port Said), Rhapsodie and Finale (Marquesas Islands). *Great Music* was a theatrical realization of the concept behind many nineteenth-century programme symphonies with narrative stories, such as Hector Berlioz's autobiographical *Symphonie Fantastique* (1830). These dimensions were akin to those of the musical *Midsummer Madness* from a few months earlier: both looked to earlier genres for inspiration (the symphony for *Great Music* and commedia dell'arte for *Midsummer Madness*) and both presented these genres in modern ways.

Top Hole, *Stepping Stones* and *Great Music* all looked to the past, recent or more remote, in some way: *Top Hole* to *Kid Boots*, *Stepping Stones* to nineteenth-century touring practices and *Great Music* to nineteenth-century narrative symphonies. *Be Yourself!* though, depicted a rural culture as lacking the sophistication of the 'modern' world. This sort of white, middle-class privilege is central to the two other musicals that opened on Broadway in early September: *The Chocolate Dandies* and *Rose-Marie*.

10 | September Sensibilities

September was a vibrant month for musical theatre. In addition to the six Broadway openings in the first four days, two very different revues debuted on either side of the Atlantic and London audiences could choose from two new adaptations of transnational properties and a new musical comedy by George Gershwin.

Performing Ethnicity for White Audiences

Beyond the four musicals to open on Broadway in early September discussed in Chapter 9, *The Chocolate Dandies*, which opened on 1 September, and *Rose-Marie*, which opened the next day, reflected an underlying sense of white privilege for their intended white, mainstream New York audiences. This sort of racial positioning has been termed 'whiteness'. Whiteness scholar and speaker Robin DiAngelo describes whiteness as those aspects of being a white person

that go beyond mere physical differences and are related to the meaning and resultant material advantage of being defined as white in society: what is granted and how it is granted based on that meaning. Instead of the typical focus on how racism hurts people of color, to examine whiteness is to focus on how racism elevates white people.[1]

This notion of affirming white culture, implicitly and explicitly, is evident in both *The Chocolate Dandies* and *Rose-Marie*.

The Chocolate Dandies

Throughout 1924, Noble Sissle (1889–1975) and Eubie Blake (1887–1983) were working on a new show to follow the success of *Shuffle Along* (see Chapter 1). They even wanted to call it *Shuffle Along of 1924*, thus ensuring

---

[1] Robin DiAngelo, *White Fragility: Why It's So Hard for White People to Talk about Racism* (Boston: Beacon Press, 2018), 25.

a connection to the past hit.[2] For the venture, Sissle and Blake teamed up with a pair of white producers: B. C. Whitney (1860–1929) and A. L. Erlanger (Abraham Lincoln Erlanger, 1859–1930). Like so many in the theatre business, Whitney and Erlanger were keen to capitalize on the popularity of Black musicals for white audiences. The result, *In Bamville*, opened in early March in Rochester, New York. After its pre-Broadway tour, it landed at the New Colonial Theatre with a new name designed to appeal to white audiences: *The Chocolate Dandies*.[3]

The thin plot, which Sissle devised with the show's star, Lew Payton (1874–1945), concerns a horse race in Bamville (Bamville being a term for a small, insignificant town, a parallel of sorts to Jimtown, the locale of *Shuffle Along*). Mose Washington (Payton) falls asleep and dreams that his horse, Dumb Luck, wins the race. Thanks to betting on the horse, he gets rich. Mose then awakens to the news that his rival's horse, Rarin'-to-Go, is the actual winner. To make matters worse, his rival also wins the hand of the town's most eligible young lady, the aptly named Angeline.

The storyline, like those of many musical comedies, was essentially a frame on which to hang songs and dances. Hence, the production was sometimes referred to as a revue. The show's new title, taken from its final number, also implied a revue. 'Dandies' sat comfortably alongside 'Scandals', 'Follies' and 'Vanities' as a moniker. Its racist descriptor, though, set it apart from those white shows and created a certain set of audience expectations, ones rooted in minstrelsy. *The Chocolate Dandies*'s visual aspect, especially Julian Mitchell's dances, also evoked the aesthetic of lavish white spectacles such as Ziegfeld's *Follies*. This was not surprising, for Mitchell had just staged *Follies of 1924*.

This emulation of white revue aesthetics was intentional. As careful observers of their white audiences in *Shuffle Along*, Sissle and Blake wanted to meet their expectations with *The Chocolate Dandies*. The show was straddling a line between offering a sophisticated Black show and giving white audiences what they wanted, problematic as this could be.

Sissle commented that 'we portray Negro characters – not try to give an imitation of whites'.[4] This goal did not always come across in performance. One Black critic in Chicago found the show 'too much white folks and not

---

[2] Carlin and Bloom, *Eubie Blake*, 174.

[3] For more on the pre-Broadway tour, see Carlin and Bloom, *Eubie Blake*, 178–186.

[4] Floyd C. Calvin, '*In Bamville* Opening', *Pittsburgh Courier*, 29 March 1924; quoted in Carlin and Bloom, *Eubie Blake*, 179.

enough "African"'.[5] The critic for *Variety* similarly noted that Lottie Gee (1886–1973) as the female lead 'in action and manner might be a Dillingham prima donna', and that Ivan H. Browning (1891–1978), one of the Four Harmony Kings, 'has all the posing tricks of a soulful tenor in a Winter Garden musical comedy'.[6] The Associated Negro Press suggested that it was the scenery and the costumes, not the performances, that disappointed the Chicago critic. Its response continued: 'The production shows that colored America has more than arrived in musical entertainment. . . . The show is accepted by the theatre going public strictly on its merit, and it merits much.'[7]

The creators nonetheless did include several racist depictions that many in the white audience expected from Black shows. Some of the actors, including the dancer Josephine Baker (1906–1975), performed partly in blackface. The title song played on the minstrel figure of Zip C—n, while 'Dancing Pickaninnies' depicted carefree Black children living on an 'idyllic' plantation.[8] Johnny Hudgins (1896–1990), in his character of Joe Dolks, performed, according to the *New York Times* critic, a 'regular old negro type in tattered attire' whose 'dancing was original and pleasing'.[9] Performing the stereotype is almost certainly what garnered him praise from the white press.[10]

As part of the show, the Four Harmony Kings performed a set of spirituals. While audiences applauded greatly,[11] the quartet's appearance drew the ire of several Black critics, one of whom called it 'sacrilege'[12] to perform spirituals in such a context. Spirituals, though, were part of the Four Harmony Kings's core repertory. They performed them in churches, on variety stages and over the radio as a way to reach wider audiences.[13] Their high-society attire in *The Chocolate Dandies* consisted of frock coats with black trimmings, purple and silver neckties and slate grey silk hats.[14] Perhaps it was the visual dimension of the performance clashing with the aural that the Black critics didn't like. The group's first tenor, Ivan

---

[5] Associated Negro Press, 'Sissle and Blake "In Bamville" Storm Chicago', *Buffalo American*, 10 April 1924, newspapers.com.

[6] *Variety*, quoted in Woll, *Black Musical Theatre*, 91.

[7] Associated Negro Press, 'Sissle and Blake "In Bamville" Storm Chicago'.

[8] Carlin and Bloom, *Eubie Blake*, 178.

[9] 'Good Negro Musical Play', *New York Times*, 2 September 1924.

[10] Carlin and Bloom, *Eubie Blake*, 190.   [11] 'Good Negro Musical Play'.

[12] Carlin and Bloom, *Eubie Blake*, 190.

[13] Sean Mayes and Sarah K. Whitfield, *An Inconvenient Black History of British Musical Theatre, 1900–1950* (London: Methuen, 2022), 94.

[14] 'Good Negro Musical Play'.

H. Browning, was also a columnist for Black newspapers and wrote for both the *New York Amsterdam News* and *The Chicago Defender*. Sean Mayes and Sarah K. Whitfield call him a 'performer-activist', for he worked diligently on behalf of Black performers and against the use of racist discourse in the press.[15]

The Chocolate Dandies featured several prominent performers in significant supporting roles. Josephine Baker (1906–1975) was cast as 'That Comedy Chorus Girl', a role in which she fabulously displayed her physical humour, idiosyncratic eye crossing, bodily contortions and comic manoeuvres in oversized shoes. Baker, who became the highest-paid Black performer later in the decade, had caught the attention of Sissle and Blake in 1922 when she joined the chorus of *Shuffle Along*'s tour. Her antics in *Shuffle Along* as the comic end girl, which David Krasner describes as 'at once graceful and uncoordinated, elegant and clumsy, passionate as well as comedic',[16] so pleased audiences that Sissle and Blake created 'The Comedy Chorus Girl' especially for her.[17]

The iconic singer Elisabeth Welch (1904–2003), in the role of Jessie Johnson, led 'That Charleston Dance'. This was a real coup for Sissle and Blake, for Welch had introduced the Charleston in their former partners Miller and Lyles's *Runnin' Wild*. The dance's popularity almost necessitated its inclusion in *The Chocolate Dandies*: it seemed impossible that Sissle and Blake would allow *Runnin' Wild* to be the only Black musical to have a Charleston. The pair not only co-opted the dance but also its performer.

What *The Chocolate Dandies* lacked, noted the Harlem Renaissance writer James Weldon Johnson, were 'comedians who approached the class of Miller and Lyles'.[18] Such shortcomings were more than compensated for by its musicians. These included a dynamic on-stage band, led by Joe Smith (1902–1937), described as 'a jazz cornetist with a mean blues',[19] cornetist Johnny Dunn and saxophonist Sidney Bechet.[20]

Sissle and Blake themselves appeared in the show. As one critic noted, it was 'those fingers of Mr. Blake soothing the piano keys which gives the production its real punch'.[21] They performed their own speciality in Act 2,

---

[15] Mayes and Whitfield, *An Inconvenient Black History*, 94–95.

[16] Krasner, 'Shuffle Along and the Quest for Nostalgia', 257.

[17] Peterson, Jr, *Profiles of African American Stage Performers*, 16.

[18] Johnson, *Black Manhattan*, 190.   [19] 'The Chocolate Dandies', *Variety*, 3 September 1924.

[20] Carlin and Bloom, *Eubie Blake*, 177.

[21] 'Sissle and Blake in New Comedy Offering', *Tribune* (Scranton, PA), 30 December 1924, newspapers.com.

which featured an especially curious choice of repertory, for in the midst of
The Chocolate Dandies, Sissle and Blake performed hits from *Shuffle
Along*.[22] To the ears of critics then and some writers now, the catchy
syncopated tunes of *Shuffle Along* made the comparatively staid nature of
their songs for *The Chocolate Dandies* all the more obvious.[23]

  The Chocolate Dandies was an expensive show to produce. It featured
lavish sets and costumes, a cast of 125 and an orchestra of 20, as well as
a spectacular horse racing sequence in which three actual horses were seen
running on a revolving treadmill. *The Chocolate Dandies* amassed tremendous debt during its pre-Broadway tour and continued to lose money after
it opened on Broadway.[24] It got to the point where even if every performance was sold out, the production couldn't cover its costs. So, it closed after
ninety-six performances and began touring on the Black TOBA (Theatre
Owners Booking Association) vaudeville circuit,[25] where, continually bur-
dened by severe debt, it was forced to end its run.

Rose-Marie

While *Chocolate Dandies* had a Black creative team, a white producing
team, a story set in a fictionalized Black township and a demise caused by
financial woes, *Rose-Marie*, which opened the next day at the Imperial
Theatre, was notably different.[26] Its all-white creative and producing teams,
tale of interactions between white settlers and Indigenous people in Canada
and magnificent score combined to make it the second-longest-running
Broadway musical to open during the decade, at 557 performances. It
starred the Metropolitan Opera lyric soprano Mary Ellis (1897–2003) and
the English Shakespearean actor Dennis King (1897–1971) as the star-
crossed romantic lovers.

  In Otto Harbach and Oscar Hammerstein II's highly melodramatic
tale, the chanteuse Rose-Marie La Flamme (played by Mary Ellis) sings
in the saloon at Lady Jane's Hotel in Saskatchewan. She and the miner
Jim Kenyon (played by Dennis King) are in love (see Figure 10.1).
Rose-Marie's brother, Émile, wants his sister to marry Edward Hawley,

---

[22] The 2016 Broadway musical *Shuffle Along, or the Making of the Musical Sensation of 1921 and All that Followed* also paid homage to the historic musical.
[23] Carlin and Bloom, *Eubie Blake*, 191.   [24] Carlin and Bloom, *Eubie Blake*, 194.
[25] Carlin and Bloom, *Eubie Blake*, 195.
[26] Whether the title has a hyphen (*Rose-Marie*) or not (*Rose Marie*) is a conundrum, since both versions appear on copyrighted materials. The hyphenated form will be used here. For more on *Rose-Marie*, see chapter 3, 'Envisioning the West: *Rose Marie*', in the author's *Rudolf Friml* (Urbana: University of Illinois Press, 2008), 35–55.

Figure 10.1 Mary Ellis in *Rose-Marie*. NYPL. https://digitalcollections.nypl.org/items/510d47e3-ebcb-a3d9-e040-e00a18064a99

a fur-trading businessman. Wanda, a First Nations person, invites Hawley to her cabin for a tryst, telling him that her husband, Blackeagle, is drunk and won't be home for several days. When Jim goes to the cabin to discuss a land deal with Blackeagle, he discovers Wanda and Hawley in a compromising situation. Jim leaves, but Blackeagle has also spotted his wife and her lover. Blackeagle confronts Wanda and she kills him. She and Hawley frame Jim for the murder. Hawley, knowing Rose-Marie's love for the miner, tells her that if she marries him, he will tell Sergeant Malone and his Mounties to stop tracking Jim and will also help him cross the US border into safety. Rose-Marie reluctantly agrees. Act 2 takes place one year later in Quebec. Rose-Marie is preparing to marry Hawley when Jim arrives with Wanda in tow, demanding that the truth be told. Wanda confesses, Jim is proven innocent and he and Rose-Marie are reunited.

The secondary love story, featuring Lady Jane and Herman, provides comic contrast to the emotional intensity of the first. Lady Jane runs the hotel where Act 1 takes place and manages a fancy-goods shop in Act 2. Herman, her fiancé, is, as he is described in the song 'Hard-Boiled Herman', 'a big-hearted pal of the rough-an'-ready school'.[27] We don't see their wedding, for it takes place between the two acts. The performed ease of their relationship balances the more complicated tale of Rose-Marie and Jim.

Rose-Marie had a somewhat murky process of creation. It had two composers: Rudolf Friml (1879–1972) and Herbert Stothart (1880–1959). Friml and Harbach wrote many of the score's more operetta-like numbers, including the rousing march 'Song of the Mounties' and the flowing waltz 'Door of My Dreams', as well as its most famous song, the evocative 'Indian Love Call' and the lilting title song. Stothart and Hammerstein contributed songs more in the spirit of musical comedy, such as 'Hard-Boiled Herman' and 'Why Shouldn't We?', both of which feature one or both of the comic couple. Part of what makes the score so effective is this juxtaposition of character-defining musical styles. This was most certainly intentional, for the authors included a telling remark in the playbill: 'The musical numbers of this play are such an integral part of the action that we do not think we should list them as separate episodes.' The musical numbers, though, were listed individually in the published vocal score and when the show transferred the London the next year.

On 2 June 1924, exactly three months before *Rose-Marie*'s Broadway opening, US President Calvin Coolidge signed into law the Indian Citizenship Act, or Snyder Act, which granted US citizenship to Native Americans who were born within the geographic boundaries of the United States. News coverage of this legislation certainly had an impact on how audiences, specifically white audiences, interpreted the operetta. By setting the show in Canada, the inherent racial politics between the white characters and the Indigenous ones are moved away from the immediacy of

---

[27] Otto Harbach and Oscar Hammerstein, *Rose Marie: A Musical Play* (London: Samuel French, 1924), 13.

Broadway theatre-goers.[28] The Indigenous characters who appear in *Rose-Marie* are not real people but rather products of the white imagination for white audiences. What Ted Jojola writes in relation to early portrayals of Native Americans on film also applies to *Rose-Marie*: 'The Hollywood Indian is a mythological being who exists nowhere but within the fertile imaginations of its movie actors, producers, and directors. The preponderance of such movie images have reduced native people to ignoble stereotypes.'[29] Among these stereotypes, three stand out in *Rose-Marie*: (1) children of nature, (2) violent savages and (3) gamblers and drunkards.[30] The children of nature trope suggests that, from a white perspective, the Indigenous characters are not as socially developed nor as modern as their white counterparts. This view permeates 'Indian Love Call'. Rose-Marie tells Jim the story behind the song. A young boy sang it to a young girl from the top of a hill. If she responded, that meant that she would marry him. The characters in her backstory are young people, simple children of nature. Their 'exoticism' for urban white audiences comes through musical means. In the song, Friml employs many so-called Indianist features, a catalogue of musical devices that Eurocentric composers of the nineteenth and early twentieth centuries used to communicate the idea of Native America to their listeners, whether in concert halls, theatres or 'silent' cinemas. Audiences would have known and recognized these musical codings, which include foregrounded melodic chromaticism, static harmonies (often minor chords) and pulsated drones.[31] These features infuse the beginning of the refrain, where Friml's melody ascends through a spacious gapped figure before turning around for a series of slithering chromatic descents on the famous double 'oo's ('When I'm calling you-oo-oo').

The wistful children of nature image of 'Indian Love Call' appears in stark contrast to that of Wanda, who performs the second stereotype: violent savages. Wanda, after all, murders her husband. She never really

---

[28] For more on this topic, including how these issues are presented in the film versions of *Rose-Marie*, see the author's 'Ethnic Mobilities and Representations in *Rose-Marie* on Stage and Screen', *Studies in Musical Theatre* 16, no. 3 (2022): 193–203.
[29] Ted Jojola, 'Absurd Reality II: Hollywood Goes to the Indians', in Peter C. Rollins and John E. O'Connor, eds., *Hollywood's Indian: The Portrayal of the Native American in Film* (Lexington: University of Kentucky Press, 1998), 12.
[30] For a discussion of the first two tropes as they relate to the 1925 film *The Vanishing American*, see Michael J. Riley, 'Trapped in the History of Film: *The Vanishing American*', in Rollins and O'Connor, *Hollywood's Indian*, 27–38.
[31] For more on these identifiers, see Michael V. Pisani, *Imagining Native America in Music* (New Haven, CT: Yale University Press, 2005), 229–230.

sings in the show; instead, she is represented musically by an instrumental 'Wanda Theme' marked *molto misterioso* (very mysteriously). The languid sound of parallel minor chords over repeated throbbings in the lower instruments of the orchestra offer an aural manifestation of her Otherness, morally as well as racially. Wanda has only one number in which she must intone solo lines, 'Totem Tom-Tom', which she can perform in a largely speech-singing style, since the narrow-ranged melody is doubled in the orchestra. Wanda is often cast with a dancer, which allows her physicality to become part of her violent characterization, feeding further into stereotypes of a femme fatale.

The lyrics of 'Totem Tom-Tom' lead to the third ignoble image: gamblers and drunkards. In the lavish production number, Wanda leads a chorus of white women dressed as totem poles. She tells the story of her grandparents going to a totem dance, where the dancers drank 'firewater' (alcohol), which made them dance faster and faster until they became sleepy and returned to their tipis. In other words, they passed out from being drunk. Musically, Stothart's static harmony, repeated melodic fragments and pulsating beats further distance the singers from white hegemony. This negative stereotype of gamblers and drunkards is also present at the first appearance of Blackeagle, Wanda's husband, where he is seen drunk at a gaming table.

Figure 10.2 Wanda (played by Pearl Regay) leads the female chorus in *Rose-Marie*'s 'Totem Tom'. Photo by White Studio. ©Billy Rose Theatre Division, The New York Public Library for the Performing Arts.

'Totem Tom-Tom' is being staged for tourists staying at the Totem Pole Hotel (see Figure 10.2) as a performance of negative stereotypes. In Act 2, we learn that Wanda is a member of a professional dance troupe, presumably the same one that performs this sequence. The white women who were performing 'Totem Tom-Tom' at the Imperial Theatre in New York (and elsewhere) become akin to a Ziegfeld *Follies* ensemble dressed in Indigenous-inspired fantasy costumes. This was wholly knowing artifice. Native American culture was being created and played by whites for whites as entertainment, not only for the unseen guests at the Totem Pole Hotel but also for the audience sitting in the theatre.

Rose-Marie is fundamentally about relationships between Indigenous peoples and white settlers. The former are fictionalized while the latter are romanticized. In *Rose-Marie*, the male chorus takes on the role of the Royal Canadian Mounted Police (RCMP) – the famous Mounties. This chorus is not just a group of decorative observers but a central character in the narrative. The RCMP dates from 1873, when, according to Christopher Gittings, it was established 'to facilitate the invasion and settlement of the West by whites from the East'.[32] South of the US–Canadian border, Mounties were reimagined as hypermasculine heroes who save those in distress – what Shane Peacock calls 'a sort of upscale cowboy'.[33] The reality, though, was that the Mounties were there to protect white settlers and their business dealings. If Blackeagle would have refused Jim's land deal, the Mountie presence would have guaranteed its completion. This sense of duty and self-proclaimed righteousness becomes clearly evident in the Mounties' signature tune, 'Song of the Mounties'. The rousing march is filled with words that endorse their mission, for they always get 'the man they're after now'. The song's uncomplicated harmonies and clearly defined phrases proclaim its fundamental whiteness. None of the Indianist evocations in 'Indian Love Call' or 'Totem Tom-Tom' are present here; they have been conquered by the tonal whiteness of 'Song of the Mounties', just like their real-life counterparts.

In both *Rose-Marie* and *The Chocolate Dandies*, a sense of white positioning in terms of people of colour is evident. Whether it is the promotion of negative stereotypes in *Rose-Marie* or the emulation of white revue aesthetics in *The Chocolate Dandies*, the idea of whiteness is present.

---

[32] Christopher Gittings, 'Imaging Canada: The Singing Mountie and Other Commodifications of Nation', *Canadian Journal of Communication* 23, no. 4 (1998), https://doi.org/10.22230/cjc.1998v23n4a1062, accessed 15 January 2022.

[33] Shane Peacock, 'Noble, Daring, & Dashing', *Beaver* 78, no. 3 (1998), Academic Search Premier: https://tinyurl.com/3x4m48us, accessed 15 January 2022.

Recognizing such racialized underpinnings is an important step toward better understanding and dismantling racist structures in musical theatre.

Revues Intimate and Grand

Two revues that opened in September – *The Co-Optimists* in London and *The Passing Show of 1924* in New York – reflected entirely different approaches to the malleable moneymaking genre. The former relied on its performers and their performances in the spirit of Charlot while the latter was a large, splashy affair meant to provide ample visual delights.

In 1921, the British actor Davy Burnaby (1881–1949) brought together a group of performers to create *The Co-Optimists*, described as 'an all-star "Pierrot" entertainment'.[34] On 2 September 1924, the eighth incarnation of the revue opened at London's Palace Theatre. Among the most celebrated skits was 'Missing the Bus', a humorous escapade in which newcomer Hermione Baddeley (1906–1986) portrayed a slovenly wife who, with her flamboyant husband (played by Gilbert Childs), was waiting for a late bus. When they finally realize that they have missed the last one, they began a downtrodden song and dance that delighted the audience. Among the most recognizable future stars in the revue was Stanley Holloway (1890–1982), who created the role of Alfred P. Doolittle in *My Fair Lady* on Broadway (1956), in the West End (1958) and in Hollywood (1964).

The reviewer for *The Sketch* noted the revue's combination of the familiar and the novel: 'It is a new old show, for, although the items are all fresh and there are new faces in the troupe, the spirit and the manner have not changed. This in itself is something wonderful'.[35] This was a wholly different response to the 'sameness' of the large-scale American revues such as Ziegfeld's *Follies*, which were generally being referred to as stale. Perhaps it was the reliance on the stars' individual performances rather than visual opulence that accounted for the difference in response.

Visual opulence was certainly present in the Shubert-produced *Passing Show of 1924*, which opened on Broadway at the Winter Garden Theatre on 3 September. It included a glamourous Arthurian sequence, precipitated by Min, who wishes that her husband, Jim, was a knight rather than a plumber. Jim falls asleep and dreams that he is at the court of King Arthur (see Figure 10.3). The soprano Olga Cook, as Queen Guinevere, and

---

[34] 'The Theatres', *Times* (London), 20 June 1921.
[35] 'Criticisms in Cameo', *Sketch*, 17 September 1924, BNA.

Figure 10.3 'When Knighthood Was in Flower' from *Passing Show of 1924*. The Shubert Archive.

the Australian tenor Allan Prior (1897–1949), as Sir Gawaine, move effort-lessly into Sigmund Romberg, Jean Schwartz and Harold Atteridge's grace-ful duet 'When Knighthood Was in Flower'. Jim then finds himself in a jousting match with Sir Launcelot set to Leon Jessel's well-known 'Parade of the Wood Soldiers'. The tune had become famous in the USA thanks to the popular Russian–French revue *Le Chauve-Souris* (The Bat), which had begun touring North America in 1922. The medieval sumptu-ousness of the décor provided stark contrast to that of other shows opening on Broadway in early September, particularly *The Chocolate Dandies* and *Rose-Marie*. By comparison, these two shows, with their gambling and murdering, seem rooted in some sort of relative realism.

The Passing Show of 1924 is often considered the twelfth and final instalment in the annual series, for it was the last to be produced in the long-established format. Whether or not it is actually the last *Passing Show* depends on how one treats the legacy of the name. As Jonas Westover writes, the moniker 'Passing Show' was used beyond 1924 and Shubert-produced revues bearing that name continued to appear well into the 1930s. For example, when *The Merry World* (opened at the Imperial Theatre on 8 June 1926) played its post-Broadway tour in Chicago in September 1926, it was called *The Passing Show of 1926*. *The Passing Show of 1932* began previews in Detroit under that name, but when it arrived in New York, it became *Greenwich Village Follies*. According to Westover, it was the 'sheer size of the Shubert theatrical machine' that allowed such flexibility.[36] Especially outside New York, the Shuberts were continuing to benefit from their legacy series.

Two Adaptations for London: *Poppy* and *Springtime*

Early in September, two different adaptations of works with very different pedigrees opened in London. On 4 September, an anglicized adaptation of the Broadway success *Poppy* (see Chapter 3) opened at the Gaiety Theatre. Four days later, an abridged English-language version of Franz Lehár's one-act operetta *Frühling*, billed as *Springtime*, was included on a variety programme at the Empire Theatre. When considered in tandem, these adaptations yet again reflect the diversity of not only the act and art of adaptation but also the mobility of musical theatre in 1924.

The setting of *Poppy* was changed from its original New England town to an English village, though its nineteenth-century time period remained. The huckster Eustace McGargle, the character so memorably created by W. C. Fields in New York, still wants to pass off his foster daughter Poppy (played by Annie Croft) as a missing heiress. Now, he is aided in his deceit by a local police constable. As in the original, Poppy is the true heiress. Playing McGargle was the comic character actor W. H. Berry (1870–1951, born William Henry Berry), whose antic-filled performance, according to one reviewer, 'saves the piece'[37] (see Figure 10.4). Critics and audiences on the whole remained largely indifferent. The success of other American imports such as *Stop Flirting* was not always repeatable.

When Franz Lehár's (1870–1948) *The Three Graces* opened at the Empire Theatre back in January (see Chapter 5), it seemed a mismatch between a full-length adaptation of a continental operetta and a venue described on its playbills as 'The Premier Variety Theatre & Cosmopolitan Club of the World'.[38] On 8 September, this situation was revisited when another adaptation of a Lehár operetta, the one-act *Springtime*, was included as part of a variety bill. In August, Sir Alfred Butt had started

---

[36] Jonas Westover, *The Shuberts and their Passing Shows: The Untold Tale of Ziegfeld's Rivals* (New York: Oxford University Press, 2016), 221.

[37] 'The Theatre: New Musical Comedy – "Poppy" at the Gaity', *Sportsman* (London), 6 September 1924, BNA.

[38] Playbill for Empire Theatre, Leicester Square, week commencing 8 September 1924, MM/REF/ TH/LO/EMP/13, M&M.

Figure 10.4 W. H. Berry in the London production of *Poppy*.

producing 'high-class variety' at the Empire and wanted to include some-thing along this line in his offerings.[39]

The German original, *Frühling*, from 1922, featured a book and lyrics by Rudolf Eger. Arthur Anderson adapted the story for its London presenta-tion, reducing its length to about half an hour.[40] Rather than a full-length offering, here was a sort of operetta sketch, something more attuned to the needs of the Empire Theatre. Marie (Hedwig in the original) is typing a libretto, which she imagines playing out in her head as she types. It is about a shy musician, Francois, who has fallen in love with a woman whose apartment he rents while she is at work and whom he has never met. He knows her only through her belongings. The plot addresses contemporary

---

[39] 'Lehar's New Work', *Sporting Times* (London), 6 September 1924, BNA.

[40] 'New Operetta: Song That is Likely to Prove Popular', *Daily News* (London), 9 September 1924, BNA.

concerns, namely the urban housing shortage, and features just five characters, all of whom are working class. It thus plays into issues that the
Labour government was facing at the time. Starring as Marie was
Blanche Tomlin (1889–?) and as Francois the noted tenor Courtice
Pounds (1861–1927), who at the time was in his sixties. Lehár's score,
like that of *Cloclo*, features a wide musical palette that includes waltzes,
foxtrots and even a shimmy. Here was an operetta adaptation that
included syncopated dances being included on a variety programme in
the British capital. It was certainly an amalgamation of the established
and the innovative.

Gershwin in London: *Primrose*

For several years, London's Winter Garden Theatre had been home to
a series of musical comedies by George Grossmith, Jr, P. G. Wodehouse
and Jerome Kern that starred Grossmith, Dorothy Dickson and Leslie
Henson. After the third of these, *The Beauty Prize* (see Chapter 2), opened
in 1923, Kern shifted his focus back to Broadway. Grossmith and his co-
producer at the Winter Garden, J. A. E. Malone, were now in need of a new
composer. They liked the charm – and the profits – that the mixture of
British and American talent brought to the Winter Garden. To succeed
Kern, they invited another American, George Gershwin (1898–1937), to
write the music for their next project. Originally called *The Clinging
Vine*, it was rechristened as the more poetic *Primrose*. Rather than
Wodehouse, they engaged the British-born American playwright Guy
Bolton (1884–1979) as librettist, writing under Grossmith's supervision
(Grossmith was listed as co-author), and Desmond Carter (1895–1939)
as lyricist. Gershwin was impressed with Carter, writing to Ira that
'This boy Carter writes some of the neatest lyrics I've seen. He is a nice
quiet chap who doesn't look as though he was capable of writing
lyrics.'[41] In addition to someone to succeed Kern, they also needed
someone to succeed Dickson. At the time, she was preparing to star in
Patricia and was therefore unavailable.

   Gershwin arrived in London in July, and rehearsals for *Primrose* began
two weeks later.[42] The composer was certainly excited by the new venture,

---

[41] George Gershwin to Ira Gershwin, London, 22 July 1924, Gershwin Correspondence, box 140,
   folder 2, George and Ira Gershwin Collection, LC.
[42] For more on Gershwin's London career, see James Ross Moore, 'The Gershwins in Britain', *New
   Theatre Quarterly* 10, issue 37 (February 1994), 33–48.

writing to his brother: 'Everything that can be done is being done for the production, although it seems very difficult to get a leading-lady. There is a very fine conductor at the Winter Garden and we are to have an orchestra of thirty, which makes it just grand.'[43] As far as his music was concerned, he wrote, 'Grossmith is tickled with the tunes & the first act opening'.[44] Grossmith had intended to play Hilary, one of the male leads, as had been his custom with the Kern shows, but Gershwin wanted a more operatic voice for the role, so Grossmith deferred. Hence, they cast the baritone Percy Heming (1883–1956), who was considered the finest Scarpia (the villain in Puccini's *Tosca*) of his day. Heather Thatcher (1896–1987), a dancer and singer known for her exotic and glamourous attire, became leading lady. *Primrose* opened on 11 September and enjoyed a very respectable run of 255 performances.

In Bolton's libretto, the writer Hilary Vane (Heming's role) lives on a houseboat and is writing a novel about a Miss Primrose. His neighbour Joan (played by Margery Hicklin) thinks the title character is based on her, so she sneaks off with the manuscript, and when she returns it, she and Hilary fall in love. Joan's wealthy guardian, Sir Barnaby Falls, however, wants her to marry his nephew, Freddie. Freddie, though, is in love with May Rooker, who shares his passion for golf (a sport seen in other musicals playing in 1924, including *Kid Boots* and *Top Hole*).

Toby Mopham (pronounced MOP-um, Henson's role) arrives from London and wants Hilary's help to dissolve his engagement to Pinkie Peach (Thatcher's part), an aggressive social-climbing beautician also known as Madame Frazeline, whose big brother wants Toby to fulfil his promise of marriage. During lunch, Pinkie faints in Hilary's arms, which delights Toby, as he now has a reason to call off the wedding. It also devastates Joan, who thinks Hilary prefers Pinkie to her (see Figure 10.5).

Act 2 takes place at a Bastille Day party being held at the Hotel Splendide in Le Bouqet, a French seaside resort. Joan and Freddie envision living separate lives, should they be forced to marry, while she and Hilary resume their coy flirtations. Hilary suggests that Toby impersonate a medium to tell Sir Barnaby of the disaster that will occur should Freddie wed Joan. Pinkie meanwhile counsels Joan that if she really wants to please Hilary, she should become a flapper, since it's all the rage. Joan takes Pinkie's advice, but the plan backfires horrendously, though comically. Toby's mother,

---

[43] George Gershwin to Ira Gershwin, London, 25 July 1924, Gershwin Correspondence, box 140, folder 3, George and Ira Gershwin Collection, LC.

[44] George Gershwin to Ira Gershwin, London, 9 July 1924, Gershwin Correspondence, box 140, folder 1, George and Ira Gershwin Collection, LC.

Figure 10.5 Pinkie (Heather Thatcher) faints in the arms of Hilary (Percy Heming) in *Primrose*. Ira and Leonore Gershwin Trusts.

Lady Sophia, arrives, recognizes her son by his nose and exposes his disguise as the carnivalesque comedy of impersonations meld into Bastille Day celebrations.

As Act 3 begins, Lady Sophia, fearing a family financial collapse, has allowed Pinkie to convert her home into a nightclub, where a costume party is taking place. Hilary shows up as Beau Brummel, the well-known arbiter of fashion in early-nineteenth-century London, and Joan arrives as the Primrose Girl of William Ward Laing's painting. Toby, ever the master of disguise, comes as a policeman and forces the right people to be together. Since Pinkie's entrepreneurial spirit has saved the Mophams, Toby welcomes her as his bride.

Not all of *Primrose*'s songs were written specifically for the show. As was typical, older songs were recycled in new contexts. Here, the older songs all featured lyrics by Ira. Because of needing British rather than American references and also considering how the songs would fit into the plot, some lyrics needed to be rewritten. Hence, Carter wrote new verses for 'Isn't It Wonderful' and 'Some Faraway Someone' and entirely new words for 'Naughty Baby', 'Boy Wanted', 'Isn't It Wonderful', 'The Sirens' (which became 'Four Sirens We') and 'Susie' (which became 'Wait a Bit, Susie').

George ensured that Ira received co-credit – and compensation – for his original lyrics.

As for the music Gershwin wrote expressly for *Primrose*, he intended it to sound English. Gershwin told an interviewer: 'I have inserted several numbers in 6/8 time because the English are a 6/8 nation. The Americans are a 4/4 nation and their music is essentially the fox-trot.'[45] He succeeded so effectively in this regard that the London *Times* reviewer thought an English composer had written the score.[46] Following his own dictate, Gershwin wrote two buoyant songs in 6/8 for Toby: 'When Toby Is Out of Town', his entrance song, and 'Mary, Queen of Scots', a duet with Freddie. Leslie Henson, who played Toby, was truly honoured when Gershwin said he was 'the most musically-minded low comedian he had every met'.[47] Likewise, Gershwin wrote the rollicking 'This is the Life for a Man' (called 'The Countryside' in the playbill) for Hilary, also in 6/8, in which the writer proclaims his love of rural England. Not everything was in 6/8, thankfully. Gershwin and Carter wrote a delightfully comic patter song in the grand British tradition for Henson as Toby, 'That New-Fangled Mother of Mine', in which he describes Lady Sophia as a great fan of liquor and nightlife. Her new-fangledness is represented musically through the sounds of syncopated ragtime. And for Heming as Hilary, he created the drinking song 'Beau Brummel', which Gershwin biographer Richard Crawford calls a 'pompous cast of British patriotic music'.[48]

There were hopes that the show would transfer to Broadway. Unfortunately, that didn't happen. It wasn't until 2003 that *Primrose* finally had its New York debut in a production by Mel Miller's Musicals Tonight![49]

While in London, Gershwin was working on the new show for the Astaires. He signed his contract with its producers, Alex A. Aarons and Vinton Freedley, on 30 September. It read, in part, 'Whereas the Managers desire to secure the services of the Composer, for the purpose of composing the complete score for a Musical Comedy, in which the Managers desire to present Fred and Adele Astaire.'[50] The focus of the new work was definitely the Astaires.

[45] Quoted in Howard Pollack, *George Gershwin: His Life and Work* (Berkeley: University of California Press, 2006), 323.
[46] Pollack, *George Gershwin*, 323.
[47] Leslie Henson, *Yours Faithfully: An Autobiography* (London: John Long, [1948]), 14.
[48] Crawford, *Summertime*, 138.   [49] N.B.: The exclamation mark is part of the series title.
[50] Quoted in Crawford, *Summertime*, 149.

11 | An Abundant Autumn

One of the most significant events of this resplendent September, which included the premieres of *The Chocolate Dandies* and *Rose-Marie*, was the return of Adele and Fred Astaire to New York. As Fred tells it, their producers, Alex A. Aarons and Vinton Freedley, came to meet their ship. Aarons was telling the siblings about ideas for the new show as the Astaires were going through customs. Aarons admitted that the working title, *Black-Eyed Susan*, was terrible and would be changed. George Gershwin had already showed them some of the songs in London, and the Astaires had verbally agreed to star in the show. The producers had a meeting with backers that evening and needed written contracts from the stars. As Fred recalled, 'We signed the contacts on a trunk lid while the customs men were going through our baggage.'[1]

When they were not rehearsing, the Astaires were taking in the sights and sounds of New York. Gershwin took them to see a lot of shows, which Fred thought 'looked mighty good to us'.[2] They also went to nightclubs, where they saw George Raft dance the Charleston. Fred called him 'the neatest, fastest Charleston dancer ever'.[3]

Several of the shows that opened at the start of September were still going strong as the month progressed and October began. A plethora of revues debuted alongside them, along with book musicals and significant new productions of *Gräfin Mariza* in Europe. It was truly an abundant autumn.

September Revues

When *Earl Carroll's Vanities* opened at the Music Box Theatre on 10 September, it was the first time the producer had added his name to the title; this was not just *Vanities*, as it was in the past year, but *Earl Carroll's Vanities*. Carroll (1893–1948) not only produced the lavish spectacle but also created its songs and co-authored its sketches with Ralph Spence. To distinguish his revues from those of his rivals, he opted for sheer quantity in the number of chorus girls (108) and the exact opposite in terms of costuming.

---

[1] Astaire, *Steps in Time*, 124.   [2] Crawford, *Summertime*, 142.   [3] Astaire, *Steps in Time*, 125.

Decency laws allowed full frontal nudity, but only if the subjects did not move. To challenge these limits, Carroll devised three pasties for each chorus girl – one for each nipple and one for the pubic area – for the opening 'The Spirit of Vanities' number in what became known as the 'Pastie Parade'. The women moved, but were not fully naked. On the second night, Tom O'Leary of the vice squad noticed one chorus girl swinging back and forth across the stage completely naked on a pendulum. Technically, she was not moving, but O'Leary raced on to the stage to try to cover her with a blanket. The woman screamed and ran off stage. Chaos and mayhem followed, with Carroll giving a curtain speech about censorship.[4]

Physicality, whether naked or clothed, was paramount in the production. Sophie Tucker (1886–1966), familiar to audiences from vaudeville, was the featured singer and delighted audiences with her powerful delivery and slightly risqué material. Her physical appearance was in distinct contrast to that of the unclothed women in the chorus.

While *Earl Carroll's Vanities* relied on its commodification of bodies, the sixth edition of the *Greenwich Village Follies*, which opened at the Shubert Theatre on 16 September, showcased a wide range of talent. Staged by John Murray Anderson (1886–1954), its stars included the identical twins the Dolly Sisters (Rosie, 1892–1970; Jenny, 1892–1941), the ballerina Anna Ludmilla (1903–1990), the vaudevillian blackface comics George Moran (1881–1949) and Charles Mack (1888–1934) and Vincent Lopez (1895–1975) and His Orchestra. Ludmilla went on to be prima ballerina with the Chicago Lyric Opera and Lopez became one of the leading band leaders of the era.

As was the norm, the show was revised during its run. Eventually all but one of Cole Porter's (1891–1964) original songs were dropped, the exception being 'Make Every Day a Holiday', which was retitled 'Let Every Day Be a Holiday'.[5] Owen Murphy and Jay Gorney were brought in to balance Porter's 'esoteric' numbers with ones that one writer claims were 'more accessible but less likable'.[6]

Hassard Short's Ritz Revue showed a different approach when it opened the next evening at the intimate Ritz Theatre. Short (1877–1956) had been an actor before turning his attention to directing and lighting design. His approach to the revue was similar to that of Charlot with its emphasis on the talents of specific performers. These included the limber dancer and comedian Charlotte Greenwood (1890–1977), the British operatic tenor

[4] Davis, *Scandals and Follies*, 217.
[5] Norton, *A Chronology of American Musical Theater, Volume 2*, 377.
[6] Davis, *Scandals and Follies*, 218.

Tom Burke (1890–1969) and the versatile dancer Albertina Vitak (1904–1993). Among the most heralded sketches was 'Her Morning Bath',[7] in which Greenwood tries to enjoy a nice bath only to be interrupted over and over again. One critic noted her 'deft handling of a towel', adding that 'handling it amateurishly would have spelled disaster and censorship'.[8] Greenwood would go on to delight film audiences in roles such as Binnie Crawford in *Down Argentine Way* (1940) and Aunt Eller in *Oklahoma!* (1955).

Critics repeatedly mentioned the show's visual loveliness,[9] which was accomplished largely through Short's lighting effects. And here came one of the producer's contributions to the history of theatre: a single lighting control board. Short worked with the electrical engineer James C. Masek of Westinghouse to install a master switchboard with a 2,000 switch capacity from which one person could control all the lighting cues through-out the show.[10] Such devices might seem nearly commonplace (or out-dated) to many who have worked on the technical side of theatre, but in 1924 this was something new.

After eight successful months on Broadway, *André Charlot's Revue of 1924* closed on 20 September and began to prepare for its tour. Three days later, in London, the latest version of *Charlot's Revue* opened at the Prince of Wales's Theatre. Once the North American tour began, Charlot had two versions of his eponymous revue playing to very different audiences.

The London version featured new sketches, mostly by Ronald Jeans, a regular supplier of material for Charlot. Songs and dances both familiar and new filled out the programme. More prominent than the material, though, were the stars, who included Maisie Gay (1883–1945), Phyllis Monkman (1892–1976), Henry Kendall (1897–1962) and Morris Harvey (1877–1944).

The revue, as was typical for Charlot, began with something novel. Here, it was the satirical sketch 'Fool's Paradise'. All sorts of people inhabit 'Fool's Paradise', including some easily identifiable caricatures of politicians, who live their lives completely according to their own desires. They become angry when Truth, played by Maisie Gay, shows up. In the playbill, she's called 'The Unwelcome One', a sure indicator of the attitudes of those who dwell in Fool's Paradise. Towards the end of the scene, 'Illusions'

---

[7] By Norma Mitchell and Ralph Bunker.
[8] 'New Revue is Ocular Feast', *Baltimore Sun*, 28 September 1924, newspapers.com.
[9] 'New Revue is Ocular Feast'.
[10] 'New Board Gives Central Control of 2,000 Switches', *Daily News* (New York), 7 September 1924, newspapers.com.

enter to attack and destroy her. She threatens to expose their lies, but they succeed in driving her out and literally dance for joy. She re-enters to tell them the truth about their dancing: 'I can tell you what I think it is – it's absolutely – ',[11] at which point the Illusions utter a loud shriek. They do not want to hear the truth, and the censor would not want the audience to hear the almost-certain expletive.

From the start, Gay was pure delight. She showed off her acting abilities in the opening sketch and her musical talents in later ones (though she did have a small song in 'Fool's Paradise'). As Miss Fancy Robinson, a parlour singer who wants to share selections from her repertoire for those whom she calls '*my* public', she gave a series of perfect imitations of what one reviewer called 'the stilted mannerisms of mediocre concert-singers'.[12] To do such convincing parodies of bad singing requires an enormous amount of true talent. In the revue's penultimate scene, 'Love, Life and Laughter' by Noël Coward, Gay played 'La Flamme', a French cabaret singer, and performed three songs by Coward in character: 'The Roses Have Made Me Remember', 'A Little Slut of Six' and 'The Girl I am Leaving in England To-day'.

Demonstrating the wide aesthetic range within the revue was the ballet *Karma* by Cyril Scott (1879–1970). Scott, a British modernist composer, was especially known for his free use of rhythm and his expansion of small musical kernels into larger organic structures. Reflective of Scott's interest in mysticism, the ballet, according to the composer, 'represents the soul-history of three characters, two women ULA and WAJA, and one man JAHNU, together with their deeds and the consequences of those deeds'.[13] As with the ghost scene in *Dinah* (discussed in Chapter 1), the cultural popularity of mysticism and afterlives is again evident here. Featuring the modern dance talents of Phyllis Monkman, Juliette Compton and Henry Kendall, the ballet reflects how Charlot was pitching his revues at a more intellectual audience than some of his New York contemporaries.

In his London revues, Charlot favoured sketches that made people think rather than those that offered spectacle or voyeurism. Perhaps the most affecting sketch in *Charlot's Revue* is the tragic 'Me Pink 'At', written not by Jeans but by Dorota Flatua (1874–1947), an Australian-born author of novels and children's books. The Chinese drug dealer Chung

---

[11] *Charlot's Revue 1924* (first edition), André Charlot Papers (Collection 1318), box 2, folder 6, UCLA Library Special Collections, Charles E. Young Research Library, University of California Los Angeles.

[12] 'Jingle', 'Charlot's Revue at the Prince of Wales', *Bystander*, 29 October 1924, BNA.

[13] *Charlot's Revue 1924* (first edition).

(Kendall) lives in a dilapidated house in Pennyfields, the heart of East London's Chinese community. He maintains a downtrodden servant, Lill (Monkman), whom he physically mistreats. When Chung goes to an illicit meeting, he leaves a pound for Lill to give to Ali, a lascar (a sailor of Asian heritage), who will come to deliver a packet. Vi'let, who deals in old clothes, stops by and shows Lill a pink hat and handkerchief, which Lill longingly admires. Vi'let leaves and in comes Bill. He's going to a party with some friends. He'd love to take Lill, but her clothing is so tattered that she wouldn't be welcome. Lill decides to use the money Chung left for Ali to buy the pink hat and handkerchief so that she can join Bill and his friends. Ali comes to deliver the package. Lill looks for the coin and truly cannot find it. She tells him that Chung must not have left it. After Ali leaves, she finds the coin and buys the hat and handkerchief from Vi'let, along with some curling tongs. Chung and Ali return: Chung is livid. He notices Lill's curling tongs, asks where she got them and opens the cupboard to discover the hat and handkerchief. He starts to tear up the hat, at which moment Lill grabs a knife and stabs Chung as the joyous sounds of Bill and the revellers are heard off-stage.[14]

The sketch, far from the farces one might expect to find in revues, furthers negative stereotypes of Asians and raises issues concerning the urban poor. Chung is a violent drug dealer, while Ali is also involved in drug trafficking. Both speak in a feigned pidgin English. Women are driven to destructive and dishonest behaviours in order to survive. Vi'let buys clothes from women who have been sent to prison and sells them on, while Lill commits murder. Anti-Chinese sentiment was rampant at the time, largely because recent Chinese immigrants were seen as taking jobs away from British-born workers. The sketch also connects to the problematic representation in Gertrude Lawrence's 'Limehouse Blues', a song that she continued to perform in later editions of this revue in London.

Meanwhile, back in the USA, only two of *André Charlot's Revue of 1924*'s three original headlining stars, Beatrice Lillie and Gertrude Lawrence, were still with the production as it began its post-Broadway tour. (Jack Buchanan had left the show in April to begin rehearsals for *Toni*.) The production received accolade after accolade as it played cities including Boston, Toronto and Detroit. This was in large part because of the consistently strong and enthusiastic performances of its two leading ladies – at least until one of them became ill. In early December, while in Toronto, Lawrence developed

---

[14] A typescript for the sketch is in *Charlot's Revue 1924* (first edition).

pneumonia, was hospitalized and had to leave the tour. When she was well enough, she returned to England to continue her recuperation.

Countess Maritza Continues to Triumph

On 20 September, Emmerich Kálmán's *Gräfin Mariza*, which was still playing to enthusiastic audiences in Vienna, opened at the Metropoltheater in Berlin. The production was transferred in its entirety, aside from some cast changes. An exception was Hubert Marischka as Tassilo, though he returned to Vienna after two months. Playing Zsupán was Max Hansen, who soon became a major star in the Berlin firmament. The Hungarian coloratura soprano Emmy Kosáry (1889–1964) triumphed in the title role. One reviewer noted her performance as having 'that natural, a bit brutal, sensuality that's characteristic of red-white-green women'.[15] Paul Morgan (1886–1938), one of the great stars of Berlin cabaret and co-founder of the famed 'Kadeko' in Berlin, played Penizek. Morgan, who was Jewish, was interred at Buchenwald, one of the largest Nazi camps, where he died of exhaustion. Adele Sandrock (1863–1937), the *grande dame* of the Berlin stage and early cinema, charmed as Tassilo's aunt. Along with her darkly hued voice, she brought a nervous disorder to the role that made her cry when she wanted to laugh and laugh when she wanted to cry.[16]

Following its Berlin success, three different European versions of *Gräfin Mariza* opened on three successive evenings in October. The international appeal of Kálmán's operetta was unstoppable. On 16 October, *Hrabina Marica* opened in Warsaw, followed the next evening by *Contessa Mariza* in Venice and, finally, on 18 October, by *Marica Grófnő* in Budapest. Other *Maricas* to open in 1924 included *Kreivitär Mariza* in Finland and *Marica* in the USSR. It would not be until 1926 that an English-language version opened on Broadway, and even longer for productions in Paris or London.[17]

The Budapest production at the Király Szíház (King's Theatre) deserves special comment, since the operetta is, after all, set in Hungary and written by a Hungarian-born composer. In the adaptation by Zsolt Harsányi, the production starred Juci Lábass as Marica (see Figure 11.1), Ferenc Kiss as Tassilo and Márton Rátkai as Zsupán. The contemporary Hungarian

---

[15] Frey, *'Laughter under Tears'*, 158–159.   [16] Frey, *'Laughter under Tears'*, 159.
[17] For a full list of premieres, see Frey, *'Laughter under Tears'*, 307–308.

Figure 11.1 Juci Lábass, star of *Marica Grófnő*, the Hungarian version of *Gräfin Mariza* (Countess Maritza).

situation was directly addressed when the words of the catchy foxtrot 'Komm mit nach Varasdin' (Come with me to Varasdin) became 'Szép város Kolozsvár' (Kolozsvár [Cluj] is a beautiful town). Four years after the Treaty of Trianon, Budapest audiences were hearing the name of a Transylvanian town lost as a result of the treaty in this overtly Hungarian operetta.[18] Kolozsvár/Cluj (part of Romania in 2023), in addition to being a picturesque locale, plays an important role in the history of Hungarian theatre. In 1792, a Hungarian Theatre was founded there as the first Hungarian theatre company in Transylvania. The operetta's reference to Kolozsvár, rather than Varasdin, therefore, remains a source of pride for many Hungarians a century later.

---

[18] My thanks to Péter Bozó for this important insight.

An Inauspicious Debut

Among the many future stars of musical theatre who made their credited Broadway debuts in 1924 was the prolific lyricist Howard Dietz (1896–1983).[19] Dietz later achieved fame working with composer Arthur Schwartz and being in charge of publicity at MGM for more than thirty years. Dietz's Broadway debut was low key, though it could have been much more, since he was working with Jerome Kern (1885–1945), the first and only time the two would do so. The show, *Dear Sir*, opened on 23 September at the Times Square Theatre and lasted just fifteen performances. It simply did not take off.

Edgar Selwyn's predictable book concerns a playboy, Laddie Munn (played by Oscar Shaw), who seeks revenge on socialite Dorothy Fair (played by Genevieve Tobin) after she publicly humiliates him and his lifestyle. He wins her services as a maid-for-a-week at a charity auction, and, in true musical comedy fashion, the two end up falling in love. A loveable downtrodden vaudevillian posing as a millionaire, Andrew Bloxom (played by Walter Catlett), helps bring them together. Dietz's talents were evident in his lyrics for 'A Mormon Life', a song for Bloxom's character, where he cleverly rhymes 'bigamy', 'polygamy' and 'make a pig o' me',[20] and 'My Houseboat on the Harlem', a satiric reversal of the domestic-bliss type of song such as Kern's own 'A Cottage in Kent' in *The Beauty Prize* and 'Mr. and Mrs. Rorer' in *Sitting Pretty*. Here, the couple can only revel in such urban delights as their residence being mud-bound.

October Revues

Among the London producers who embraced Charlot's approach to the revue was Albert de Courville (1887–1960). This modesty was evident in *The Looking Glass*, which opened at the Vaudeville Theatre on 2 October. De Courville and Edgar Wallace provided the words and Frederick Chappelle the music. The most successful sketch concerned a couple stuck in traffic for

---

[19] According to Joan Kennedy Taylor, Dietz was not credited for his lyrics for the song 'Alibi Baby' in *Poppy* (1923) on the playbill or the sheet music due to lyricist Dorothy Donnelly's 'iron-clad contract' (Joan Kennedy Taylor, 'The Life of Howard Dietz', unpublished carbon copy typescript, Howard Dietz Papers, JPB 06–31, box 2, folder 5, Music Division, New York Public Library). In 2023, Dietz is credited as lyricist for the song on the Internet Broadway Database (www.ibdb.com/broadway-production/poppy-9261#Songs, accessed 2 December 2023).

[20] Thomas Hischak, *The Jerome Kern Encyclopedia* (Lanham: Scarecrow, 2013), 136.

Figure 11.2 Ed Wynn, signed photograph to theatre critic and journalist
J. Willis Sayre, 1924.

ten years, during which they marry, bring up a son and raise chickens. In
another, the versatile Shakespearean comic actor D. Hay Petrie (1895–1948)
delighted audiences with his song 'Oh Shakespeare You're the Best of All but
You Can't Fill the Fourteen Shilling Stall', in which he metatheatrically
confesses that the only way he can earn a living in the theatre is to perform
in revues. Shakespeare doesn't sell tickets; revues do. Another feature was the
intimate staging for the quasi-Victorian sentimental ballad 'Winter Rose':
a round cameo medallion with two singers seated at a piano. But there was
only one Charlot, and this imitation just did not have the spark of the
original and closed after six weeks.

　　Likewise, there was only one Ed Wynn (1886–1966). Few stars could
carry an entire show as well as he could, and even fewer could create the
book, music and lyrics for their own revue (see Figure 11.2). But that's
exactly what Wynn did in *The Grab Bag*, which opened at the Globe
Theatre on 6 October. Wynn himself starred in each of the revue's scenes,
donning a different funny suit for each. When he was changing costumes,
he offered vaudeville-style turns to other performers to display their talents,
including the Ormond Sisters singing Scottish songs, Ralph Riggs and
Katherine Witchie dancing, Janet Adair performing a music hall routine
and a Russian male octet called the Volga Boys singing Russian folksongs.

The Grab Bag, though, was really all about Ed Wynn. As Gilbert Seldes wrote about him in *The Seven Lively Arts*, 'It is Ed Wynn's pleasure to make everything seem utterly haphazard.'[21] Wynn was among those comics who would rhythmically talk their way through songs, with the melody in the orchestra, thus creating an aural illusion that they were singing. As a creator, when he didn't actually write a song, he invented its title, as he did for the faux-lament 'She Might Have Been a School Teacher, But She Hadn't Any Class'.[22] Wynn's gifts as a performer were matched only by the complete wholesomeness of his material, something that set his shows apart from so many other revues. As one critic noted, '"The Grab Bag" hasn't one line that is not as cheery as Thanksgiving and as clean as Christmas, and there are no scenes at which anyone could blush. Three cheers for Ed Wynn!'[23] Wynn's family-friendly reputation continued through the decades, and in 1964, forty years after he starred in *The Grab Bag*, he played Uncle Albert in the film *Mary Poppins*, delighting generations of audiences with his song, appropriately titled 'I Love to Laugh'.

On 15 October, a revue at the opposite end of the wholesomeness spectrum opened at the Astor Theatre: the second edition of the Shuberts' *Artists and Models*. This particular brand was known for its scantily clad women, whose costumes became so minimal that, as one reviewer noted, they 'can be carried in a vanity case'.[24] Numerous 'artists and illustrators' again contributed sketches, and, as was typical for Shubert revues, staff writers provided the music, this time Sigmund Romberg and J. Fred Coots, and the lyrics, now Clifford Grey and Sam Coslow.

Artists and Models opened with a self-referential prologue in which a group of New York artists descend on a rural New Hampshire town. These modern city residents listen to 'the vile shrieking phonograph', 'bob their hair' and use 'paint and powder'[25] – all things to be avoided. In the sketch, called 'Ain't Nature Grand', Sally Gump, a local spinster who is president of the local purity league, and Tony Comstock, the puritanical mayor, are unnerved because, as Comstock states, 'A plague is descending on this town'. These morally upright individuals have names that audiences would have recognized, though not for their purity. Sally Gump was

[21] Seldes, *The Seven Lively Arts*, 183.   [22] Davis, *Scandals and Follies*, 219.

[23] Brett Page, 'What's New Along Broadway', syndicated column, 18 October 1924, *Great Falls Tribune*, 19 October 1924, newspapers.com.

[24] Uncited clipping, 'Shubert Revue Plays to Every Variety of Taste', *St Louis Star*, Artists and Models Show File, Shubert Archive.

[25] All quotes are from the unpublished typescript for 'Ain't Nature Grand', Passing Show of 1924 script, Shubert Archive.

a common term for a prostitute, and Comstock shares his names with the famous Comstock Laws, which criminalized the transportation of obscene materials and contraceptives across state lines. These characters are not what they seem. By the end of the scene, everyone is so captivated by the modern world that they perform a production number as they race 'Off to Greenwich Village'.

Among the revue's most celebrated sketches was 'The Unveiling', in which Sally finds herself talking to a gallery owner. He is preparing to unveil the statues entered into his competition 'for the reproduction of the perfect human form'. Sally wants to see them before they are presented to the public, for, as a self-described 'stickler for purity and propriety', she is concerned that they may turn out to be nudes. The gallery owner/competition sponsor tells her 'You can rest assured they are works of art.' Since he wants the winning sculpture to be placed in Central Park, a public place, he wants the public (i.e., the audience in the theatre) to select the winning sculpture. And, in a splendid piece of theatricality that required additional rigging, he throws the cords for each set of statue drapes into the audience and asks their recipients to 'pull sharply at the count of three'.[26] Seventeen 'statue girls' are thus revealed. Given the elegance of the scene, the music notes call for 'something very classical and flowery'.[27] Romberg dutifully provided such an atmosphere with the song 'Pull Your String'.

A Play with Musical Connections

Though not a musical, Edwin Justus Mayer's play *The Firebrand* has significant ties to the musical theatre. The fictionalized tale about the real-life Renaissance sculptor Benvenuto Cellini opened on 15 October at the Morosco Theatre, where it played into the next year. Its premise was not unlike that of the operetta *Madame Pompadour* – a fiction about a historical title character. The play featured the song 'The Voice of Love', referred to as 'Cellini's Love Song', with music by Robert Russell Bennett (1894–1981) and Maurice Nitke (1879–?) and lyrics by Ira Gershwin (1896–1983). Bennett was a prolific orchestrator whose credits included *Sitting Pretty* (see Chapter 7), while Nitke was an acclaimed theatre violin soloist, music director and composer. The song is in the style of an Italian serenade, a man singing to his beloved: in this case,

---

[26] Unpublished typescript for 'The Unveiling', Passing Show of 1924 script, Shubert Archive.
[27] 'Artists and Models Musical Nos.', 8 August 1924, Shubert Archive.

Benvenuto to Angela. *The Firebrand* connected not just Bennett and Gershwin but also Kurt Weill (1900–1950), who wrote the score for its musical adaptation, *The Firebrand of Florence* (1945), with lyrics by Gershwin.

Dixie to Broadway

Revues sometimes focused on the extraordinary talents of one individual, such as Ed Wynn's *The Grab Bag*. For the Black revue *Dixie to Broadway*, which opened at the Broadhurst Theatre on 29 October, that individual was the charismatic Florence Mills (1895–1927). Mills had played in vaudeville, and when she replaced Gertrude Saunders in the original company of *Shuffle Along*, it began her rapid rise to fame.

Mills was a phenomenon. The Harlem Renaissance writer James Welton Johnson called her 'indefinable'. He described her famous upper vocal range as 'full of bubbling, bell-like, bird-like tones'.[28] Recalling how she used it in her signature song, 'I'm a Little Blackbird Looking for a Bluebird', Johnson remarked, 'it [was] with such exquisite poignancy as always to raise a lump in your throat'.[29] Sadly, no recordings, either audio or visual, of Mills's extraordinary abilities are known to exist. What do survive are the universal accolades for her unique synthesis of the dramatic and the comedic, the naive and the sophisticated, the garish and the contained. Unlike her contemporary Josephine Baker, the only African American artist of the time more heralded, Mills, according to historian David Krasner, 'remained steadfastly within the bounds of decorum'.[30] While Baker often performed nearly nude in a jungle stage setting to overplayed stereotypes, Mills, when she appeared in the 'jungle number' in *Dixie to Broadway*, offered what Krasner describes as 'a counterintuitive element that cut against the grain of the caricature'.[31] Even as Mills was performing racist stereotypes, she was transcending the degradation.

Before George White produced *Runnin' Wild* or B. C. Whitney and A. L. Erlanger *The Chocolate Dandies*, another white impresario, Lew Leslie (born Lew Lessinsky, 1888 or 1890–1963), was already promoting African American artists on Broadway musical stages. Capitalizing on the success of *Shuffle Along* and the white audience's fascination with Black artists, in

---

[28] Johnson, *Black Manhattan*, 199.   [29] Johnson, *Black Manhattan*, 199–200.
[30] Krasner, '*Shuffle Along* and the Quest for Nostalgia', 285.
[31] Krasner, '*Shuffle Along* and the Quest for Nostalgia', 285.

the early 1920s Leslie staged the *Plantation Revue* at the Plantation Club, formerly the Café de Paris, above the Winter Garden Theatre. Such venues were popular with theatre patrons, who would follow an evening performance with a visit to one of these sites for dining and cabaret-style entertainment. The revue's title, alas, did not resonate with ideas of the Harlem Renaissance but rather harkened back to the days of minstrelsy. The programme even carried the subtitle 'Night Time Frolics in Dixieland'.[32] Mills's biographer Bill Egan considered the Plantation Room and its revue a step backwards after the progress of *Shuffle Along*.[33] The second edition, from 1922, was built around Mills and her husband, the acrobatic dancer Ulysses 'Slow Kid' (U. S.) Thompson (1888–1990). The forty-five minute, single-act production quickly became popular with its affluent white clientele.

Mills dreamed of performing for her friends and neighbours in Harlem, many of whom could not afford the prices at the Plantation Room. So, Leslie expanded his *Plantation Revue* into a full-length entertainment which played two weeks in July 1922 at the Lafayette Theatre in Harlem. This was in essence a tryout for a Broadway production, which opened at the 48th Street Theatre on 28 July for a brief run.[34] As was typical of revues, material was changed and a revised version opened in October.

The English impresario Charles B. Cochran (1872–1951) had seen Mills in *Shuffle Along* and was deeply impressed with her stage presence and distinctive talents. He desperately wanted to bring her to London in an all-Black revue, believing that she would delight his audience.[35] As a vehicle, Cochran would feature Mills in a revised, single-act version of *Plantation Revue* which he would combine with a single-act, all-white revue to create *Dover Street to Dixie*. The segregated entertainment would consist of two halves: the first white (Dover) and the second Black (Dixie). When the show opened on 31 May 1923, Mills was catapulted to international stardom and immediately joined the Astaires as the toasts of London (see Figure 11.3).[36] Her fans included the Prince of Wales, who saw the show multiple times, and a young drama student named John Gielgud.[37] After the show closed on 1 September, Mills and her husband visited Paris before

---

[32] Bill Egan, *Florence Mills: Harlem Jazz Queen* (Lanham: Scarecrow, 2004), 65.

[33] Egan, *Florence Mills*, 67.   [34] Egan, *Florence Mills*, 70.   [35] Egan, *Florence Mills*, 79.

[36] For more on *Dover Street to Dixie*, see David Linton and Len Platt, '*Dover Street to Dixie* and the politics of cultural transfer and exchange', in Len Platt, Tobias Becker and David Linton, eds., *Popular Musical Theatre in London and Berlin, 1890–1939* (Cambridge: Cambridge University Press, 2014), 170–186.

[37] Egan, *Florence Mills*, 91.

Figure 11.3 Florence Mills in *Dover Street to Dixie*.

returning home to Harlem. In February, she returned to the Lafayette Theatre for two weeks in the *Plantation Revue* before embarking on the extensive pre-Broadway tour for what would become her next success, *Dixie to Broadway*. The new show's title was a declaration of Mills's continuing success after *Dover Street to Dixie*: She had gone from 'Dover Street to *Dixie*' to Broadway.

Dixie to Broadway was a two-act revue that consciously avoided any sort of plot. Although the entire cast was Black, the producer, Lew Leslie, and the multiple creators were white.[38] People came to the theatre not to watch a narrative unfold but to be in the presence of talented performers. Besides Mills, the cavalcade of top-notch artists included Will Vodery (1885–1951) and his Plantation Orchestra; the composer and arranger William Grant Still

---

[38] Music was by George W. Meyer and Arthur Johnston, lyrics by Grant Clarke and Roy Turk, and book credited to Walter De Leon, Tom Howard, Lew Leslie and Sidney Lazarus.

(1895–1978); singers Aida Ward (1900–1984), Lillian Brown (1885–1969) and Cora Green (1895–after 1949); and a plethora of dancers including Mills's husband, U. S. Thompson, and Maude Russell (1897–2001), who had famously danced the Charleston in *Liza* back in 1922. One reviewer vividly described the overall effect of the dances and the songs: 'the agreeable manipulation of harmony and counterpoint, horizontal and vertical effects at the same time, cross-word puzzle stuff in music that makes sense both ways. The old plantation melodies emerge only at the end of the show, a mere fugitive motif in the wilderness of polytonic jazz.'[39] Here was a sophisticated musical score, with just enough minstrel elements to play to its white audience's expectations.

This showcase for Florence Mills's extraordinary and wide-ranging talents began with an educational pageant, stemming from an established African American tradition, in which the history of Black people in the USA was presented. It began in Africa, moved to periods of enslavement and emancipation in the USA and ended in the present day with actors encircling a statue of Abraham Lincoln with raised prayer hands.[40] A regression to minstrel clichés followed, with 'Put Your Old Bandana On' and Mills's first song, 'Dixie Dreams', a ballad she performed costumed as a lonely wanderer in overalls carrying a small bundle over her shoulder. The song and its performance echoed 'Down among the Sleepy Hills of Ten-Ten-Tennessee', her entrance number in *Dover Street to Dixie*. Other songs included 'Jungle Nights in Dixieland', in which she appeared as a Zulu dancer in an elaborate feathered costume (not nearly naked, as Baker may have done), and 'Mandy, Make Up Your Mind', where she played a groom waiting for his tardy bride. But the musical and dramatic high point was her final song in the revue, 'I'm a Little Blackbird Looking for a Bluebird'. This exquisitely beautiful number became Mills's impassioned plea for racial tolerance.[41]

Several scenes and songs in *Dixie to Broadway* reinforce negative stereotypes, especially as the show was created by whites for whites. According to Egan, Leslie would have argued that this was a commercial decision, since such scenes were 'stock-in-trade' and what his white audiences were paying to see. Mills did not express any views on the issue publicly, though she did say that Black critics tended to be too generous in their praise for Black shows.[42] It is entirely possible that Mills was not in a position where she

[39] 'Little Colored Artiste a Big Hit', uncited article, MG 599, Professional Papers, Scrapbook, box 2, Helen Armstead-Johnson Theater Collection/Florence Mills Papers, Schomburg Center for Research in Black Culture, NYPL.
[40] Egan, *Florence Mills*, 110.   [41] Egan, *Florence Mills*, 110–111.
[42] Egan, *Florence Mills*, 122.

could express her true thoughts, for she was a Black woman working in a white, male-dominated industry. Furthermore, Leslie had provided employment for a significant number of Black performers in his revue, something he had promised Mills he would do.[43] She may have felt that any negative remarks could have been seen as damaging to the producer behind her success.

Dorothy Dickson Returns in *Patricia*

A star vehicle of a very different sort opened on 31 October at His Majesty's Theatre in London. *Patricia* featured the American-born Dorothy Dickson (1893–1995) of Winter Garden Theatre fame in the title role (see Chapter 2). Produced and directed by Charlot-protégé Dion Titheradge (1889–1934), the musical comedy featured book and lyrics by Denis Mackail, music by Geoffrey Gwyther and additional lyrics by Greatrex Newman.

Dickson (see Plate 14) played a young American woman who comes to England to live with her wealthy uncle, Augustus Wentworth (played by Arthur Chesney), and his family. After a raucous party, Patricia's cousin, Elizabeth (played by Mary Leigh), cannot find her diamond bracelet. Furthermore, her uncle's secret plans for his latest invention – one that will make him and his partner very wealthy – also disappear. To find the missing items, the Wentworths hire the bumbling detective Peter Rumble (played by Ambrose Manning), who is comically assisted by Augustus's worldly secretary, Miss Smythe (played by Cicely Debenham). Suspicion falls on Patricia, especially after she is seen in an amorous embrace with her driving instructor. It turns out that the instructor, John Bradshaw (played by Philip Simmons), had been an engineering student in the United States and that he and Patricia had been romantically involved. After their unexpected reunion, the two immediately marry. Elizabeth's smarmy suitor Ogden Scales (played by Billy Leonard) realizes that he accidentally scooped up the plans for the invention along with some other papers, and Elizabeth finds her bracelet. John, meanwhile, is still accused of stealing the plans for the invention, since Rumble uncovered a copy of them in his house. Finally, it is revealed that Augustus and John have been developing a wireless television, which is why John had a copy of the plans, and that a prototype is underway.

---

[43] Egan, *Florence Mills*, 123.

Musical highlights included John's wistful waltz 'If I Had Only Known' and Patricia and John's perky 'Every Second Monday', in which they imagine their own version of domestic bliss (a popular theme in 1924 musicals). Cicely Debenham (1891–1955), as Miss Smythe, provided the show's comic numbers, including the delightfully droll 'Finish Your Education', in which she encourages Elizabeth's friends to go to London to learn what they really need to know, such as how to smoke and drink, and 'Millions of Men', added after the show opened, in which she offers one extraordinarily racist description after another of the various men she's encountered.

Thus, in the latter part of September and throughout October, audiences were treated to a variety of new offerings. The co-existence of revues that focused on performers or bodies, operettas with added political resonances and musical comedies that went beyond the overused plots continued to draw audiences to theatres in London, New York, Budapest and elsewhere.

12 | November Pairings

Many of the musicals that opened in November exhibited some sort of paired connection, whether it was between players and producers, adapted works and their sources or different takes on the same genre. When one of these shows opened, another was often lurking in the background, visible or not. It was an eventful month, and Adele and Fred Astaire, along with the Gershwins, would have been keenly observing what was happening around them on Broadway as they were preparing for their new musical to open at the start of the next month.

Two Stars and Two Star Vehicles: *Annie Dear* and *Peter Pan*

The same day that US President Calvin Coolidge was re-elected to office (4 November), Billie Burke (1884–1970), the dramatic actress married to Florenz Ziegfeld (1867–1932), opened in her first leading role in a musical: the title character in *Annie Dear*. Two days later, Ziegfeld's former headliner Marilyn Miller (1898–1936) debuted in her first leading dramatic part, the title role in *Peter Pan*. This was an especially curious juxtaposition, for it was as if each actor was staking a claim in the other's theatrical territory. Burke was known for her acting, not her dancing and singing, so her appearance in a musical might have surprised some. Miller, on the other hand, was known for her dancing and singing, not her acting, so taking on a role that Maude Adams had made iconic carried a substantial amount of professional risk.

Ziegfeld was, as one would expect, a central figure in the story, as was his rival Charles B. Dillingham (1868–1934). On 17 December 1923, Miller's lawyers sent a telegram to the New York newspapers stating: 'Miss Marilynn Miller has authorized us to announce that she has cancelled her contract with Mr. Florenz Ziegfeld and will not appear again under his management.' Ziegfeld responded with his own telegram to the papers later in the evening: 'If that statement is any satisfaction to her, I am satisfied. I simply refer to my letter to her attorneys, dated last Friday, and ask them to publish it.' *The New York Times* concluded its coverage with mentions of ongoing problems between Miller and Ziegfeld, including his 'alleged interference' when she married the actor Jack Pickford several years earlier.[1] The next day, the *Times* reported that Ziegfeld's office said it was 'professional jealousy' toward Mary Eaton, who was appearing in *Kid Boots*, that brought about Miller's departure from Ziegfeld.[2] As 1924 progressed, Miller was missing the stage terribly and knew she needed to find another producer to promote her, and that producer would be Dillingham.

Dillingham, though, was having problems of his own. His wife, the former Eileen Ann Kearney, a dancer, had become romantically involved with another man. The Dillinghams divorced in August, and Eileen re-married in October. To complicate matters, the former Mrs Dillingham and Billie Burke were lifelong friends. Thus, there must have been some level of recompense for Dillingham in that he could feature Ziegfeld's former favourite, Miller, in one of his own productions.

The multi-talented Clare Kummer (1873–1958) was working in the Dillingham fold when Ziegfeld contracted her to create *Annie Dear* as a vehicle for Burke. The previous year, Kummer had adapted Maurice Yvain's *opérette Ta bouche* for Dillingham as *One Kiss* (see Chapter 2), and at the time was preparing another adaptation for Dillingham, *Madame Pompadour*. Kummer wrote the libretto, the music and the lyrics for *Annie Dear*, basing the story on one of her own comic plays, the popular *Good Gracious Annabelle* from 1916.

The play's premise is that the title character, Annie Leigh, has been separated from her husband for so long that she doesn't recognize him when he re-enters her life. Years earlier, in the western part of the USA, as her father was dying, a bearded man kidnapped Annie and took her to his cave. He brought in someone to marry them, after which she escaped. Her unknown husband tracked her down and sends her money every three months, which she receives through an agent. She enjoys the high life and, having spent her entire allowance and still in need of money, she and a group of her friends take jobs at the estate of James Wimbledon, all under assumed names. None of them have any experience at their new jobs, which leads to plenty of comic mishaps. Visiting the estate is John Rawson, whom Annie had already noticed in town. She fantasizes about marrying him, but her western marriage, and its monetary benefit, keep her from pursuing the daydream. She is disappointed to learn, and likewise comforted in a strange way, that Rawson is also married. Relief and joy come in the play when Rawson tells Annie that he is man who rescued her

[1] 'Marilynn Miller, Star of "Sally", Quits', *New York Times*, 18 December 1923.
[2] 'Thinks Actress Jealous', *New York Times*, 19 December 1923.

(not kidnapped her) from what appeared to be a desperate situation all those years ago and that they are in fact already married to each other. He has reformed his ways, is now a wealthy mine owner and – importantly – has shaved his beard. Kummer included three of her own songs, all in a domestic parlour style, in the play – 'Somebody's Eyes', 'Other Eyes' and 'Just You and I' – each of which was published separately.

Transforming the play into a Ziegfeld musical spectacle meant that a lot of music had to be added. There's no evidence that any of the three songs Kummer included in *Good Gracious Annabelle* made it into *Annie Dear*. Ziegfeld, though, thought that Kummer's score for his wife's musical debut needing bolstering, so he brought in Sigmund Romberg and Clifford Grey to create several additional songs for the show.

When it comes to the storyline, Kummer expanded Annabelle's circle of friends. Among the new characters is Twilly, who is in charge of the servants at the Wimbledon estate. Twilly was played by the character actor Bobby Watson (1888–1965), who scored tremendous success as the over-the-top faux-French dressmaker 'Madame Lucy' in *Irene* (1919). That role was probably performed as an effete gay man, endorsing negative stereotypes. This characterization was continued in *Annie Dear*, for Wimbledon at one point tells Twilly that he thought he was a woman. Twilly responds that he actually is a cowboy who fell off his horse, broke his voice and became a costume designer and interior decorator.[3] Further gay stereotypes are thus presented, namely a distinctive voice and a career in design. Twilly is also a playwright, and his woodland fantasy, 'Rainbow's End',[4] becomes the extended final sequence in *Annie Dear* in which Annie's friends, as well as Wimbledon and his 'real' employees, take on costumed roles. There's more to Twilly, for he confesses to Annie that he was one of the ruffians who carried her from her father's cabin. This shows Twilly as a character who goes beyond stereotype.

The extended 'Rainbow's End' sequence, subtitled 'A Comedy Fantasy – Words and Music by Clare Kummer' in the playbill, evokes a gentle panto spirit with its nursery-rhyme characters, including Little Boy Blue (played by Burke as Annie) and a giant who holds the gold at the end of the rainbow (played by Marion Green as Rawson). In the final tableau, the giant, wearing a fake beard, is holding Little Boy Blue, who has fainted.

---

[3] Clare Kummer, 'Annie Dear Script', *T-Mss 2001–0004, box 1, folder 4, Victor Finizio Research Materials on Clare Kummer, Billy Rose Theatre Collection, NYPL.

[4] The title of the sequence carries a meaning today that wouldn't have been there in 1924, for the eight-colour Rainbow Flag, a symbol of the LGBTQ community, didn't come into existence until 1978.

Annie looks up and, thanks to the beard, recognizes the man who is holding her as her husband. The denouement, which becomes like that in *Good Gracious Annabelle*, now ends with Annie's delight at already being married to the man she loves. Billie Burke, as the star, gets the last word.

'Rainbow's End' functions in the same way as its precedent in *Kid Boots*: a revue-style 'show-within-the-show' to allow Ziegfeld spectacle to feature in a book musical. Not all found it effective, with one critic noting that 'the whimsey becomes heavy-handed and persistent: 'Oh, look, how fanciful and fantastic we are', Miss Kummer seems to say, and she raises her voice a little. That is a mistake. You must never shout at a fantasy.'[5]

Since Burke was not primarily a singer, the score conveniently avoids her having any solo numbers. She instead has three duets: two with Rawson and one with Wimbledon. The last, it so happens, is the title song. Its legato, mostly step-wise melody features a gradual overall ascent, an indication of Annie's sense of optimism. The song's charm led to it being recorded in a foxtrot instrumental version by Fred Waring and the Pennsylvanians.[6]

So as not to make the fact that the star of the musical does not have any solo songs too obvious, Rawson only gets one, and it wasn't by Kummer but rather by Romberg and Grey: 'Whisper to Me'. Perhaps not surprisingly, given that this was a Ziegfeld production with a star not famous for her singing, most songs are ensemble numbers of various sorts, many of which feature Twilly. Since Twilly has written the show-within-the-show, his abilities as a performer can easily become part of his character.

The Ziegfeld production sequence at the show's end is not the only self-referential nod to the man behind the musical. *Annie Dear* opens with a sort of metatheatrical scene in a ticket line for Broadway shows. *Kid Boots* and the *Follies* are sold out – both Ziegfeld shows – and when someone asks about *Annie Dear*, the ticket agent gleefully responds, 'Not till next year! All sold out!'[7] The line reflected a bit of hopeful hyperbole, for *Annie Dear* only played to the end of January 1925 and actually closed before *Kid Boots*.

The critics adored Billie Burke, even though several did note her small-sized voice. Kelcey Allen, for example, opined,

Billie Burke never looked so beautiful or so slender as she did last night, and her performance as Annabelle Leigh was delightful. The part gives her faunlike grace and effervescent personality full scope. She does not possess a powerful singing

---

[5] Heywood Broun, 'Seeing Things at Night', syndicated column, *Boston Globe*, 16 November 1924, newspapers.com.

[6] Victor 19544, recorded 9 December 1924.   [7] Kummer, 'Annie Dear Script'.

voice when she sings, but she renders her songs in a pleasing manner. Whether she sings or acts, Billie Burke is fascinating.[8]

Burke herself was far more candid: '[T]he plain truth of the matter is that I did not have enough voice really to do my share musically. I could sing smaller songs successfully enough, but the burden of carrying a big musical with whopping big song numbers is one that can be hoisted only by professional singers with voices like pipe organs.'[9] Burke carried no delusions about not being in that category (see Plate 15).

Her charm carried far beyond the footlights. The reviewer for the *New York Post* revelled in the star's glory, especially in the final scene:

If there has been anything more gloriously beautiful than Billie Burke as Little Boy Blue in the final scene on this stage in years it has been outside of this town. She certainly topped all the Ziegfeld beauties that manager has ever given us. . . .

A word about the settings. The scenic effects were artistic and restful in their colorings and the gowns – they were gowns – were in exquisite taste. . . . It was a real Ziegfeld finale, full of color and beauty, with Billie Burke, in that wonderful Gainsborough 'Blue Boy' dress, a perfect picture in a perfect setting.[10]

With the gowns 'in exquisite taste' – created by the New York fashion salon owner Madame Frances (Spingold) – and the 'gloriously beautiful' Billie Burke, one almost cannot help but think of Burke's entrance in what became her most famous role: Glinda in the 1939 film *The Wizard of Oz*. Could Kummer's sylvan caprice in *Annie Dear*, with Karl Koeck's evocative scenic designs, have served in some way as a precursor for those iconic first impressions of Oz? Or, as theatre historian Ethan Mordden ponders, could they have been not-so-subtle competition to the fantastic Never Land sets in J. M. Barrie's *Peter Pan*, which was playing down the street at the Knickerbocker Theatre, starring Ziegfeld's former favourite and now Billie Burke's rival, Marilyn Miller?[11]

The revival of *Peter Pan*, which was decidedly not a musical, opened at the Knickerbocker Theatre on 6 November. J. M. Barrie's play debuted at the Duke of York's Theatre in London on 27 December 1904 and became a hit in New York the following year with the legendary Maude Adams (1872–1953). Barrie's play did not feature any songs, though John Crook did write

---

[8] Kelcey Allen, 'Dainty Billie Burke Shines in Georgeous [sic] Musical Play', uncited clipping, *T-Mss 1987–010, Series III: Clippings, box 14, folder 1, Flo Ziegfeld-Billie Burke Papers, Billy Rose Theatre Collection, NYPL.

[9] Billie Burke , with Cameron Shipp, *With a Feather on My Nose* (London: Peter Davies, 1950), 171.

[10] Uncited article, 'The Play', *New York Post*, 5 November 1924, *T-Mss 1987–010, Series III; Clippings, Box 14, folder 1, Flo Ziegfeld-Billie Burke Papers, NYPL.

[11] Ethan Mordden, *Ziegfeld: The Man Who Invented Show Business* (New York: St. Martin's, 2008), 219.

incidental music for the original production. (Crook's music was used in the 1924 revival.) Until 1924, Adams had been the only person to play Peter Pan on Broadway, with revivals in 1912 and 1915. Barrie wanted to do one more revival with Adams, but she was in her early fifties and happy to pass along the role. It was Dillingham who suggested to Miller that she play Peter Pan, to which she agreed and of which Barrie approved.

Miller was a brilliant dancer who possessed a great deal of classic femininity. These attributes, which would be assets in other contexts, proved detrimental to her success in *Peter Pan*. Two dances were added to the production expressly for her: 'Indian Dance' in Act 2 and 'Pillow Dance' in Act 3. Both were arranged by the noted Russian ballet dancer and choreographer Alexis Kosloff (*c.*1888–1983), who at the time was working with the Metropolitan Opera Company. The two dances, as would be expected, exuded a tone of refinement and were brilliantly performed. This was exactly what bothered so many observers: 'There are few in all the world who can dance like Marilyn Miller, and Peter Pan should not be one of them. He dances because he is happy and gay and not because he has been to a ballet school.'[12] The polished performances seemed overly out of character for the boy who won't grow up. Apparently, it was too much of a stretch for audiences to imagine the dazzling former Ziegfeld star as a boy.

There were other fundamental problems. Many reviewers were aghast at a children's fantasy being turned into a vehicle for a musical comedy star. But audiences loved Marilyn Miller. When she'd get stuck flying over the middle rows of the orchestra, which happened more than once, she'd start laughing and the audience would join in.[13] Another indication of her public adoration was the song 'Peter Pan (I Love You)' by Robert King and Ray Henderson. The adoring tribute to the actor who played the role is not brilliant in terms of music or lyrics, unlike the cover (see Plate 16), for here is Miller at her most enchanting as Peter Pan.

Annie Dear played its last performance on 31 January 1925, and *Peter Pan* followed two weeks later, on 14 February 1925. While both stars were praised for their willingness to expand their horizons, the general consensus was that they were better off as they were: Burke in drama and Miller in musical comedy. Once they returned to their respective domains, their careers continued to flourish.

---

[12] Heywood Broun, 'Seeing Things at Night', syndicated column, *Boston Globe*, 16 November 1924, newspapers.com.

[13] Harris, *The Other Marilyn*, 127.

Another Sort of Adaptation: Zarzuela in London

When *The First Kiss* opened at the New Oxford Theatre on 10 November, it was the first time an English-language adaptation of a Spanish zarzuela had played in London. *The First Kiss* was a radically altered version of Pablo Luna's *El asombro de Damasco* (The Wonder of Damascus), a success when it opened in Madrid in 1916. Antonio Paso and Joaquín Abati's Orientalist libretto tells the tale of Zobeida, who comes to Damascus to ask a doctor to whom her husband loaned money years ago to repay the debt, since her husband is ill and needs to pay for a cure. In response, the doctor, the Cadi of Damascus and the Grand Vizier all show sexual interest in Zobeida. Following the advice of a passing Dervish, Zobeida invites all three men to a banquet at the home of her friend Fahima without telling any of them that she has also invited the other two. As the suitors arrive and discover that they won't be spending the evening alone with Zobeida, a nefarious outlaw captures the house. All three men plead for mercy from the masked intruder. Zobeida, however, recognizes him as the Dervish who suggested the ploy. When he reveals himself to be the Caliph, who has been travelling throughout his kingdom *incognito*, he strips the lust-seeking trio of their titles and wealth, only to bestow the latter on Zobeida, whom he calls 'the wonder of Damascus'.

The score, as musical theatre historian Andrew Lamb and zarzuela scholar Christopher Webber have shown, leans towards the sound worlds of Edwardian musical comedy and French cabaret and tends to minimize the traditional dance rhythms associated with zarzuela. This suggests that the zarzuela's creators, from the beginning, could have been envisioning a London transfer.[14] This makes sense in the transnational world of musical theatre before and after the Great War, where, as we've seen, bringing continental operettas to London and New York was big business.

In 1922, plans to bring *El asombro de Damasco* to the United Kingdom were well underway. The American-born impresario William J. Wilson (*c*.1873–1936) committed to producing the work, renamed *The First Kiss*. Boyle Lawrence (1869–1951), a former journalist and drama critic, crafted the book and lyrics, which were said to come 'from the Spanish of Paso Y Abati'. The issue here is that no single individual named Paso Y Abati exists. Antonio Paso and Joaquín Abati were two separate people, and in Spanish 'y' means 'and', and at some point, the two surnames were fused,

---

[14] Andrew Lamb and Christopher Webber, *'De Madrid a Londres': Pablo Luna's English Operetta 'The First Kiss'* (London: Couthurst Press, 2016), 3–4.

along with a middle initial, to create a 'new' librettist, who in some places was even called 'Paso Y. Abati'.

As required by law, a script for *The First Kiss* was submitted to the Lord Chamberlain's Office for approval before it could be staged, and a licence was granted on 18 December 1922. On 1 January 1923, *The First Kiss* opened at the Harrogate Opera house in Yorkshire. From evidence in the typescript, Lawrence kept some of the basic plot points, such as having various suitors vying for Lalila (formerly Zobeida)'s attention at the home of Fateema (formerly Fahima), a widowed beauty specialist. Significantly, though, the entire action was moved to Seville, and Lalila is now single, which means she can be matched with a re-envisioned third suitor, the Caliph's son, and the show, called 'a comedy operetta', can now have the romantic happy ending that English audiences would expect.

By moving the action to Spain, the operetta's exotic elements were refocused. No longer is the Orientalist realm the chief domain but rather Spain. Those very Spanish aspects that Luna, Paso and Abati had tried to minimize in *El asombro de Damasco* were now being foregrounded.[15] This change could well have been done to lessen the work's overt comparisons with the Orientalist hit *Chu Chin Chow*, along with the play *Kismet* and the various *Arabian Nights* pantomimes. Wilson and Lawrence may have thought that the imaginary of the Middle East had oversaturated the West End.

The new script required far more music than the original.[16] Hence, interpolations by various songwriters were added, including from Luna himself. Lamb and Webber suggest that some of the music Luna wrote for *The First Kiss*, including the trio 'Laws of the Prophet', travelled back to Spain to appear in his zarzuela *Benamor* that same year.[17] Such connections mark a fascinating cultural exchange in both directions between Spain and the United Kingdom.

To bring the newly created love story to life, Wilson secured two exceptional singers for the romantic leads. Désirée Ellinger (1893–1951), who played Lalila, was a noted opera singer perhaps most famously known for singing the title role in Puccini's *Madama Butterfly* with Thomas Beecham's opera company. The light opera baritone Gregory Stroud (1892–1974) played the Caliph's son. He had toured Australia in the

---

[15] Lamb and Webber, *'De Madrid a Londres'*, 17.

[16] Andrew Lamb and Christopher Webber, "'*The First Kiss*" – Pablo Luna's English Musical', www.zarzuela.net/ref/feat/first-kiss.htm, 21 September 2016, accessed 1 April 2022.

[17] Lamb and Webber, *'De Madrid a Londres'*, 19–21.

Orientalist fantasy *Chu Chin Chow* and, in 1922, appeared opposite Ellinger in Adrian Beecham's opera *The Merchant of Venice*.

The First Kiss toured until early April 1923, when some of its cast, including Ellinger, moved to another Wilson touring production, *The Early Girl*,[18] until *The First Kiss* tour resumed that August. Another hiatus came in February 1924, when, as previously, company members joined other Wilson-produced tours. Ellinger took on the title role in Kálmán's *The Gipsy Princess*.

On 10 November, *The First Kiss* opened in London at the New Oxford Theatre. The plot bore little resemblance to what had been submitted to the Lord Chamberlain's Office nearly two years before, and even less to the Spanish original.[19] Before the action begins, the infants Princess Mariposa (the former Lalila character) and Prince Nurriden, son of the Tunis-based Caliph, were promised to each other in marriage. The infant princess was kidnapped, taken to Seville and sold into slavery. Given her name, which means butterfly, we know that her true identity and destiny will ultimately emerge. (Lamb and Webber suggest that her name may refer to Ellinger's most celebrated role as Madama Butterfly.[20]) Now a young adult, Prince Nurriden travels to Spain on a pilgrimage and falls for a woman he purchases in Seville's Square of the Crooked Streets. The horrific practice of human trafficking is glossed over in the libretto. The pair fall in love while the two remaining suitors from the earlier versions now vie for Fateema. The villainous pirate Zu-far surrounds and invades Fateema's house, and when the Caliph arrives Zu-far is able to save himself through a deus ex machina reminiscent of Gilbert and Sullivan by revealing that Mariposa is the long-lost princess betrothed to the infant prince.

Continuing and furthering operetta tropes, the love duets for the romantic leads in *The First Kiss* are waltzes. Their first kiss becomes the basis for the Act 1 finale, where it is inspires a luxuriant duet with chorus, 'The First Kiss of Delight', that simultaneously evokes the expansiveness of a ballad with the sweeping flow of a waltz.[21] Other waltz duets include Act 1's 'Kismet, 'tis Written', the title of which includes a reference to one of the most famous Orientalist plays of the era, and Act 2's 'A Thing of Dreams',

---

[18] Lamb and Webber, *'De Madrid a Londres'*, 6. For a list of all tour dates, see Lamb and Webber, *'De Madrid a Londres'*, 28.

[19] No scripts are known to survive for the 1924 version. The plot description comes from press reports and information included on programmes.

[20] Lamb and Webber, *'De Madrid a Londres'*, 7.

[21] This effect is accomplished through the number's 12/8 time signature. The four beats per measure suggest the ballad, while the triple division of each beat evokes the flavour of a waltz.

in which Luna creates a faint sense of expanse through the use of hemiola. Critics noted the score's cosmopolitan style and comparative absence of Spanish clichés. One wrote, 'Hardly, indeed, does the composer give us more than a fugitive hint here and there of anything suggesting Spanish rhythms.'[22] Even if the music itself did revel in ethnic identifiers, sheet music covers certainly did. There, a woman is shown in Spanish costume, and her veil adds a sense of mystery and Otherness. The phrase 'from the Spanish' further cements the work's distinctive origin.

The First Kiss played a six-week, forty-three performance limited run in London (see Plate 17). During its second week, *Tatler* reported it was to play only another four weeks, after which it was supposed to transfer to the USA.[23] Wilson also produced in the USA, so the transfer, though it didn't happen, was plausible. Furthermore, as was often the case in December, theatres would be booked well in advance for seasonal pantomimes.[24] Rather than going to the USA, *The First Kiss* toured the United Kingdom until April 1925, with stops in Stoke Newington, Southport, Manchester and Birmingham.

With *The First Kiss* being so different from *El asombro de Damasco*, Lamb and Webber ask if it really is an adaptation.[25] Aside from some of the music, the source had indeed become nearly unrecognizable.

Madame Pompadour Goes to Broadway

From its Berlin premiere in 1922, Leo Fall's *Madame Pompadour* was a box office smash. Productions opened all over Europe, and the British adaptation starring Evelyn Laye (see Chapter 3) delighted audiences throughout 1924. Among those who adored the London production was the New York producer Martin Beck (1868–1940). After seeing other productions on the continent he decided to open his eponymous theatre at 302 West 45th Street with the sumptuous operetta.[26]

In 1924, Beck was at a professional crossroads. He'd achieved theatrical prestige and prominence in the early decades of the century as a booking manager and eventually head of the Orpheum Circuit, an important network of vaudeville theatres spread across the USA. Decades of leadership come with a price, even if Harry Houdini is one of your star

---

[22] 'New Oxford Theatre: "The First Kiss"', *Daily Telegraph* (London), 11 November 1924.
[23] Lamb and Webber, 'De Madrid a Londres', 9.
[24] *Dick Whittington* came to the New Oxford.
[25] Lamb and Webber, 'De Madrid a Londres', 25.   [26] In 2024, it is the Al Hirschfield Theatre.

attractions. In 1923, a boardroom coup resulted in Beck being deposed as the organization's president. Needing to redefine himself, and knowing the commercial appeal of operetta adaptations, Beck sought to make himself known as a purveyor of operettas. His hope was that *Madame Pompadour* would solidify his reputation in that realm.

Beck faced four significant challenges in bringing *Madame Pompadour* to New York. First, Charles B. Dillingham, who also realized the potential appeal of *Madame Pompadour* for North American audiences, had already secured the US rights to Fall's operetta. Dillingham had hoped to bring it to New York during the 1923–1924 season, but when he couldn't cast the demanding title role, he decided to wait.[27] Beck knew he could solve the rights problem. He approached Dillingham about co-producing the operetta, and Dillingham agreed.

Second was the book. Beck and Dillingham seemed to have been unable to secure the rights to the English translation by Frederick Lonsdale and Harry Graham that was playing in London. This problem, like the first, was solvable. The producers commissioned a new adaptation from Clare Kummer.

A third challenge concerned Leo Fall (1873–1925), the composer. Fall travelled to New York for rehearsals and reportedly to conduct performances. This was Fall's first trip to the USA, and, according to Fall's biographer Stefan Frey, Fall thoroughly enjoyed the lifestyle of an international artiste who would make appearances at performances of his works.[28] *Madame Pompadour* provided him with the opportunity to do so in New York. Rehearsals did not go smoothly. Fall didn't like one particular scene and voiced his concern. Beck rose and asked who was interfering. After being told 'the composer Leo Fall', Beck is said to have given Fall a disapproving look along with the curt reply, 'The composer has nothing to say.'[29] According to press reports, Fall, extremely angry at Beck's dismissive treatment, stomped out, breaking his hat on the way. Beck, in response, refused to allow the composer entrance into his new namesake theatre.[30] (A similar incident took place during the rehearsals of *Pippin* in Washington, DC, where the show's director, Bob Fosse, barred its composer, Stephen Schwartz.[31])

---

[27] Leo A. Marsh, 'Much-Sought-For Title Role of "Pompadour" Goes to Hope Hampton', 5 August 1924, incomplete citation, T-Mss 1952–002, box 62, Madame Pompadour Scrapbook, R. H. Burnside Collection, Billy Rose Theatre Collection, NYPL.

[28] Frey, *Leo Fall*, 196.   [29] Frey, *Leo Fall*, 196–197.

[30] James Muir, 'Public alone is master of stage tastes', *Dayton Daily News*, 30 November 1924, newspapers.com.

[31] Paul R. Laird, *The Musical Theatre of Stephen Schwartz: From 'Godspell' to 'Wicked' and Beyond* (Lanham: Rowman & Littlefield, 2014), 360.

The fourth challenge was casting the title role. Many singers were rumoured to have been considered, including Metropolitan Opera star Geraldine Farrar and Fritzi Massary, the original Madame in Berlin.[32] Eventually, the silent film starlet Hope Hampton (1897–1982) was chosen, and her debut on the live musical stage was eagerly anticipated. Could she sing? Hampton had already been contracted to star in an English-language version of Franz Lehár's *Cloclo*, which had opened in Vienna in February (see Chapter 6).[33] Hampton was released from *Cloclo* in order to appear in *Madame Pompadour*, and the planned Broadway production of *Cloclo* never materialized.

According to reviews for the operetta's two-week pre-Broadway tryout in Philadelphia, Hampton's dynamic stage presence made up for any problems with her singing.[34] She was, after all, a film actress, which at the time meant she would have relied heavily on physical gesture as a means of expression. But problems were mounting. On 7 November, just four days before the New York premiere, Hampton was informed that the following evening's performance, the last in Philadelphia, would also be hers in *Madame Pompadour*. This must not have come as a complete surprise, for one newspaper account mentioned that Hampton's husband, Jules Brulatour, had asked some theatrical friends to come watch the show in Philadelphia so that they could offer expert testimony in court, should it become necessary. Brulatour promised 'fireworks' over his wife's dismissal.[35] None happened, at least publicly.

Hampton's replacement was Wilda Bennett (1894–1967), star of two previous operetta adaptations: *The Riviera Girl* (1917, an adaptation of Emmerich Kálmán's *Die Csárdásfürstin*) and *The Lady in Ermine* (1922, an adaptation of Jean Gilbert's *Die Frau im Hermelin*). Those roles lie closer to musical comedy than continental operetta, and the vocal demands of *Madame Pompadour* seemed to exceed Bennett's abilities. The critic Helen Klumph remarked, 'It is a part that would tax the powers of a Jeritza so it is not surprising that a newcomer proved unsatisfactory in the role.'[36]

---

[32] Frey, *Leo Fall*, 195.

[33] Uncited article, 'Hope Hampton is to appear in "Clo-Clo" and Leo A. Marsh, 'Much-Sought-For Title Role of "Pompadour" Goes to Hope Hampton', 5 August 1924, incomplete citation, Madame Pompadour Scrapbook.

[34] '"Madame Pompadour" Arrives in America', *Evening Ledger* (Philadelphia), 28 October 1924, Madame Pompadour Scrapbook.

[35] 'Out of Opera', *Buffalo Times*, 9 November 1924, newspapers.com.

[36] Helen Klumph, 'Play Premiere without Hope', *Los Angeles Times*, 16 November 1924.

As for the work itself, Philadelphia critics lauded Fall's music, and Kummer's book garnered generally good reviews. Linton Martin, writing for the *Philadelphia North American*, wrote, 'First attention is devoted to the music, because it is the outstanding feature of the production. But high commendation must follow closely for Clare Kummer's felicitous adaption of the book and lyrics.'[37] He was glad that Kummer hadn't succumbed to any of the 'heavy handedness and boiler plate obviousness'[38] that other adapters infused into their work. Other reviewers were more guarded about the book, though they still appreciated its merits. They offered comments such as, 'Some of the numbers she has translated delightfully, but in attempting to remove the ultra-raciness she has made certain portions rather milk-and-water.'[39] One instance of this 'milk-and-water' occurs in Act 2's 'Serenade', when the soldiers (the male chorus) sing to the title character. In the British version, which follows the German original, the soldiers pine to see her 'dear little garter'. In Kummer's version, they only ask her to save them a kiss. Such softening of sexual references was not unique to *Madame Pompadour*. New York critics, however, heaped heavy criticism on the book, something that hadn't happened in Philadelphia. The main reason behind this, according to a letter from the German theatrical agent Hans Bartsch to Dillingham, was because so many scenes had been cut.[40] The critics simply did not see the totality of Kummer's work.

The Dillingham–Beck production of *Madame Pompadour* lasted just eighty performances. Nonetheless, the New York production of *Madame Pompadour* holds a significant place in the performance history of the popular operetta. The 11 January 1925 performance, since it started five hours after its sister in London, became the 10,000th performance of any version of the work to be seen worldwide. London would have staged number 9,999. According to the press release, 78 different companies had performed *Madame Pompadour* since its Berlin premiere in 1922,[41] and it was the New York one that reached a performance milestone.

---

[37] Linton Martin, 'Forrest: Hope Hampton Emerges as Prima Donna in "Mme. Pompadour"', *Philadelphia North American*, 28 October 1924, Madame Pompadour Scrapbook.

[38] Martin, 'Forrest: Hope Hampton'

[39] 'Waters', uncited review, 'Madame Pompadour', Madame Pompadour Scrapbook.

[40] Hans Bartsch, typed letter to Charles Dillingham, 4 December 1924, Correspondence, 1924–1926, Box 24, A-E, Charles B. Dillingham Papers. Manuscripts and Archives Division. The New York Public Library. Astor, Lenox, and Tilden Foundations.

[41] '"Pompadour" Played 10,000 Times by 78 Companies', *Graphic*, 12 January 1925, Madame Pompadour Scrapbook.

A London Revue and Two New York Musical Comedies Round Out the Month

As the month drew to a close, London theatre-goers were elated when the Russian–French touring revue *La Chauve-Souris* (The Bat) landed at the Strand Theatre on 24 November for four weeks. Directed by Nikita Balieff, who also acted as emcee and introduced each segment, most of the company's material originated from its early days in Russia prior to the 1917 Revolution. Like other revues, this one included material from earlier incarnations alongside new sketches and songs. The audience favourite 'The Parade of the Wooden Soldiers', performed to Leon Jessel's 'Die Parade der Zinnsoldaten' (The Parade of the Tin Soldiers), was a highlight, as was a musical retelling of the 'Legend of the Volga'. Here was Russian culture being performed in its glamourous splendour.

In New York, a pair of musical comedies opened on successive evenings. First was *My Girl* on 24 November at the Vanderbilt Theatre. With a slight book and lyrics by Harlan Thompson (1890–1966) and music by Harry Archer (1888–1960), it was in essence a revue-like string of comic scenes and sprightly songs. The unifying thread concerned a family from Omaha, Nebraska (the Astaires' home town) who want to join New York's swanky Rainbow Club. They host a party, which has to be dry because of Prohibition and is utterly boring until a bootlegger (played to great delight by Roger Gray) arrives and needs a place to hide fourteen cases of Scotch. Of course, one of the cases finds its way into the party. The score's hit was 'You and I', whose descending scalar melody over a rhythmically active accompaniment accounted in part for its popularity on dance floors and on record.[42]

The Magnolia Lady, with book and lyrics by Anne Caldwell (1867–1936) and music by Harold Levey (1894–1967), opened at the Shubert Theatre the next evening. It was based on A. E. Thomas's 1916 play *Come Out of the Kitchen*, a dramatization of Alice Duer Miller's novel of the same name. In the musical comedy, a proud but impoverished Virginia family, the Ravenels, must lease their mansion and then become servants in the household of the Englishman who becomes their landlord. The romantic leads – Ruth Chatterton (1893–1961) as Lily-Lou Ravenel and Ralph Forbes (1904–1951) as

---

[42] Jack Shilkret recorded 'You and Me' on 23 January 1925, on Victor 19571.

the Englishman Kenneth Craig – were both known as dramatic actors. Critics noted that they were following in the footsteps of Madge Kennedy (in *Poppy*) and Billie Burke (in *Annie Dear*) as dramatic actors taking on leading roles in musicals and agreed that both were better suited for spoken plays, although they sang and danced just fine.[43]

[43] Burns Mantle, 'The Magnolia Lady and Ruth Chatterton', *Daily News* (New York), 26 November 1924, newspapers.com.

PART IV

From December Onwards

The First Day of the Last Month of 1924

In many Broadway musicals, 11 o'clock numbers are those dramatically unforgettable star turns that take place as the show approaches its conclusion. They were called this because, with musicals starting at 8:30 and lasting until about 11:30, they generally happened around 11 o'clock. These were often show-stopping songs – literally, the applause would have to subside before the action could continue.

In 1924, the first weekend of December became the 11 o'clock number for that year's musical theatre. Four new musicals opened on Broadway, each of which had its own unmistakable flavour. Each showcased trends that had been appearing throughout the year and brought them into sharp focus.

Three of the year-defining musicals opened on 1 December and the fourth came one day later. First was *Lady, Be Good!*, formerly known as *Black-Eyed Susan*, which opened at the Liberty Theatre with Adele and Fred Astaire playing a sibling dance duo who find themselves in various romantic entanglements. Second was another musical comedy, *Princess April*, this one featuring the well-trodden rags-to-riches scenario, which opened at the Ambassador Theatre. Third was Irving Berlin's *Music Box Revue*, which captivated audiences at the Music Box Theatre. The next evening, the romantic operetta *The Student Prince in Heidelberg*, known more commonly as *The Student Prince*, opened at Jolson's Theatre. Thus, on two successive evenings, Broadway welcomed four quintessential examples of musical theatre: two strikingly different musical comedies, one revue and one operetta.

Musical Comedy, Astaire Style: *Lady, Be Good!*

The synchronous careers of George Gershwin (1898–1937) as musical theatre composer and pianist-composer had remained closely intertwined since the premiere of *Rhapsody in Blue* in February. In November, his latest musical, *Lady, Be Good!*, began its pre-Broadway tour in Philadelphia on 17 November, and just ten days later, on 27 November, he performed his *Rhapsody in Blue* with Paul Whiteman at the Academy of Music in the same city. Then, on 1 December, *Lady, Be Good!* opened at the Liberty Theatre.

Plans for *Lady, Be Good!* were well underway earlier in the year. Gershwin met with the show's stars, Adele and Fred Astaire, when they were all in London that summer, and the producers, the newly formed team of Alex A. Aarons and Vinton Freedley, kept the project moving ahead on both sides of the Atlantic.

In many ways, *Lady, Be Good!* could be thought of as a game of pairs: the stars, Adele and Fred Astaire; the songwriters, George and Ira Gershwin; the producers, Aarons and Freedley; the book writers, Guy Bolton and Fred Thompson; and the two-piano team whose contribution helped define the sound of the work, Victor Arden and Phil Ohman.

Lady, Be Good! crowned the Astaires as Broadway royalty and cemented the Gershwins as a songwriting team. Alex A. Aarons (1890–1943) and Vinton Freedley (1891–1969), well versed in the business and artistic sides of Broadway, had management styles that complemented one another, and their partnership, which began with *Lady, Be Good!*, led to further successes with the Gershwins and others.[1] In 1927, they opened their own Alvin Theatre, its name taken from the first letters of their first names, **Al**ex and **Vin**ton, to promote their own sophisticated brand of musical comedy.

Guy Bolton (1884–1979) had worked with Jerome Kern and P. G. Wodehouse on the famous 'Princess Theatre' musicals in the teens and 1924's *Sitting Pretty* (see Chapter 7), and with Gershwin on *Primrose* (see Chapter 10). He and the London-born librettist and actor Fred Thompson (1884–1949) crafted a book that was erudite without being pretentious and clever without being fussy.

Victor Arden (1893–1962, born Lewis John Fulks) and Phil Ohman (1896–1954, born Fillmore Wellington Ohman) began their work as 'duetting pianists' in 1922 (see Figure 13.1). As members of the orchestra, the sound of the piano, Gershwin's own instrument, was inscribed into the sonic fabric of *Lady, Be Good!* But there was more. During intermission, Arden and Ohman would improvise on tunes introduced in the first half of the show.[2] The pianists also featured prominently in the exit music, which

---

[1] For more Aarons and Freedley, see Jennifer Ashley Tepper and William A. Everett, 'Alexander A. Aarons and Vinton Freedley: The Smart Sophisticates', in *The Palgrave Handbook of Musical Theatre Producers*, ed. Laura MacDonald and William A. Everett (New York: Palgrave Macmillan, 2017), 119–125.

[2] Todd Decker, 'Broadway in Blue: Gershwin's Musical Theater Scores and Songs', in *The Cambridge Companion to Gershwin*, ed. Anna Harwell Celenza (Cambridge: Cambridge University Press, 2019), 93.

Figure 13.1 Victor Arden and Phil Ohman, the 'duetting pianists' of *Lady, Be Good!*
LC.

many in the audience stayed behind to hear. As Fred recalled, 'Often too, when the exit music was completed, Phil and Vic would put on an impromptu concert for the fans who refused to go home. This happened many times and I was convinced that the new sound of Ohman and Arden's two pianos in the pit had a lot to do with the overall success of *Lady, Be Good!*[3] Recapturing this distinctive sound creates some challenges, for, like their intermission features, most of what Arden and Ohman did during the show itself was improvised and therefore very much of the moment and not for posterity.

The dynamic talents of Adele (1896–1981) and Fred (1899–1987) Astaire shaped the essence of *Lady, Be Good!*, though they were surrounded by formidable talent. The siblings played the brother-and-sister dance team Dick and Susie Trevor. Since the Trevors cannot pay their rent, they are

---

[3] Astaire, *Steps in Time*, 129.

kicked out of their apartment thanks to the heiress Josephine Vanderwater (played by Jayne Auburn), who wants Dick to marry her and sees eminent eviction as a way to force him to do so. Dick, of course, is in love with someone else, the down-to-earth Shirley Vernon (played by Kathlene Martyn). Rather than dwell on their misfortune, they sing and dance their optimistic vow of support, 'Hang on to Me', as musical comedy characters are wont to do in such situations. This song is in the mode of other platonic pledges such as 'Someone Loves You After All' from *Kid Boots* (1923) and the classic 'Till the Clouds Roll By' from *Oh, Boy!* (1917).

The Vanderwaters host a glamourous party at which Arden and Ohman showcase their pianistic talents to the diegetic delight of the on-stage guests and the adoring in-theatre audience. The Trevors enter, as does the unscrupulous lawyer J. Watterson Watkins, better known as Watty (played by Walter Catlett). Dick decides to go ahead and marry Jo; Susie vehemently disagrees. Their arguing is interrupted when the party performer Jeff White starts to sing. White was played by audience favourite Cliff Edwards (1895–1971), better known as 'Ukelele Ike' (see Figure 13.2).[4] Playing a performer, Edwards introduces one of the most famous of all Gershwin songs, 'Fascinating Rhythm'. This context matters, for 'Fascinating Rhythm' is presented as a popular song, which it will quickly become.

The rhythmic construction and overlap of melody and accompaniment is, as the title says, fascinating. The refrain is cast in a somewhat unusual AABAAC form, and it is the A section melody that generates a metric layering far more complicated than typical syncopation. The melody here consists of seven half-pulses (six eighth notes plus an eighth rest) that play out over eight half-pulses in the orchestra. Such trickiness, according to Ira's self-reflexive lyric, can threaten a person's sanity. Gershwin had played with such metric layerings elsewhere, including in 'Jijibo' from *Sweet Little Devil*, but here it reaches a new level.

Edwards sang the verse and refrain, accompanying himself on ukulele. The Astaires then joined him for a second refrain before performing their virtuosic dance break. But how does one end such a dynamic showpiece? As Fred recalled, he and Adele needed a 'climax wow step to get us off'. Gershwin came to watch a rehearsal, and as Adele and Fred reached their final move, the composer directed them, 'Now travel – travel with that one'. They began their last step, positioned in the middle of the stage, and kept

---

[4] Edwards is perhaps most famous for voicing Jiminy Cricket in Walt Disney's *Pinocchio* (1940) and introducing the song 'When You Wish Upon a Star'.

Figure 13.2 Cliff Edwardes, 'Ukelele Ike', who introduced 'Fascinating Rhythm' and 'Little Jazz Bird' in *Lady, Be Good!*

repeating it as they travelled to the side and into the wings.[5] Fred described the move:

The step was a complicated precision rhythm thing in which we kicked out simultaneously as we crossed back and forth in front of each other with arm pulls and heads back. There was a lot going on, and when George suggested traveling, we didn't think it was possible.[6]

But this was the Astaires, so of course it was possible.

A mysterious figure then arrives at the party, one who appears destitute (played by Alan Edwards). He professes his love to Susie, and although she has no idea who he is, she is immediately smitten, as they sing in the duet 'So Am I'. Watty, meanwhile, is setting up a scam. If he can find the widow of Jack Robinson, who reportedly has died in Mexico, 'Señora Robinson' will receive a substantial sum, and he, of course, will get a cut. Pedro Manuel Estrada (played by Bryan Lycan) enters, claiming that his sister Juanita is

[5] Astaire, *Steps in Time*, 134.   [6] Astaire, *Steps in Time*, 135.

Jack's widow, and that he has come to collect her inheritance. Watty becomes very worried. Pedro threatens the attorney, who quickly needs to find someone to 'become' Juanita. He hopes Susie might be interested, and tries his best to convince her in the almost title song 'Oh, Lady Be Good'.

With its bluesy and cleverly placed minor chords, 'Oh, Lady Be Good' became another song from *Lady, Be Good!* to become popular in its own right. It undergoes a dramaturgical shift in its presentation as it moves from being closely related the plot – Watty uses it to get Susie to be part of his scheme – to becoming a wholly independent number. As Gershwin scholar Larry Starr has noted, Ira's lyrics start to make less and less sense to the plot as the song morphs into a large-scale production number. It becomes the big moment in the show for Walter Catlett (1889–1960), the superb physical comedian who played Watty (see Figure 13.3).[7] The song-and-dance (literally) works, for

Figure 13.3 Jayne Auburn as Josephine and Walter Catlett as Watty in *Lady, Be Good!*

[7] Larry Starr, *George Gershwin* (New Haven, CT: Yale University Press, 2011), 65–66.

Susie agrees to play Juanita. The job will give her enough money to pay the rent and to keep Dick from having to marry Jo.

Act 2 begins at a swanky hotel. Watty and Susie prepare to put their scheme into action while Dick and Shirley, very much in love, lament Dick having to marry Josephine in the satirical 'The Half of It, Dearie, Blues'. ('You don't know the half of it, dearie' was a phrase popular from Ziegfeld's *Follies* that Ira cleverly used as the verbal hook for the song.[8]) This number, like so much of the show, is significant in that it features Fred's first solo dance routine; all his previous ones had included Adele. While her brother bemoans his fate, Susie entertains the male guests in full costume as Juanita, the pugnacious widow of the presumably deceased Jack. Enter Susie's mysterious suitor, who introduces himself as the very much alive Jack Robinson, with news that he just inherited a fortune from his uncle. Watty's deception is revealed, and Watty and Susie are arrested for fraud. Jack, though, says that Susie didn't deceive anyone, for she really is his wife. Susie is elated.

The final scene takes place at the Eastern Harbor Yacht Club, another entertainment venue that provides another opportunity for a new song to be introduced in a diegetic context. White (Edwards/'Ukelele Ike') returns, this time with 'Little Jazz Bird'. Dick tells his sister he's found a job and doesn't need to marry Jo. Susie, wearing a Swiss costume, tells her brother that she too found a job. She's a yodeller and ready to go on stage. Fred quicky changes and joins her for 'Swiss Miss'. Susie, no longer impersonating a person of colour from Mexico but rather a white woman from Switzerland, performs quintessential European – that is, white – rectitude alongside her brother in the diegetic number. The polka-style music, touristic costumes and cliché-filled lyrics all point to a revue speciality. But there may be another reason for the song. Susie must redeem herself after her 'transgressive' ethnic behaviour in impersonating a woman of colour, though her agency as a white person allowed her to do so. She must prove her whiteness in 'Swiss Miss' and, in terms of gender dynamics, cannot be trusted to do this on her own but rather must do so under the watchful eye of her brother.

All ends well, as it must. Jack sings a reprise of 'Oh, Lady Be Good' to Susie, taking over what had been Watty's invitation to a scam and making it a declaration of love. 'Fascinating Rhythm' becomes 'fascinating wedding' as four couples come together at the end: Susie and Jack, Dick and Shirley, Jo and Watty, and two friends of Jo's, Daisy and Bertie. 'Fascinating

[8] Starr, *George Gershwin*, 58.

Rhythm', which began as a diegetic popular song performed at a party, has, through clever musical dramaturgy, become wedded to the plot.

Another Gershwin standard originated in *Lady, Be Good!* but was removed during the pre-Broadway tryout: 'The Man I Love'. The song came early in Act 1 to feature Adele, though with such an internalized song appearing in such an extroverted show, along with its style not showing off Adele's strengths, it was ultimately cut.[9] The ballad was published and recorded soon after *Lady, Be Good!* opened and took on a life of its own. The Gershwins tried to include it in two later shows – *Strike Up the Band* (1927) and *Rosalie* (1928)[10] – but it didn't work in either instance. The song had become too well known, and its interpolation would disrupt the overall musical-dramatic flow of any musical to which it might be added. Of course, when the song is used in a twenty-first-century jukebox-style musical that features Gershwin's music – namely, *An American in Paris* (2014, Paris; 2015, Broadway) – it fits perfectly.

Lady, Be Good! delighted audiences and critics. The opening-night audience demanded numerous encores from the siblings, which led one critic to quip that the audience must have thought 'that there was no limit to their endurance'.[11] Most reviewers agreed that it was the Astaires who carried the show,[12] especially Adele. The *New York Times* review on 2 December was even titled 'Adele Astaire Fascinates' and the first half focused entirely on her. Fred finally gets a mention in the fourth paragraph, and neither Gershwin brother appears until the sixth.[13]

Princess April

Although its title suggests some sort of Ruritanian romance, *Princess April*, which shares the date of its premiere at the Ambassador Theatre with *Lady, Be Good!*, was a predictable rags-to-riches musical comedy with a predictable Irish immigrant title character. Its subtitle, 'A Musical Comedy of Youth, Vitalizing the American Girl', alluded directly to Ziegfeld and his moniker 'glorifying the American girl'. Thus, the three

---

[9] Crawford, *Summertime*, 148.   [10] Neimoyer, 'After the *Rhapsody*': 110.
[11] 'Astaires Warmly Greeted in New Musical Comedy', *Daily News* (New York), 2 December 1924.
[12] Pollack, *George Gershwin*, 332.
[13] 'Adele Astaire Fascinates', *New York Times*, 2 December 1924.

principal strands of popular musical theatre at the time – operetta, musical comedy, revue – are all evoked in the show's title and subtitle.

Tessa Kosta (1890–1981) played the title role of April Daly, an aspiring actress of Irish descent who lives on the New Jersey coast. She falls in love with a wealthy young man, Roger Utley (played by Nathaniel Wagner), but his family approves of neither her class nor her profession. When April saves Roger's sister from an embarrassing situation, the family changes its opinion. Though *Princess April* on the whole lacked originality, it did feature two notable secondary characters. First is April's father (played by Harry Allen), who calls his daughter his 'princess', hence the title of the musical. His quasi-Irish ballad 'An Irish Rose for Me' was the score's highlight. The other illustrious character, in the spirit of a satirical revue, was the critic, cleverly named A. Sharpe Quill (played by Harry Clarke).

Princess April's reviews were mediocre, given William Carey Duncan (1874–1945) and Lewis Allen Browne (1876–1937)'s recycled plot points and Monte Carlo and Alma Sanders's (see Chapter 5) similarly styled songs. The show didn't even make it to the end of the year; the clichés had overrun their course.

Music Box Revue

The same evening as the premieres of *Lady, Be Good!* and *Princess April*, the fourth annual edition of Irving Berlin's *Music Box Revue* opened at the Music Box Theatre. The star line-up who performed Berlin's words and music was most impressive. It included opera singer Grace Moore (1898–1947); comic actor Oscar Shaw (1887–1967); the Brox Sisters close-harmony trio; dancers Tamiris (Helen Tamiris, 1905–1966), Carl Randall (1898–1965) and Ula Sharon (1905–1993); and the inimitable comedian, dancer and singer Fanny Brice (1891–1951). John Murray Anderson (1886–1954) staged the revue, having taken over from Hassard Short (1877–1956) during rehearsals. Earlier, Short had replaced Anderson as director of *Greenwich Village Follies*, so this was a directorial swap of sorts.

To bridge the past and present, a salient feature of musical theatre in 1924, the *Music Box Revue* opened with a self-referential prologue. In the Catskill Mountains, Washington Irving's Rip Van Winkle is awakened by a climber. 'Mountain Climber', as he is called, brings Rip to New York, where together they watch a parade featuring a 'Broadway stepper' who is 'jazzing her life away'.[14] Rip longs for his New York of long ago, so he goes to the Music Box Theatre, where he watches the new revue from the wings. There, he is treated to twenty-nine glamour-filled scenes.

Among these is 'Tokio Blues' (envisioned by Short), which featured a spectacular pink-hued set. The Brox Sisters,[15] presented the song, with its distinctive Orientalist parallel chords, in yellowface. Berlin's lyrics, which exhibit strong racist imagery, evoke the singers' nostalgic feelings for their Japanese homeland. Although there is a certain hint of Gertrude Lawrence's 'Limehouse Blues', here the singers are missing what they had rather than bemoaning their present. Once the siblings finished their performance, the modern dancers Tamiris and Margarita offered a kinetic interpretation of the scenario. 'Tokio Blues' was a prime example of the visual opulence associated with the *Music Box Revue*. The set magnificently unfolded into a stage-enveloping pagoda, which returned to its compact state at its end.[16]

Special visual effects returned in the Act 1 finale: another racist number titled 'The Call of the South'. The sequence opened 'in one' – that is, in front of the curtain. Oscar Shaw stood at one side, singing longingly for the land of 'Mammy songs', and Grace Moore, on the opposite side, entered with Stephen Foster's 'Old Folks at Home' as a countermelody. The curtain then parted to reveal Fanny Brice leading the company in 'Bandanna Ball'. Racist lyrics continued to pour from the stage when a special lighting effect, also seen in other revues of the year, made the all-white chorus appear Black. By having Rip Van Winkle positioned as a keen observer of the number in full view of the audience, Berlin, according to musical theatre scholar Jeffrey Magee, 'brought the minstrel spirit into the jazz age' and 'allowed Berlin to restore minstrelsy's nineteenth-century roots in this climactic number'.[17] In a sense, the advancements made in Black musicals, including *Shuffle Along* and the legacy of Florence Mills, were being eradicated here in a knowing return to the previous century.

In addition to the counterpoint song at the start of the Act 1 finale, Moore and Shaw delighted audiences with two duets: 'All Alone' and 'In

---

[14] Irving Berlin, 'Broadway Scene', 'Music Box Revue of 1924', box 173, folder 16, Irving Berlin Collection, LC.

[15] Lorayne (born Eunice, 1901–1993), Bobbe (born Josephine, 1902–1999) and Patricia (born Kathleen, 1904–988).

[16] Gillette, 'The New Plays: "Music Box Revue"'.

[17] Jeffrey Magee, *Irving Berlin's American Musical Theatre* (New York: Oxford University Press, 2012), 143.

the Shade of a Sheltering Tree'. In the former, a languid waltz that was added after the show opened, the singers stood on opposite sides of the stage, both dressed in black evening attire. Each held a telephone with a small light emanating from a mouthpiece that would show their faces. The minimal stage effect, evoking Charlot, was mesmerizing and added to the emotive energy of the song's inherent loneliness. This was in contrast to the lilting 'In the Shade of a Sheltering Tree', where, in a more visually grand fashion, chorus members dressed as various trees furnished a gently swaying visual backdrop.

But it was Fanny Brice who scored the biggest accolades. She brought her characteristic blend of tragedy and comedy to every one of her sketches. In 'Don't Send Me Back', she played 'The Immigrant', who pleaded not to be forcibly returned to her native Petrograd (St. Petersburg). One critic noted that she was able to change the song's mood from pathos to comedy 'by the utterance of a single word ("terrible") as only she in the world can utter it'.[18] The song drew tears of sympathetic sorrow from more than one critic. In another sketch, she played Madame Pompadour, the title character in the operetta that at the time was struggling to stay afloat on Broadway. According to reviewer Alan Dale, she burlesqued the part 'in a way that would have paralyzed the classic Martin Beck'.[19] Brice brilliantly displayed her physical comedy in 'I Want to Be a Ballet Dancer', a parody of the classical style Randall and Sharon demonstrated when they went about ordinary household tasks in 'Ballet Dancers at Home'.

After these and other delights, Rip Van Winkle is invited back to the stage. He is the guest of honour at the company's celebratory banquet. It is not just the literary character who is being feted, according to Magee, but also New York City's white past. The racial realities of nineteenth-century New York have been erased and the plights facing immigrants, especially those who are Japanese and Russian, have been left unresolved. As Magee put it, 'The show's version of the city's past downplayed conflict in order to evoke a picture of racial homogeneity and social stability.'[20] This was the past being used to project a particularly whitewashed image of a troubled present.

One thing to be noted about *Music Box Revue*, especially within the context of other revues playing on Broadway at the time, was its sensual

---

[18] Uncited review, Project Files, box 268, folder 11, Irving Berlin Collection, LC.

[19] Alan Dale, 'Irving Berlin's "Music Box" Opens', *New York American*, n.d., Project Files, box 268, folder 11, Irving Berlin Collection, LC.

[20] Magee, *Irving Berlin's American Musical Theatre*, 141.

decency. One reviewer thought it 'the cleanest and most fully clothed' of any of the recent revues. He continued: 'The humor, too, has been pretty thoroughly disinfected.'[21] As was typical for revues, songs and sketches were added and removed during the run, which played for 184 performances before closing on 9 May 1925. It was the final edition of the series.

[21] Uncited review, Project Files, box 268, folder 11, Irving Berlin Collection, LC.

14 | In the Days and Weeks that Followed

While the musicals that opened on 1 December extolled the present and delighted their audiences with a mixture of comic antics and popular song, the show that opened the next evening – Sigmund Romberg and Dorothy Donnelly's' *The Student Prince in Heidelberg* (to give the work's full name) – offered something substantially different.[1] *The Student Prince* (to use the more familiar name), called 'a spectacular light opera' on publicity and printed materials, resided squarely in the world of operetta, American style. The story is almost like a fairy tale: a beautiful young woman, a commoner in a far-off European kingdom, dreams of marrying a prince and living happily ever after. By the end of the first act, it seems her wish is being granted, without any Cinderella-esque magic, though, following the American Cinderella paradigm (see Chapter 2), she is employed. The following act, however, presents a different story altogether, as dreams give way to reality (at least in terms of musical theatre fantasy) and the storyline's focus shifts to the devastating yearning for what can never be. Audiences devoured the sentimental tale, and *The Student Prince* went on to become the most popular Broadway musical of any type to open during the 1920s, playing an astounding 608 performances in its original run.

The Student Prince was the second of four collaborations between librettist-lyricist Dorothy Donnelly (1880–1928) and composer Sigmund Romberg. Donnelly was born into a New York theatrical family; her father managed the Grand Opera House. She began her career as an actor, appearing on stage and in a handful of silent films before turning to writing libretti, including *Poppy* (see Chapter 3)

Donnelly's first collaboration with Romberg was *Blossom Time* (1921), which in 1924 was still immensely popular with multiple touring companies crisscrossing each other on the road. On 19 May 1924, the Shuberts brought it back to the Jolson Theatre, where *The Student Prince* would enjoy its record-long run, for twenty-four performances. *Blossom Time* is a fictionalized tale featuring the Viennese composer Franz Schubert

---

[1] For more on *The Student Prince*, see William A. Everett, *Sigmund Romberg* (New Haven: Yale University Press, 2007), 124–149.

(1797–1828). He falls in love with Mitzi, an attractive young woman, but is too shy to tell her of his feelings.[2] So, he gets his good friend Baron Schober to sing exquisite songs to her on his behalf (a sort of Cyrano de Bergerac scenario). Predictably, Mitzi and the Baron fall in love. Shubert becomes despondent and dies of a broken heart. Romberg's score included reworkings of several famous Schubert melodies, perhaps most famously the second theme of the Eighth Symphony, the 'Unfinished', as the recurring waltz 'Song of Love'.

Blossom Time's success helped rehabilitate Austrian culture after the Great War. With the USA and the former Austrian-Hungarian Empire on opposite sides of the conflict, strong resentment toward German-speaking Central Europeans remained after Armistice. Here, though, was a benign Vienna filled with beer gardens and song. This was a culture steeped in nostalgia and waltzes with no signs of malevolent political manoeuvring.

Something similar happened with German culture and *The Student Prince*. Although the Shuberts remained concerned about producing another show set in German-speaking Europe amidst lingering post-war anti-German sentiments, they trusted Donnelly and Romberg enough after the success of *Blossom Time* to make it work. And that they did. Nineteenth-century Heidelberg, like the Vienna of *Blossom Time*, was made politically benign: the only dangers that could be found anywhere concerned affairs of the heart. In Donnelly's libretto, Karl Franz, crown prince of mythical Karlsberg, goes with his tutor Engel (literally his guardian angel, since Engel means angel in German) and valet Lutz to study in Heidelberg. Lutz is a gentle-hearted chum who even brings along his own valet, Hubert. Soon after arriving in Heidelberg, Karl Franz finds his way to the Inn of the Three Golden Apples, where he falls in love with Kathie, a waitress who works there. The couple cannot be together since Karl Franz must enter an arranged marriage to Princess Margaret, who in turn must forfeit her own true love, Captain Tarnitz. As the operetta concludes, Karl Franz returns to Heidelberg one final time to bid farewell to his youth and to his first love, Kathie.

Donnelly based her libretto on the popular play *Alt-Heidelberg* (Old Heidelberg) by Wilhelm Meyer-Foerster, which had its premiere in Berlin in 1901. The play's US premiere, in German, took place on 5 March 1902, at the Pabst Theatre in Milwaukee, and the first New York production, also in

---

[2] *Blossom Time* was an adaptation of Heinrich Berté, Alfred Maria Willner and Heinz Reichert's Viennese operetta *Das Dreimäderlhaus* (The House of the Three Maidens, 1916), itself a retelling of Rudolf Hans Bartsch's novel *Schwammerl* (1912). The British adaptation, *Lilac Time* (1922), was also a success. For more on these adaptations, see Scott, *German Operetta*, 80–84.

German, took place on 21 October that same year at the Irving Place Theatre. The play was performed for the first time in English at the Princess Theatre in New York on 15 December 1902 in a version prepared by the actor Aubrey Boucicault for himself, which he titled *Heidelberg*. Another actor, Richard Mansfield, saw Boucicault's performance and subsequently created his own version, *Old Heidelberg*, to inaugurate the Lyric Theatre on 12 October 1903. The popular tale was filmed in two silent versions. The first was in 1915, with Wallace Reid and Dorothy Gish, and the second in 1927 (after the appearance of the operetta), with Ramon Novarro and Norma Shearer. In all these versions, the prince is called Karl Heinrich, and his tutor Juttner. It is in the Donnelly–Romberg version that the names Karl Franz and Engel first appear. *Old Heidelberg* was a well-established theatrical property, and, as such, a musicalized version would play on nostalgic yearnings for the many fans of the old play.

On 27 October 1924, Romberg and Donnelly's new operetta, called at the time *In Heidelberg*, had its world premiere at the Apollo Theatre in Atlantic City – the same theatre where the Shuberts' fleshy revues *Innocent Eyes* and *Artists and Models of 1924* had played earlier in the year. But when the producers realized that many people mistook the new musical for a revival of *Old Heidelberg*, they quickly renamed it *The Student Prince in Heidelberg*, keeping their original title as part of the new one. The paeon to youth, though, quickly became known as simply *The Student Prince*.

Playing the ill-fated romantic leads were the German-born soprano Ilse Marvenga (1896–?) and the American tenor Howard Marsh (1888–1969). J. J. Shubert, in a highly successful marketing ploy, decided to have Marvenga play the opening night of every major *Student Prince* company. As a result, she performed the taxing role more than 3,000 times. Kathie is one of those musical theatre roles that requires tremendous technique and stamina. Not only does it have more than its share of high notes, some of which are sustained, but it also requires a two-octave range that must be spanned in less than three seconds, along with some especially challenging coloratura passages. To be more precise, Kathie must sing nineteen high As, four B-flats, two B-naturals and sixteen Cs, and that number doesn't include any encores, which were typical at the time.[3]

Howard Marsh (see Figure 14.1) was no stranger to Romberg's expansive lyricism, for he created the role of Baron Schober in *Blossom Time*. Like the role of Kathie for sopranos, that of Karl Franz offers ample challenges for tenors and high baritones. 'Serenade', which features in the Act 1 finale,

---

[3] Mordden, *Make Believe*, 50.

Figure 14.1 Howard Marsh, star of *The Student Prince*.

is notorious in this regard. Karl Franz must be on stage observing the action and remaining silent for some minutes, meaning there is no chance to warm up the vocal cords. Then, after just two chords in the orchestra, he must immediately negotiate a treacherous arpeggio that encompasses an octave and fourth in just five notes and spans the low and high ends of his register. The arresting passage reappears in the midst of the number, while at the very end he must sustain the same high note (an E-flat) that he sang in the arpeggiated opening with a sonorous resonance that can be heard above the full male chorus and orchestra.

Appearing alongside Kathie and Karl Franz is the male chorus, which in *The Student Prince* functions as a major character (see Figure 14.2). As Karl Franz's fellow male students, they have accepted him as one of their own and personify the prince's 'fitting in' and being part of a community. The male chorus links to the *Männerchor* movement, a long-standing singing tradition in the German-speaking world with roots in the nineteenth century, the time period of *The Student Prince*. The Latin student song 'Gaudeamus igitur' (So let us rejoice) was part of the *Männerchor* core repertory, and by including it in *The Student Prince*, Romberg adds a touch of historical authenticity, at least musically, to the work. The song endorses not just the male choral tradition but also the need to savour the fleeting joys of youth.

This male chorus consists of university students who like to drink beer, lots of it. One of the most popular numbers in *The Student Prince* is the

Figure 14.2 Ilse Marvenga and the male chorus in *The Student Prince*. The Shubert Archive.

'Drinking Song', which opens with a treble utterance of its key command: 'Drink, drink, drink'. Here, Romberg creates a student drinking song in a rollicking triple metre with uncomplicated harmonic underpinning and an easily singable and memorable melody. It became popular not only because of its close resemblance to an actual German drinking song but also because *The Student Prince* appeared during Prohibition, when doing what was happening on stage was *verboten* outside the theatre. Audience members found themselves becoming vicarious participants in the on-stage revelry.

To provide an aural picture of *The Student Prince*'s Teutonic Ruritania beyond the male chorus, Romberg crafted a sensuous array of waltzes along with a rousing set of marches. Four distinct waltzes occur in Act 1 alone, two of which celebrate youth and vitality in the present and two that venerate the power of nostalgic memory. Marches both regal and boisterous appear throughout the work.

The celebratory waltzes both occur amidst larger musical scenes. These are not stand-alone dances but firmly imbed themselves within the musical storytelling. In both instances, they represent a shared sense of community. 'I'm Coming at Your Call' is part of the extended sequence during which we first meet Kathie. Her exuberance is conveyed through her waltz, in which she is joined by her appreciative male chorus. She shows herself to be a vital part of their social life. The choral paean 'When the Spring Wakens Everything' takes place during the expansive Act 1 finale and grounds the entire sequence in an atmosphere of communal joy.[4] The exuberance of these waltzes sets them apart from the two other in the act, which are more introspective and reflective in tone.

In 'Golden Days', the second musical number in the score, Engel tells his young charge about his own student days. Karl Franz joins his mentor in the flowing duet, and this is the first time we hear the prince's singing voice. The future king is learning the importance of remembering and honouring the past from his guardian angel. Donnelly's evocative lyrics implore us, when it comes to the 'Golden days full of innocence and full of truth', to 'remember them all else above'.[5] This invitation to nostalgia, remembering the past not as it was but as we wish it had been, runs throughout *The Student Prince*, and the music of a waltz, yet again, serves as a conduit for memory.

It is the tear-filled duet for Karl Franz and Kathie, 'Deep in My Heart, Dear', that becomes the principal recurring waltz of *The Student Prince*. Musically expansive, with three highly distinctive sections in the verse, it is the refrain, marked 'molto espressivo' (very expressive), that lies at the heart of the work. Its slower tempo – when compared with the more buoyant waltzes – and long musical lines – there are no rests indicated – make it highly distinctive. As Karl Franz and Kathie realize, in a prescient manner, that 'our paths may sever', they iterate the work's central theme: 'I'll remember forever'.[6] To reinforce this mandate, the refrain appears in each act's finale. Its treatment at the end of Act 2 is especially poignant, for it is played in the orchestra after Karl Franz leaves behind a heartbroken Kathie, whose emotional state is so shattered that she is no longer capable of singing. Words – indeed, any sort of vocal utterance – have failed her, and it is only the sheer power of purely instrumental music that can convey the intensity of the moment. This is the same sort of thing that happens in several especially dramatic moments in many musicals, including those of Rodgers and Hammerstein, such the 'Bench Scene' in *Carousel* (1945, which

---

[4] For more on the finale, see William A. Everett, 'Golden Days in Old Heidelberg: The First-Act Finale of Sigmund Romberg's *The Student Prince*', *American Music* 12, no. 3 (fall 1994): 255–282.

[5] Sigmund Romberg and Dorothy Donnelly , *The Student Prince: A Spectacular Light Opera* [vocal score] (New York: Harms, 1932), 9–10.

[6] Romberg and Donnelly, *The Student Prince*, 62.

includes 'If I Loved You'), 'Twin Soliloquies' in *South Pacific* (1949) and 'Do I Love You Because You're Beautiful' in *Cinderella* (1957).

To add to the pathos of this moment, Romberg places two character-defining waltzes, one for Karl Franz and one for Kathie, earlier in the sequence. Karl Franz's mournful 'Farewell to Youth' is the only minor-mode waltz in the score. Before Karl Franz was summoned back to Karlsberg, he and Kathie had been planning a trip to Paris. Kathie sings of her elation in the jubilant 'We're Off to Paris'. The waltz, like her happiness, is short-lived, for Karl Franz must inform her of his impending royal duty. This pair of waltzes, with their evocations of sadness and joy, leads up musically and dramatically to the emotive reprise of 'Deep in My Heart, Dear' that concludes the act.

The romance of Karl Franz and Kathie is not the only one that royal duty keeps from being realized. Princess Margaret, whom Karl Franz must marry, loves Captain Tarnitz. The princess and the captain have their own waltz of regret: 'Just We Two'. The association of the waltz with memory and separation becomes even more poignant thanks to Donnelly's emotive lyric in which 'the waltz swells and halts' and is 'ending too soon' as 'we say adieu'.[7] Romberg stresses the intimacy of this waltz and its lyric by placing it within a larger musical sequence along the lines of what he did in Act 1. Here, the privacy of Margaret and Tarnitz's waltz is contrasted with the large ensemble numbers that surround it. Significantly, the music for these outer sequences, with their various sorts of metric accentuations and perky rhythmic underpinnings, point ever so slightly, but ever so importantly, to the 'modern' world of musical comedy and revue. Couples who want to be together but cannot is not a problem exclusive to those who inhabit a Ruritanian operetta. The modern world of 1924 was filled with such realities.

Waltzes, though they are of extreme significance in *The Student Prince*, are not the only type of music in the operetta. Marches feature prominently as well, especially ones for the male chorus. The steadfastness of the refrains of 'By Our Bearing So Sedate', in which the male chorus play attendants at court, is contrasted with verses filled with jaunty dotted rhythms and slightly syncopated passages – musical identifiers of 'modern' revues and musical comedies – in which the young men offer insights into the less formal sides of themselves, namely the amorous passions and boisterous behaviours of youth. These come to the fore when the male chorus become students in Heidelberg and celebrate their sense of community in lively

---

[7] Romberg and Donnelly, *The Student Prince*, 132–133.

marches such as 'Students Marching Song' ('To the Inn We're Marching'), and 'Come, Boys, Let's All be Gay, Boys'. Kathie joins them in the latter to sing some of the most difficult music she has in the entire score. And, of course, there's the immortal 'Serenade' – not a march – in which, in the midst of the Act 1 finale, Karl Franz, accompanied by a trio of his closest friends as well as his larger community, the entire male chorus, declares his love to Kathie. We know, as do they, that the love they are celebrating will have to be sacrificed for royal duty.

Like *Blossom Time* and other operettas Romberg wrote for the Shuberts, *The Student Prince* ends sadly. It does not have the feel-good finale of *Lady, Be Good!* or so many of the other shows that were playing in 1924. Audiences, nonetheless, were captivated by the anguish and kept *The Student Prince* alive for decades. But what would have happened if there had been just one more scene, one where Kathie follows Karl Franz to Karlsberg and the two are reunited for a happy ending? This is the sort of thing that happens at the end of the chamber musical *Girlfriend* (2010, book by Todd Almond, music and lyrics by Matthew Sweet), which tells the story of two recent high school graduates in Nebraska in the 1990s, Will and Mike, who are in love.[8] In the penultimate scene, Mike leaves for college while Will remains behind. This is akin to the end of *The Student Prince*. Then, during the final scene, Will moves to the city where Mike has gone to college, gets a job at a local retail store and finds Mike at a club. A happy ending ensues with the reluctant lovers reunited. Romberg and Donnelly deny Karl Franz and Kathie such a reconciliation, which makes the ending of *The Student Prince*, where one lover leaves the other behind, so emotionally gripping and such a powerful final image amongst the quartet of musicals that collectively make up 1924's 11 o'clock number.

The Year Draws to a Close

As the year drew to a close, another slight flurry of openings began. On 20 December, the famed Moulin Rouge reopened in Paris after being destroyed by fire in 1915. In another example of a transnational connection, the inaugural production was *New York Montmarte*, described as 'distinctly American in character'.[9] Jacques-Charles Gesmar (1900–1928)

---

[8] *Girlfriend* was developed and had its tryout at the Berkeley Repertory Theatre in 2010 and is performed at regional theatres across the USA. A jukebox musical, its music comes from Matthew Sweet's 1991 album of the same name.

[9] 'Finest Music Hall in Europe with Semi-American Revue', *Variety*, 24 December 1924, 3.

produced the revue, whose American features included former Ziegfeld girls as well as the Gertrude Hoffman Girls.

In New York, *Topsy and Eva*, a retelling of Harriet Beecher Stowe's anti-slavery novel *Uncle Tom's Cabin* (1852), opened on 23 December at the Sam H. Harris Theatre. It was the brainchild of the Duncan Sisters (Rosetta (1894–1959) and Vivian (1897–1986)), who not only played the title characters but also wrote the musical's songs. Before arriving on Broadway, the show enjoyed an extensive and highly successful tour. The sisters had been slated to appear in the original production of the musical comedy *Sitting Pretty*, but the unexpected success of *Topsy and Eva* necessitated their withdrawal. Catherine Chisholm Cushing (1874–1952) refocused Stowe's narrative to emphasize the characters of Topsy (which Rosetta played in blackface) and Eva (Vivian's part). Cushing also added a romantic plot between George Shelby (played by Robert Halliday (1893–1975)) and a newly invented character called Mariette (played by Nydia d'Arnell (d. 1970)).[10] The Duncan Sisters, with pianist Phil Ohman (of *Lady, Be Good!* fame) recorded the show's hit, the wistful 'Rememb'ring'.[11] Particularly fascinating are the sisters' vocal imitations of instrumental riffs and their exquisite two-part counterpoint. The show played for about four months on Broadway before resuming its tour. In 1927, the sisters made a silent film of their property and continued to play Topsy and Eva well into the 1950s.

On Christmas Day, *Betty Lee* opened at the 44th Street Theatre. Otto Harbach's book, based on the 1909 play *Going Some* by Paul Armstrong and Rex Beach, told of Wallingford (Wally) Speed (played by Hal Skelly), a Yale alumnus, who wants to impress the attractive Betty Lee (played by Gloria Foy). A group of college students are coming to the Chapin Ranch, and the cowboys who work there hope that one of them is a good runner, for they want to win back the phonograph they lost to the Centipede Ranch in the last race. Earlier, Wally found a record of the song 'Betty Lee' at a friend's house and sent it to its namesake. When he arrives, she asks him what the song sounds like, so he sings it for her. The cowboys join in, then exclaim that that's the song on their favourite record, but they cannot play it because the Centipede ranchers have their phonograph! Betty begs Wally to race Skinner, the cook from the Centipede Ranch, in a rematch and win

[10] 'The Duncan Sisters in *Topsy and Eva*', 'Uncle Tom's Cabin and American Culture', http://utc .iath.virginia.edu/onstage/duncanhp.html, accessed 30 March 2023.
[11] Victor 19206-A, recorded on 19 November 1923. The sisters also recorded two other songs from their show with Edna Fisher as pianist: 'I Never Had a Mammy' (Victor 19206-B) and 'Um-Um-Da-Da' (Victor 19311-A).

it back. Wally, who despite his surname is anything but athletic, agrees. Since Wally is friends with a real athlete, Culver Covington, who is on his way to the ranch, Wally will conveniently get sick the day before the race and have Culver run in his place. Culver can surely outrun Skinner, and Wally will get sympathy from Betty. Berkley Fresno, however, also likes Betty and, knowing that Wally is a fraud, schemes to thwart the plan. He has his fraternity brothers assault Culver, injuring him and forcing Wally to race. Skinner, needing money, throws the race, which allows Wally to win the contest, the phonograph and Betty's heart.

Most of the music was by Louis A. Hirsch (1887–1924), who passed away on 13 May before finishing the score. Con Conrad (1891–1938) completed what needed doing, including the perky title song. This title song is of particular significance in a metatheatrical sense, for a large portion of the plot centres on a record of the song and being able to play it. The song is inferred to be a popular song, not associated with a musical, but in reality (i.e., outside of the musical itself), it is a song from a musical. It's similar to 'Fascinating Rhythm' and 'Little Jazz Bird' from *Lady, Be Good!* in this regard. But in *Betty Lee*, the connections and commercial mobilities between the recording and theatre industries take centre stage.[12]

Harbach also commented in a metatheatrical sense on the relationship between plot and music, the idea of integration that was stated in the playbill for *Rose-Marie* and which was of concern to the creators of *Kid Boots*. In *Betty Lee*, Betty and Wally are talking when they hear the cowboys singing the refrain of the title song:

BETTY: (LISTENS TO SINGING) THATS THE COWBOYS. THEY'RE SINGING THE SONG
      OF THEIR FAVORITE RECORD.
SPEED: (LISTENS) ISNT IT FUNNY HOW THOSE WORDS FIT?
BETTY: THE MUSIC?
SPEED: (WITH FEELING) NO! THE SITUATION, MY MOOD, MY MIND, OH, BETTY.[13]

Speed lets us know that 'Betty Lee' is integrated into the plot both as a physical object (the record) and as a character-defining song.

Not all musical theatre presentations to appear in 1924 (or indeed in any year) were professional productions, as we saw with the two musical comedies that appeared in March with music by Richard Rodgers. The

---

[12] For more on earlier musical theatre works that feature phonographs and gramophones, see Eva Moreda Rodríguez, 'Talking Machines in Spanish Commercial Musical Theatre, 1888–1913', *Arti musices* 53, no. 2 (2022): 343–354.

[13] Otto Harbach, 'Betty Lee', unpublished script, *T-Mss 1993–038, Series III – Scripts, box 9, folder 3, Otto Harbach Papers, Billy Rose Theatre Collection, NYPL.

amateur revue *Vanity Fair of 1924* is another case in point. Described in *The New York Times* as 'one of the best amateur society productions in New York',[14] the revue had two performances, on 26 and 27 December, in the grand ballroom of the Waldorf-Astoria Hotel. The revue was a fund-raiser for the Mineola Home, a cardiac facility in Irvington-on-Hudson, and presented by the Junior League of the Cardiac Committee of the Public Education Association. Among the listed producers were composer Sigmund Romberg and Regina (Mrs Clarence) Millhiser, granddaughter of the founder of Gimbel's Department Store. The revue's many highlights included a 'rhapsody in blue' that paid homage to George Gershwin's famous composition from earlier in the memorable year. The scene featured a stunning silver-blue gauze décor and models adorned in various shades of blue.

The final musical to debut on Broadway in 1924 was another revue, this one of Russian origin: *Seeniaya Ptitza* (The Blue Bird), which opened at the Frolic Theatre on 29 December. Assembled and hosted by Yasha Yushny, in many ways it emulated *La Chauve-Souris*, which opened in London the previous month and was extremely popular in the USA. Especially memorable scenes included a staged performance of the 'Volga Boatmen' song, which Stark Young described in *The New York Times* as possessing 'a thrilling timbre to the voices, terrible pathos, strange, dying, folk tragedy and despair'.[15] Another haunting sketch involved an elderly Jewish rabbi instructing two younger pupils and the three of them joining together in song.

Seeniaya Ptitza reflected many of the defining trends of musical theatre in 1924. First, it was a revue. The genre's popularity with producers and audiences was immense. Second, it represented the transnational currents that facilitated the movement of musical theatre on both sides of the Atlantic. Here was a Russian revue brought to New York via Germany by the American journalist–producer–ethnologist Wendell Phillips Dodge (1883–1976). Third, it was produced in repertory at the Frolic Theatre, a roof theatre above Ziegfeld's New Amsterdam Theatre not unlike the Plantation Room above the Shuberts' Winter Garden Theatre. It thus represents the various venues where musical theatre performances took place. Fourth, it closed during its run and reopened in a revised version. Such reworking of material, especially in revues, was commonplace. Fifth, it simultaneously looked forwards and backwards. It was new to

---

[14] '"Vanity Fair of 1924" a Colorful Pageant', *New York Times*, 27 December 1924.
[15] Stark Young, 'The Play: Yushny's Revue', *New York Times*, 29 December 1924.

US audiences, novel in its content, and it offered something different for audiences, even pointing towards the avant-garde. It also paid tribute to the Russian culture that was being eradicated under the new regime and, like *The Student Prince*, emphasized the vital importance of the undeniable power of memory.

So, why does 1924 matter? It was, after all, just a year. But it was a year that marked an extraordinary confluence of the old and the new, the established and the innovative. It reflected the vitality of a transnational web of musical theatre production and genres that extended beyond New York and London to include Berlin, Budapest, Buenos Aires, Madrid, Manchester, Milan, Paris and Vienna, among other nexuses. The past came into the present not just through the reappearance of stars such as Mistinguett but also in the continuing careers of the likes of Marie Tempest, José Collins, Betty Fischer, Louise Kartousch, Fred Stone, Hubert Marischka, F. E. Miller, Aubrey Lyles, Leslie Henson and many more. Legacies were happening.

The year also pointed towards the future. New stars were being made brighter, as in the cases of Evelyn Laye and Florence Mills. After *Madame Pompadour* closed in 1925, Laye created the role of Marianne, the female lead in Sigmund Romberg's *The New Moon*, when the operetta transferred to London's Drury Lane Theatre in 1929. That same year, she made her Broadway debut in Noël Coward's *Bitter Sweet*. Her reputation was such that the Austrian director Max Reinhardt wrote to her in 1932: 'You are that rare and Holy Trinity of the stage, a great singer, a great actress, and a great beauty.'[1] Laye subsequently appeared in a handful of early film operettas, including *One Heavenly Night* (1931) and *The Night is Young* (1935), as well as in the 1936 London production of Lehár's operetta *Paganini* opposite the legendary tenor Richard Tauber. Her career spanned decades, and in 1979 Laye returned to the stage as the professional courtesan of long ago, Madame Armfelt in a revival of *A Little Night Music* directed by Richard Digby Day. In that production, the nearly eighty-year-old actor sang 'Liaisons', a saga of past loves that bore a scent of the role that made her famous, Madame Pompadour.

After *Dixie to Broadway* closed on Broadway, Mills led its tour before returning to the Plantation Room for *Black Birds of 1925*. When that show

---

[1] Quoted in Michael Thornton, 'Evelyn Laye: "Queen of Musical Comedy"', liner notes for *Evelyn Laye: 'Queen of Musical Comedy'* (Avid Entertainment AMSC 977, 2009), 6.

was expanded into a full-length theatrical offering as *Black Birds of 1926*, many songs and dances from *Dixie to Broadway* were reprised. Even though the star's health was starting to fail, Mills headlined *Black Birds of 1927* and continued to perform until her tragic and untimely death of complications from pelvic tuberculosis on 1 November 1927. The producer Lew Leslie then cast Adelaide Hall, a featured performer in *Runnin' Wild*, as her replacement and, in doing so, he created another star.

Adele and Fred Astaire continued to reign as musical theatre royalty. They appeared together in several Broadway musicals throughout the 1920s, and in 1932, Adele left the stage when she married Lord Charles Arthur Francis Cavendish (1905–1944) and moved to Lismore Castle in Ireland. Fred, of course, went on to have a highly successful career in Hollywood, delighting millions with his exquisite dancing.

Then there are the legacies of the shows themselves. After *Kid Boots* closed in New York, Eddie Cantor led its cast on a highly successful tour. Among those who saw the production in Chicago was the British actor Leslie Henson, star of *The Beauty Prize* and *Primrose* in 1924. Henson took Cantor's role when the show played at London's Winter Garden Theatre in 1926 and on its subsequent UK tour. Cantor came to see the show in London, and Henson recalled him coming backstage afterwards: 'When he came round to the dressing-room he congratulated me, assuring me that I was not only a comedian but an actor; a compliment very dear to the Henson heart.'[2]

Also in 1926, Paramount released an hour-long film called *Kid Boots* with Cantor in title role. The film featured highlights of the stage production and included versions of the salesman and osteopath scenes, along with some comic incidents on the golf course. In one of these, Kid is seen cleaning up the course by picking up golf balls everywhere he finds them. This greatly annoys the golfers, who Kid thinks are waving 'hi' to him as they try to tell him to stop.

Despite its continued appearances on Italian stages, *Il paese dei campanelli* has had only a modest international legacy. Attempts were made in the 1930s to take the work to Germany as part of a Nazi plan to promote German–Italian solidarity.[3] It thus was being used as an example of 'soft power', where cultural products are employed to achieve socio-political goals. Soft power was also evident when *Il paese* made it to Broadway in

---

[2] Henson, *Yours Faithfully*, 84–85.

[3] Kevin Clarke, 'Italian Sex Spectacles: Operettas by Carlo Lombardo & Co.,' *Operetta Research Center*, 20 August 2014.

1935, sung in Italian. Produced by The Permanent Italian Theatre and directed by Cesare Sodero, it played five performances between 9 and 12 May at the Majestic Theatre. The work's setting was slightly changed to be 'The Town Square on the Seacoast of a Legendary Country – The Land of Bells'. Due to inter-war realities, its locale was no longer specifically Dutch. The performances were staged primarily for the Italian community in New York, and, according to newspaper accounts, many 'smart and socially prominent Italians'[4] were seen there on opening night, displaying the soft-power presence of Italian Americans in New York culture and politics. One of the operetta's most important legacies, though, remains the 1954 film co-released by Alba Film and Valentia Film and directed by Jean Boyer. In addition to its delectable musical performances, the film featured the iconic Sophia Loren as Bombon (see Plate 18).

The saga of *Madame Pompadour* in America did not end with the ill-fated adaptation by Clare Kummer produced by Martin Beck and Charles B. Dillingham. The Shuberts, well known for their highly successful productions of operettas, became interested in mounting their own version of the property. On 21 May 1926, they acquired the rights to produce *Madame Pompadour*.[5] From documents in the Shubert Archive, it appears that they were planning to use a new adaptation by Marie Armstrong Hecht.[6] That production never seems to have materialized, for when Milton J. Shubert produced *Madame Pompadour* at the St. Louis Municipal Opera Theatre in the summer of 1930, he used the adaptation by Frederick Lonsdale and Harry Graham, the same one that played throughout 1924 in London.

Gräfin Mariza kept playing throughout continental Europe. Even though it took it a while to reach New York, Paris and London, it eventually became Kálmán's greatest international hit.[7] In 1925, plans were underway to bring the work to Broadway in an adaptation by Otto Harbach and Oscar Hammerstein II with Hope Hampton, who had been fired from *Madame Pompadour*, in the title role.[8] The project never materialized. So, when *Countess Maritza* opened on Broadway on 18 September 1926, it was not

[4] Danton Walker, 'Voices Ring the Bell in Italian Music Show', *Daily News* (New York), 10 May 1935, newspapers.com.

[5] Letter from Hans Bartsch to Shubert Theatrical Corporation, 21 May 1926, Show Files, folder 849-A, 'Madame Pompadour', Shubert Archive.

[6] Copies of the script are in the Scripts Collection, box 40, in the Shubert Archive.

[7] Stefan Frey, *'Laughter under Tears': Emmerich Kálmán – An Operetta Biography*, translated by Alexander Butziger (Culver City: Operetta Foundation, 2014), 161.

[8] Mark Eden Horowitz, compiler and editor, *The Letters of Oscar Hammerstein II* (New York: Oxford University Press, 2022), 10.

a Harbach–Hammerstein creation but rather a Shubert production at their namesake theatre. Harry B. Smith's adaptation and lyrics added lots of antics to the plot, along with interpolated songs by Harry K. Morgan and Al Goodman. It took longer for the work to appear in France and the United Kingdom. Titled *Comtesse Maritza* and adapted by Max Eddy and Jean Marietti, the French version debuted in Mulhouse at the Théâtre Municipal on 27 February 1930 and in Paris at the Théâtre des Ambassadeurs on 7 May 1931. Its London premiere, as *Maritza*, took place at the Palace Theatre on 6 July 1938 in an adaptation by Robert Layer-Parker, Eddie Garr and Arthur Stanley.[9]

The operetta was filmed three times in Germany. The first, a silent version, was released by Terra-Film in 1925. The second, from Rot-Film in 1932, starred Dorothea Wieck as Mariza and Hubert Marischka as Tassilo, the role he immortalized on stage. The third, from Carlton-Film, was released in 1958 and featured Christine Görner as Mariza, Rudolf Schock as Michael (a renamed Tassilo) and Hans Moser, who created Penizeck in the original 1924 production, as a renamed Ferdinand.[10]

Soon after *Rose-Marie* opened in New York in September 1924, the London producer Alfred Butt sent a cablegram to Charles B. Dillingham asking if he recommended the show for Drury Lane.[11] Dillingham responded the next day: 'All Englishmen ... say Rosemarie sure success England.'[12] Dillingham's informants proved absolutely correct in their prediction: *Rose-Marie* turned out to be a huge hit in London, where it opened at the Theatre Royal, Drury Lane, on 20 March 1925 with Edith Day, the star of *Wildflower* on Broadway in 1923 and 1924, in the title role. Hammerstein was elated about the London production, writing to Harbach on 15 March that 'In some ways this looks like the best of all Rose Maries. Edith Day is a positive joy.'[13]

MGM filmed the operetta three times. First was a silent version starring Joan Crawford that was released in 1928. Crawford was no stranger to the musical stage, having appeared in *Innocent Eyes* and *The Passing Show of 1924*. That film is now considered lost. The second version, from 1936, was reworked to be a showcase for the singing talents of Nelson Eddy and

---

[9] Frey, *'Laughter under Tears'*, 307–308.   [10] Frey, *'Laughter under Tears'*, 308.

[11] Alfred Butt, Cablegram to Charles Dillingham, 29 September 1924, Correspondence, 1924–1926, box 24, A-E, Charles B. Dillingham Papers. Manuscripts and Archives Division. The New York Public Library. Astor, Lenox, and Tilden Foundations.

[12] Charles Dillingham, Cablegram to Alfred Butt, 30 September 1924, Correspondence, 1924–1926, Box 24, A-E, Charles B. Dillingham Papers, NYPL.

[13] Horowitz, *The Letters of Oscar Hammerstein*, 9.

Jeanette MacDonald, MGM's famed duo (see Plate 19),[14] and the third, from 1954, was filmed in wide-screen colour CinemaScope, which made the spectacular scenery as much a star as Ann Blyth, Howard Keel and Fernando Lamas.[15] The plots for both films were radically changed from Harbach and Hammerstein's original, and new music was included, though the title song, 'Indian Love Call' and 'Song of the Mounties' still featured prominently. After all, these are what made the operetta famous and drew audiences to the cinema.

Lady, Be Good! travelled to London, again starring the Astaires, where it opened at the Empire Theatre on 14 April 1926 and played for 326 performances. A new number, 'I'd Rather Charleston' was added for Adele. Fred called it 'one of Ira's best comic ideas suited to Adele'.[16] It also promoted the emblematic dance, which had featured in several Black musicals in 1924, as it crossed into white culture.

A film by the name of *Lady Be Good* (without the exclamation point) was released in 1941. It had nothing to do with the original show, other than its title, the title song and 'Fascinating Rhythm' appearing as a production number. Race featured prominently in terms of Eleanor Powell's tap dancing and athletic display in the title song, which connect her to the Berry Brothers, an African American trio that performed similar steps earlier in the film. In 'Fascinating Rhythm', Powell and the brothers perform together. Here was a cinematic rendering of the white appropriation of Black dance.

Finally, *The Student Prince* continued to be heard for decades in many productions, both professional and amateur, and remained a favourite with summer light opera companies. The operetta sparked a number of studio recordings by some of the most renowned singers of subsequent decades, including Nelson Eddy and Doretta Morrow in the 1940s and Dorothy Kirsten and Gordon MacRae in the 1950s. In 1954, MGM released a lavish technicolour film version starring a massive male chorus, the splendid soprano Ann Blyth, Edmund Purdom's handsomely chiselled looks and Mario Lanza's glorious tenor voice.[17]

---

[14] The 1936 film was directed by W. S. Van Dyke and produced by Hunt Stromberg. Frances Goodrich and Albert Hackett created the screenplay.

[15] The 1954 film was directed and produced by Mervyn LeRoy. Ronald Millar and George Froeschel crafted the screenplay, which was based somewhat on the Harbach and Hammerstein original, enough that Harbach and Hammerstein are named in the credits.

[16] Astaire, *Steps in Time*, 135.

[17] The film was directed by Richard Thorpe and produced by Joe Pasternak, with a screenplay by William Ludwig and Sonya Levien, and three additional songs with music by Nicholas Brodszky and lyrics by Paul Francis Webster.

The musicals that appeared in 1924 radiated glamour through their juxtapositions of different artistries and aesthetics, both old and new. Waltzes and Charlestons became companions, leading the way to both dances' centrality in Emmerich Kálmán's *Die Herzogin von Chicago* (The Duchess of Chicago, 1926). Operetta was alive and thriving on both sides of the Atlantic, alongside revue and musical comedy. Progressive attitudes towards race were emerging, though racist structures and depictions remained firmly in place. While most plots emphasized heteronormative romance, a prominent character in *Kid Boots* is most likely gay, and a lesbian couple were responsible for much of the innovations happening at the Neighborhood Playhouse, where *The Grand Street Follies* played. The omnipresence of social class was keenly felt in ever so many plots, and characters, both male and female, were challenging and subverting established gender norms. It was a year filled with the continuing legacies of luminaries such as Noble Sissle and Eubie Blake, Ed Wynn, Marie Tempest, José Collins, Hubert Marischka and Franz Lehár. It was also a year filled with the establishment of major figures in New York such as George and Ira Gershwin, Richard Rodgers, the Marx Brothers, Adele and Fred Astaire, Gertrude Lawrence, Josephine Baker and Florence Mills. Such extraordinary confluences, operating in various transnational contexts, opened up new potentialities for the musical theatre not just in the USA and the United Kingdom but also in Spain, Italy, Austria, France, Hungary, Germany and elsewhere. Taken as a whole and pointing in all sorts of directions – temporal, geographical and aesthetic – 1924 surely could be called the year that made the musical.

Select Discography and Videography

This list includes only recordings available on CD or DVD. It does not include those available on other media, including 78 rpm records or LP albums.

Cloclo (Franz Lehár, Béla Jenbach)

Ohio Light Opera, English translation by Steven A. Daigle, conducted by Steven Byess. Ohio Light Opera 2018 Summer Festival production. With Caitlin Ruddy, Daniel Neer and Yvonne Trobe. Operetta Foundation Operetta Archives OA 1028, 2019. DVD.

Lehár Festival Bad Ischl, conducted by Marius Burkert. Lehár Festival Bad Ischl 2019 production. With Sieglinde Feldhofer, Gerd Vogel and Susanna Hirschler, Chor des Lehár Festivals Bad Ischl, Franz Lehár-Orchester. CPO 777 708–2, 2020. 2 CDs.

Doña Francisquita (Amadeo Vives, Federico Romero, Guillermo Fernández Shaw)

Conducted by Antoni Ros-Marbá. Recorded 1993. With Alfredo Kraus and Maria Bayo. Polifónico Choir, Reyes Bartlet Choir, Choir of the University of La Laguna, Rondalla of Tenerife, Orchestra Sinfonica of Tenerife. Naïve Classique V 4893, 2002. 2 CDs.

George White's Scandals of 1924

'Somebody Loves Me' (George Gershwin, B. G. De Sylva, Ballard MacDonald). Tom Patricola, of original cast. Recorded 1924. On *The Ultimate George Gershwin – Volume 1*. Pearl GEM 0113, 2001. CD.

Gräfin Mariza/Countess Maritza (Emmerich Kálmán, Julius Brammer, Alfred Grünwald)

Conducted by Willy Mattes. Recorded 1971. With Anneliese Rothenberger, Kurt Böhme, Willi Brokmeier, Olivera Miljakovic and Edda Moser, Chor des Bayerischen Staatsoper München, Symphonie-Orchester Graunke. EMI Classics 50999 0 82359 2 3, 2011. 2 CDs.

Seefestspiele Mörbische 2004 production, revised text by Michaela Ronzoni, conducted by Rudolf Bibl. With Dagmar Schellenberger, Nikolai Schukoff, Julia Bauer, Marko Kathol and Natela Nicoli. Videoland VLMD 011, 2004. DVD.

Seefestspiele Mörbische 2018 production, conducted by Guido Marcusi, artistic direction by Peter Edelmann. With Vida Mikneviciute, Roman Payer, Rinnat Moriah, Christoph Filler and Mila Janevska. Videoland VLMD 024, 2018. DVD.

Conducted by Ernst Theis. Recorded 2018. With Betsy Horne, Mehrzad Montazeri, Lydia Teuscher, Jeffrey Treganza and Pia Viola Buchert, Konzertvereinigung Wiener Volksopernchor, Müncher Rundfunkorchester. CPO 777 399–2, 2021. 2 CDs.

Ohio Light Opera, English-language version by Nigel Douglas, conducted by Steven Byess. Ohio Light Opera 2003 production. With Julie Wright, Brian Woods, Betha Curtis, Anthony Maida, Boyd Mackus and Amy Pfrimmer. Operetta Archies OA 1006, 2004. 3 CDs.

Lady, Be Good! (George Gershwin, Ira Gershwin, Guy Bolton, Fred Thompson)

The Leonore S. Gershwin – Library of Congress Recording and Publishing Project. Restored by Tommy Krasker, conducted by Eric Stern. Recorded 1992. With Lara Teeter and Ann Morrison. Elektra Nonesuch 79308–2, 1992. CD.

2015 Encores! Cast Recording. Conducted by Rob Fisher. With Danny Gardner and Patti Murin. Ghostlight Records 8–4491, 2015. CD.

Madame Pompadour (Leo Fall, Rudolph Schanzer, Ernst Welisch)

Volksoper Wien, conducted by Andreas Schüller. Recorded 2012. With Annette Dasch, Mirko Roschkowski and Boris Pfiefer, Orchestra and Choir of the Volksoper Wien. CPO 777 795–2, 2014. CD.

English-language version by Frederick Lonsdale and Harry Graham. Original London production, conducted by Arthur Wood. Recorded 1924. With Evelyn Laye, Derek Oldham, Huntley Wright, Elsie Randolph, Daly's Theatre Orchestra. On *The Dubarry – Madame Pompadour*. Pearl GEMM CD 9068, 1993. CD.

Primrose (George Gershwin, Desmond Carter, Ira Gershwin)

Original London production, conducted by John Ansell. Recorded 1924. With Leslie Henson, Heather Thatcher, Percy Heming and Margery Hicklin, Winter Garden Theatre Orchestra. On *The Ultimate George Gershwin – Volume 1*. Pearl GEM CD 0113, 2001. CD.

Rose-Marie (Rudolf Friml, Herbert Stothart, Otto Harbach, Oscar Hammerstein II)

Conducted by Lehman Engel. Recorded 1958. With Julie Andrews and Giorgio Tozzi. Includes selections from the original 1925 London cast featuring Edith Day, Derek Oldham and the Drury Lane Theatre Orchestra conducted by Herman Finck. Sepia 1140, 2009. CD.

Media Theatre Cast Recording, conducted by Scott F. Bradley. Recorded 1999. With Maureen Francis and Kyle Gonyea. Rockwell IND99222, 1999, CD.

Sitting Pretty (Jerome Kern, P. G. Wodehouse, Guy Bolton)

Conducted by John McGlinn. Recorded 1989. With Judy Blazer, Paige O'Hara, Davis Gaines and Jason Graae. New World Records 80387–2, 1990. 2 CDs.

Stop Flirting (various)

'The Whichness of the Whatness' (William Daly, Paul Lannin, Arthur Jackson) and 'Oh, Gee! Oh, Gosh!' (William Daly, Ira Gershwin [as Arthur Francis]). Fred and Adele Astaire, original cast. Recorded 1923. On *Fred Astaire: The Complete London Sessions*. EMI 7243 5 20045 2 2, 1999. CD.

The Student Prince (Sigmund Romberg, Dorothy Donnelly)

Conducted by Stefan Gyártó. Recorded 1979–1980. With Erik Geisen, Celia Jeffreys and Dieter Hönig, Members of the Hamburg Stage Opera Chorus and Orchestra. Bayer Records 150 005, 1990. CD.

Conducted by John Owen Edwards. Recorded 1989. With David Rendall, Marilyn Hill Smith and Norman Bailey, Ambrosian Chorus, Philharmonia Orchestra. TER Classics CDTER2 1172, 1990. 2 CDs.

Conducted by John Mauceri. Recorded 2012. With Dominik Wortig, Anja Petersen and Frank Blees, WDR Rundfunkchor Köln, WDR Funkhausorchester Köln. CPO 555 058–2, 2016. 2 CDs.

Sweet Little Devil (George Gershwin, B. G. De Sylva)

Restored and produced by Tommy Krasker, conducted by Sam Davis. Recorded 2012. With Bethe Austin, Danny Burstein, Philip Chaffin, Sara Jean Ford, Jason Graae, Rebecca Luker and Sally Wilfert. PS Classics PS-1207, 2012. CD.

Permissions

Select Bibliography

Libraries, Archives and Special Collections

British Library. Lord Chamberlain's Plays.
Library of Congress. Music Division. Washington, DC.
New York Public Library. Billy Rose Theatre Division, Music Division, New York
    Library for the Performing Arts; Schomberg Center for Research in Black
    Culture; Manuscripts and Archives Division.
Shubert Archive, New York.
University of Bristol (UK), Theatre Collection.
University of California, Los Angeles Charles E. Young Research Library Special
    Collections.
Wisconsin Historical Society, Madison, WI.

Books and Book Chapters

Astaire, Fred. *Steps in Time: An Autobiography.* New York: Harper & Brothers, 1959.
Bañagale, Ryan Raul. *Arranging Gershwin: 'Rhapsody in Blue' and the Creation of an American Icon.* New York: Oxford University Press, 2014.
Banfield, Stephen. *Jerome Kern.* New Haven: Yale University Press, 2006.
Baranello, Micaela. *The Operetta Empire: Music Theatre in Early Twentieth-Century Vienna.* Oakland: University of California Press, 2021.
Bax, Clifford. *Midsummer Madness: A Play for Music.* London: Ernest Benn, 1923.
Block, Geoffrey. *Richard Rodgers.* New Haven: Yale University Press, 2003.
Bolitho, Hector. *Marie Tempest.* Philadelphia: Lippincott, 1937.
Bordman, Gerald. *American Musical Revue: From 'The Passing Show' to 'Sugar Babies.'* New York: Oxford University Press, 1985.
    Days to Be Happy, Years to Be Sad: The Life and Music of Vincent Youmans. New York: Oxford University Press, 1982.
    Jerome Kern: His Life and Music. New York: Oxford University Press, 1980.
Burke, Billie, with Cameron Shipp. *With a Feather on My Nose.* London: Peter Davies, 1950.
Cantor, Eddie. *My Life Is in Your Hands* (1928, with David Freedman) & *Take My Life* (1957, with Jane Kesner Ardmore): *The Autobiographies of Eddie Cantor.* New York: Cooper Square Press, 2000.

Cantu, Maya. *American Cinderellas on the Broadway Musical Stage: Imagining the Working Girl from 'Irene' to 'Gypsy'*. Houndmills: Palgrave Macmillan, 2015.

Carlin, Richard, and Ken Bloom. *Eubie Blake: Rags, Rhythm, and Race*. New York: Oxford University Press, 2020.

Collins, José. *The Maid of the Mountains, Her Story: The Reminiscences of José Collins*. London: Hutchinson & Co., 1932.

Crawford, Richard. *Summertime: George Gershwin's Life in Music*. New York: W. W. Norton, 2019.

Davis, Lee. *Scandals and Follies: The Rise and Fall of the Great Broadway Revue*. New York: Limelight, 2000.

Decker, Todd. 'Broadway in Blue: Gershwin's Musical Theater Scores and Songs'. In *The Cambridge Companion to Gershwin*, edited by Anna Harwell Celenza, 80–101. Cambridge: Cambridge University Press, 2019.

Diamond, Noah. *Gimme a Thrill: The Story of 'I'll Say She Is'. The Lost Marx Brothers Musical and How It Was Found*. Duncan: BearManor Media, 2016.

DiAngelo, Robin. *White Fragility: Why It's So Hard for White People to Talk about Racism*. Boston: Beacon Press, 2018.

Dietz, Dan. *The Complete Book of 1920s Broadway Musicals*. Lanham: Rowman & Littlefield, 2019.

Egan, Bill. *Florence Mills: Harlem Jazz Queen*. Lanham: Scarecrow, 2004.

Everett, William A. *Rudolf Friml*. Urbana: University of Illinois Press, 2008.

Sigmund Romberg. New Haven: Yale University Press, 2007.

Frey, Stefan. *Franz Lehár: Der letzte Operettenkönig*. Vienna: Böhlau, 2020.

'Laughter under Tears': Emmerich Kálmán – An Operetta Biography. Translated by Alexander Butziger. Culver City: Operetta Foundation, 2014.

Frey, Stefan, with Christine Stemprok and Wolfgang Dosch. *Leo Fall: Spöttischer Rebell der Operette*. Vienna: Edition Steinbauer, 2010.

Gennaro, Liza. *Making Broadway Dance*. New York: Oxford University Press, 2022.

Harbach, Otto, and Oscar Hammerstein. *Rose Marie: A Musial Play*. London: Samuel French, 1924.

Harrington, John P. *The Life of the Neighborhood Playhouse on Grand Street*. Syracuse: Syracuse University Press, 2007.

Harris, Warren G. *The Other Marilyn: A Biography of Marilyn Miller*. New York: Arbor House, 1985.

Henson, Leslie. *Yours Faithfully: An Autobiography*. London: John Long, [1948].

Hischak, Thomas S. *The Jerome Kern Encyclopedia*. Lanham: Scarecrow, 2013.

Horowitz, Mark Eden, compiler and editor. *The Letters of Oscar Hammerstein II*. New York: Oxford University Press, 2022.

Hylton, Robert. *Dancing in Time: The History of Moving and Shaking*. London: British Library, 2022.

Johnson, James Weldon. *Black Manhattan*. New York: Knopf, 1940 (first published 1930); reprint edition, New York: Arno Press and The New York Times, 1968.

Jones, John Bush. *Our Musicals, Ourselves: A Social History of the American Musical Theatre*. Lebanon: Brandeis University Press, 2003.

Koseluk, Gregory. *Eddie Cantor: A Life in Show Business*. Jefferson: McFarland, 1995.

Krasner, David. '*Shuffle Along* and the Quest for Nostalgia: Black Musicals of the 1920s'. In *A Beautiful Pageant: African American Theatre, Drama, and Performance in the Harlem Renaissance, 1910–1927*, 239–288. New York: Palgrave Macmillan, 2002.

Lamb, Andrew. *Jerome Kern in Edwardian London*. Brooklyn: Institute for Studies in American Music, Brooklyn College, 1985.

Lamb, Andrew, and Christopher Webber. '*De Madrid a Londres': Pablo Luna's English Operetta 'The First Kiss'*. London: Couthurst Press, 2016 (available at https://www.academia.edu/26447008/De_Madrid_a_Londres_Pablo_Lunas_English_Operetta_The_First_Kiss?sm=b).

Lawrence, Gertrude. *A Star Danced*. New York: Doubleday, 1945.

Laye, Evelyn. *Boo, to My Friends*. London: Hurst & Blackett, 1958.

Leinwand, Gerald. *1927: High Tide of the 1920s*. New York: Four Walls Eight Windows, 2001.

Lewisohn Crowley, Alice. *The Neighborhood Playhouse: Leaves from a Theatre Scrapbook*. New York: Theatre Arts Books, 1959.

Linton, David. *Nation and Race in West End Revue, 1910–1930*. London: Palgrave Macmillan, 2021.

Linton, David, and Len Platt. 'Dover Street to Dixie and the Politics of Cultural Transfer and Exchange'. In *Popular Musical Theatre in London and Berlin, 1890–1939*, edited by Len Platt, Tobias Becker and David Linton, 170–186. Cambridge: Cambridge University Press, 2014.

Longobucco, Luisa. *Carlo Lombardo e 'Il Paese dei Campanelli': Breve storia dell'operetta*. Cosena: Pellegrini Editore, 2013.

Macpherson, Ben. *Cultural Identity in British Musical Theatre, 1890–1939: Knowing One's Place*. London: Palgrave Macmillan, 2018.

Magee, Jeffrey. *Irving Berlin's American Musical Theatre*. New York: Oxford University Press, 2012.

Mantle, Burns. *The Best Plays of 1923–1924 and the Year Book of the Drama in America*. Boston: Small, Maynard & Company, 1924.

The Best Plays of 1924–1925 and the Year Book of the Drama in America. New York: Dodd, Mead and Company, 1925.

Mayes, Sean, and Sarah K. Whitfield. *An Inconvenient Black History of British Musical Theatre, 1900–1950*. London: Methuen, 2022.

McNamara, Brooks. *The Shuberts of Broadway: A History Drawn from the Collections of the Shubert Archive*. New York: Oxford University Press, 1990.

Moore, James Ross. *André Charlot: The Genius of Intimate Musical Revue.* Jefferson: McFarland, 2005.

Mordden, Ethan. *Make Believe: The Broadway Musical in the 1920s.* New York: Oxford University Press, 1997.

  Ziegfeld: The Man Who Invented Show Business. New York: St. Martin's, 2008.

North, Michael. *Reading 1922: A Return to the Scene of the Modern.* New: Oxford University Press, 1999.

Norton, Richard C. *A Chronology of American Musical Theater*, Volume 2: 1912–1952. New York: Oxford University Press, 2002.

Ommen van der Merwe, Ann. *The Ziegfeld Follies: A History in Song.* Lanham: Scarecrow, 2009.

Peck, Ellen M. *Sweet Mystery: The Musical Works of Rida Johnson Young.* New York: Oxford University Press, 2020.

Peterson, Bernard L., Jr. *A. Century of Musicals in Black and White: An Encyclopedia of Musical Stage Works By, About, or Involving African Americans.* Westport: Greenwood, 1993.

  Profiles of African American Stage Performers and Theatre People, 1816–1960. Westport: Greenwood, 2001.

Pisani, Michael V. *Imagining Native America in Music.* New Haven: Yale University Press, 2005.

Pollack, Howard. *George Gershwin: His Life and Work.* Berkeley: University of California Press, 2006.

Range, Peter Ross. *1924: The Year that Made Hitler.* New York: Little, Brown and Co., 2016.

Schweitzer, Marliss. *When Broadway Was the Runway: Theatre, Fashion, and American Culture.* Philadelphia: University of Pennsylvania Press, 2009.

Scott, Derek B. *German Operetta on Broadway and in the West End, 1900–1940.* Cambridge: Cambridge University Press, 2019.

Seldes, Gilbert. *The Seven Lively Arts.* New York: Harper & Brothers, 1924; reprint ed., New York: Dover, 2001.

Stalter-Pace, Sunny. *Imitation Artist: Gertude Hoffman's Life in Vaudeville and Dance.* Evanston: Northwestern University Press, 2020.

Starr, Larry. *George Gershwin.* New Haven: Yale University Press, 2011.

Stearns, Marshall. *Jazz Dance: The Story of American Vernacular Dance.* New York: Macmillan, 1968; reprint ed., New York: Da Capo, 1994.

Stempel, Larry. *Showtime: A History of the Broadway Musical Theater.* New York: W. W. Norton & Co., 2010.

Sturman, Janet L. *Zarzuela: Spanish Operetta, American Stage.* Urbana : University of Illinois Press, 2000.

Traubner, Richard. *Operetta: A Theatrical History.* Garden City: Doubleday, 1983; paperback ed., Oxford: Oxford University Press, 1989.

Vernon, Doremy. *Tiller's Girls: The Colourful Story of the Legendary Dancing Troupe.* London: Robson, 1988.

Webber, Christopher. *The Zarzuela Companion*. Lanham: Scarecrow, 2002.

Weinstein, David. *The Eddie Cantor Story: A Jewish Life in Performance and Politics*. Waltham: Brandeis University Press, 2018.

Westover, Jonas. *The Shuberts and Their Passing Shows: The Untold Tale of Ziegfeld's Rivals*. New York: Oxford University Press, 2016.

Wodehouse, P. G. and Guy Bolton . *Bring On the Girls! The Improbably Story of Our Life in Musical Comedy with Pictures to Prove It*. Pleasantville: Akadine Press, 1997 (originally published New York: Simon and Schuster, 1953).

Woll, Allen. *Black Musical Theatre: From 'Coontown' to 'Dreamgirls'*. Baton Rouge: Louisiana State University Press, 1989.

Young, Clinton D. *Musical Theatre and Popular Nationalism in Spain, 1880–1930*. Baton Rouge: Louisiana State University Press, 2016.

Articles

Gittings, Christopher. 'Imaging Canada: The Singing Mountie and Other Commodifications of Nation'. *Canadian Journal of Communication* 23, no. 4 (1998): 507–522. https://doi.org/10.22230/cjc.1998v23n4a1062. Accessed 15 January 2022.

Lamb, Andrew, and Christopher Webber. '"*The First Kiss*" – Pablo Luna's English Musical'. www.zarzuela.net/ref/feat/first-kiss.htm, 21 September 2016. Accessed 1 April 2022.

Moreda Rodríguez, Eva. 'Singing and Speaking in Early Twentieth-Century *Zarzuela*: The Evidence from Early Recordings'. *Journal of Musicological Research* 41, no. 1 (2022): 23–49.

Morrison, Matthew D. 'Race, Blacksound, and the (Re)Making of Musicological Discourse'. *Journal of the American Musicological Society* 72, no. 3 (Fall 2019): 781–823.

Neimoyer, Susan. 'After the *Rhapsody*: George Gershwin in the Spring of 1924'. *Journal of Musicology* 31, no. 1 (January 2014): 91–138.

Peacock, Shane. 'Noble, Daring, & Dashing'. *Beaver* 78, no. 3 (1998). Academic Search Premier: https://tinyurl.com/3x4m48us. Accessed 15 January 2022.

Websites

British Newspaper Archive. britishnewspaperarchive.co.uk.

Discography of American Historical Recordings. adp.library.ucsb.edu.

Internet Broadway Database. ibdb.com.

New York Times Digital Archive. timesmachine.nytimes.com .

Newspapers.com. newspapers.com.

YouTube. youtube.com.

Index